FIERCE, FABULOUS, A

CRITICAL PERSPECTIVES ON YOUTH SERIES
General Editors: Amy L. Best, Lorena Garcia, and Jessica K. Taft

Fast-Food Kids: French Fries, Lunch Lines, and Social Ties
Amy L. Best

White Kids: Growing Up with Privilege in a Racially Divided America
Margaret A. Hagerman

Growing Up Queer: Kids and the Remaking of LGBTQ Identity
Mary Robertson

The Kids Are in Charge: Activism and Power in Peru's Movement of Working Children
Jessica K. Taft

Coming of Age in Iran: Poverty and the Struggle for Dignity
Manata Hashemi

The World Is Our Classroom: Extreme Parenting and the Rise of Worldschooling
Jennie Germann Molz

The Homeschool Choice: Parents and the Privatization of Education
Kate Henley Averett

Growing Up Latinx: Coming of Age in a Time of Contested Citizenship
Jesica Siham Fernández

Unaccompanied: The Plight of Immigrant Youth at the Border
Emily Ruehs-Navarro

The Sociology of Bullying: Power, Status, and Aggression Among Adolescents
Edited by Christopher Donoghue

Gender Replay: On Kids, Schools, and Feminism
Edited by Freeden Blume Oeur and C. J. Pascoe

Fierce, Fabulous, and Fluid: How Trans High School Students Work at Gender Nonconformity
LJ Slovin

Fierce, Fabulous, and Fluid

How Trans High School Students Work at Gender Nonconformity

LJ Slovin

University of Regina Press

© 2024 by New York University

Copublished with New York University Press, New York, www.nyupress.org

All rights reserved. No part of this work covered by the copyrights hereon may be reproduced or used in any form or by any means—graphic, electronic, or mechanical—without the prior written permission of the publisher. Any request for photocopying, recording, taping or placement in information storage and retrieval systems of any sort shall be directed in writing to Access Copyright.

Printed and bound in Canada. The text of this book is printed on 100% post-consumer recycled paper with earth-friendly vegetable-based inks.

Cover design by Duncan Noel campbell
Cover image: "School backpack on pink background," by vejaa/AdobeSTock

Library and Archives Canada Cataloguing in Publication

TITLE: Fierce, fabulous, and fluid : how trans high school students work at gender nonconformity / lj slovin.

NAMES: slovin, lj, author.

DESCRIPTION: Includes bibliographical references and index.

IDENTIFIERS: Canadiana (print) 20240363515 | Canadiana (ebook) 20240363523 | ISBN 9781779400505 (softcover) | ISBN 9781779400529 (PDF) | ISBN 9781779400512 (EPUB)

SUBJECTS: LCSH: Transsexual students. | LCSH: High school students.

CLASSIFICATION: LCC HQ77.7 .S53 2024 | DDC 371.826/7—dc23

University of Regina Press, University of Regina
Regina, Saskatchewan, Canada, S4S 0A2
TEL: (306) 585-4758 FAX: (306) 585-4699
WEB: www.uofrpress.ca

This book has been published with the help of a grant from the Federation for the Humanities and Social Sciences, through the Awards to Scholarly Publications Program, using funds provided by the Social Sciences and Humanities Research Council of Canada.

We acknowledge the support of the Canada Council for the Arts for our publishing program. We acknowledge the financial support of the Government of Canada. / Nous reconnaissons l'appui financier du gouvernement du Canada. This publication was made possible with support from Creative Saskatchewan's Book Publishing Production Grant Program.

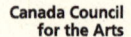

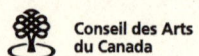

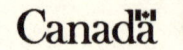

CONTENTS

Introduction: Got Trans?	1
1. East City High's Diversity Culture	35
2. Accommodating Trans Youth	64
3. The Labor of Understanding and Forgiveness	83
4. The Labor of Gender Legibility	110
5. The Labor of World-Making	137
Conclusion: From Risk to Desire	167
Acknowledgments	191
Appendix: What Grade Are You In?	193
Notes	201
Bibliography	211
Index	221
About the Author	231

Introduction

Got Trans?

It was January at East City High, and rehearsals for the Senior Theater Company's main stage production had just started ramping up. When I got to the auditorium for class, I headed to the steep, narrow steel staircase in the back that led up to the tech booth. Raeyun, a queer Filipino trans student, was carefully navigating the stairs down and paused midway.[1] He was looking for me. Raeyun was the main tech person for the play. He was the only one who knew how to program the lights and reset the gels. Most lighting work had to be done during blackouts, so often Raeyun did not have much to do during regular rehearsals. Instead, we sat in the tech booth and hung out. Sometimes he wrote fan fiction, which he referred to as his "gaymances"; other times he drew on his phone. Mostly, we talked.

Up in the booth, Raeyun pulled out his phone and started scrolling through photos of his favorite K-pop artists. He wanted me to see what he saw: beautiful, idolized, masculine men who were wearing skirts, crop tops, and eyeliner. Raeyun loved K-pop. He had a singer from NCT as the backdrop on his phone.[2] Raeyun's adoration was not just about the music. He described K-pop as a world in which men of color could engage with their gender expression and each other in ways that felt distant and not quite possible to him. As he was flicking through photos of all the fashion styles he admired and limning the possibilities of femme masculinity, I felt acutely aware of my recorder tucked into my backpack downstairs in the auditorium seats, turned off and unhelpful.

I was at East City High conducting an ethnography on the ways gender-nonconforming youth navigated their genders as they moved through different spaces and relationships at school. In my year at East City High, I accompanied youth to their classes, joined in during their extracurricular activities and clubs, ate lunch with them, attended their performances, and hung out in hallways, in tech booths, and on the peripheries of classrooms. Sometimes we skipped school together, met up in cafés, and just roamed the halls. We texted (often). They taught me how to play Dungeons & Dragons (D&D), introduced me to the world of K-pop, schooled me on what TV shows I really should have been watching all along, and read me their writing.

This project centers youth who were not regularly recognized by others as trans. Many of these young people were nonbinary and genderfluid. Sometimes they used the term "trans," though they also struggled with not feeling "trans enough." I am interested in these tensions and these dynamics. Throughout *Fierce, Fabulous, and Fluid*, I use many different words to talk about these youth because they used many different words for themselves—over the year and often within a conversation. They talked about themselves as gay, queer, bisexual, pansexual, trans, gender nonconforming, genderfluid, and nonbinary. These words overlapped and existed together, in sometimes seamless and other times uneasy ways. When speaking directly about the youth, I honor their language and follow their choices around terminology. However, I chose to ground this project in the term "gender nonconforming" since it does not rely on a young person's specific identity. Given my focus on youth who were not often recognized as trans, I am interested in the work that went into being read as trans and negotiating being misgendered. Following the trans studies scholar Toby Beauchamp, the use of "gender nonconforming" facilitates a focus on embodiment and enactment, policing and surveillance, and on the ideas, structures, and expectations that inform how people read and interact with youth's genders instead of offering an analysis about the "reality" of their genders.[3] Therefore, I most often use "gender nonconforming" and "trans," an umbrella term for any person whose gender does not align with the one they were designated at birth, to signal how the youth desired to be recognized as trans and, at times, held this desire for recognition in tension.

I began with this story about Raeyun because it illustrates the driving focus of this book: gender-nonconforming youth's labor to survive and thrive in school. Over the year I spent moving alongside six youths in grades 9–12 at East City High, I noticed that youth performed myriad forms of labor throughout a school day to exist as gender nonconforming. This labor was in response to the people, the physical environment, the curriculum, and the policies that reproduced narrow understandings of trans identity that did not have space for the capaciousness of their relationships to gender. At times, this labor was apparent and perceptible *as work*. Youth corrected adults when they were misgendered and deadnamed or spoke to teachers and administrators to secure accommodations in their classes.[4] Other times, this labor was unnoticed and devalued, as with Raeyun's sharing of K-pop photos in the tech booth. Though youth regularly engaged in small acts of resistance and rebellion by escaping into their own spaces or disappearing into their writing during classes, this behavior was not acknowledged as important, as valuable, or as a form of intervention. In *Fierce, Fabulous, and Fluid*, I take seriously their daily acts of trans life as forms of labor.[5] I consider how in the tech booth, for instance, Raeyun was engaged in not only the labor of survival but also the work of utopic world-building.[6] He was creating another world to exist in while at East City High through the work of caring—for himself, for his gender, and, ultimately, for the burgeoning trans community he was cultivating through this labor.

In this book, I explore how even though youth's labor frequently went unnoticed at East City High, it was also often demanded and required of them. To understand this complex dynamic, I consider how teachers, administrators, and staff understood trans identity. During my year at East City High, I observed many teachers respond with care and concern to the *idea* of trans youth and to the trans youth they were aware existed. This response aligns with recent scholarship on the privileging of visibility as a metric when working with and supporting trans students in schools.[7] Overwhelmingly, when East City High teachers were aware of a trans student, they endeavored to support this young person. This support was framed within an accommodations approach, which, as I explore further in chapter 2, has become the dominant strategy for pursuing trans-inclusivity in Canadian schools.[8] Teachers assisted students in accessing workarounds in physical education (PE) classes or changing their names and pronouns. At times, this support was seamless and useful. At other times, it was awkward and halting. However, it was always reactive, compelled either by adults' awareness of a trans student in their class or by a student making themselves explicitly known as trans to an adult. While there is growing critique of accommodations approaches, scholarship primarily attests to their individualistic focus and reliance on visibility.[9] Beyond these facets, I explore how accommodation-based responses are mired in an understanding of trans identity as inherently risky. At East City High, adults were quick to express care and concern for known trans youth because they believed that being trans makes a young person vulnerable, especially in a school. While educators accepted recognizable trans youth, they did not want youth to be trans. When trans identity is associated with risk, then wanting a young person to be trans is analogous to wishing a young person a hard life. Therefore, despite adults' care and support, no one ever expressed desire for a young person to be or grow up queer and trans.

As a result of the concern of adults at East City High, they were invested in helping *visible* trans students. I argue that this approach to trans-inclusivity both relied on and reproduced narrow terms of gender legibility that tethered gender nonconformity to risk, harm, and danger. While I return to this discussion later in the introduction, first, it is critical to emphasize that most of the youth I worked with were not visible as trans. They were not recognized as trans because of the ways they were racialized, their fatness, their neurodivergence, and the many ways their genders did not align with societal expectations for what it "means" and "looks" like to be trans. Furthermore, many of the youth in the study were not interested in *knowing* their genders and did not understand gender as knowable within concrete terms of identity. They looked to gender nonconformity as a way to signal ambiguity and even confusion. They wanted to be unreadable. There is an important tension here. Many youth wanted to be understood as gender nonconforming based on the ways they transgressed societal gender norms. However, youth also desired gender nonconformity precisely because it was confusing and uncategorizable. Being gender nonconforming, therefore, meant that adults in the school would not be able to place them because they were intentionally unplaceable. They both wanted to be legible as not conforming to the gender binary and understood gender nonconformity *as* illegibility. I am not intending to resolve this tension. I am pointing it out to suggest that legibility and knowability are fraught desires. *Fierce, Fabulous, and Fluid* explores how gender-nonconforming youth resisted stable categories of knowing. At times, their resistance was grounded in a fierce intention to disrupt cisheteronormative assumptions; at other times, it was others who resisted knowing them, unable to recognize the complexities of their genders.

In this book, I am not interested in making these youth and their genders stable and knowable. Rather, I ask, When educators respond to trans youth from places of risk and concern, how do youth work daily to create space to exist as gender-nonconforming young people? Though the youth I worked with regularly confronted transphobic, racist, and ableist ideas and narratives from adults, other students, the curriculum, and the physical space of the school, they intervened at East City High through their labor. I document not only the labor they performed to resist and navigate these oppressive structures but also the beauty of their world-making. I demonstrate how in building worlds outside of adult surveillance, youth were creating spaces in the school animated by their desires for genders that did not have to be legible according to others' metrics and expectations.

East City High

East City High is an imposing building that encompasses a full city block and enrolls around eighteen hundred students. It has four floors, several outbuildings, an auto shop, a turf field, a track, and tennis courts. A local nonprofit runs a community gardening program from the grounds, and in the spring, local elementary schoolchildren regularly gather there learning about seeds and plants.

East City High occupies the unceded lands of the səlilwətaʔɬ təməxʷ (Tsleil-Waututh), xʷməθkʷəy̓əm (Musqueam), and Skwxwú7mesh-ulh Temíxw (Squamish) Nations. This area, which is now known as the Lower Mainland of British Columbia, has been split into several neighborhoods, though it is often simplified into the east and west side. The west side is associated with wealth and understood as having better schools and opportunities. The east side is positioned as grittier and more politically progressive.

The administrators, teachers, and staff promoted this progressive version of the school in part through visuals. As one entered, one of the first visible images was a painted land acknowledgment expressing awareness of the Indigenous peoples on whose land the school was built. Throughout the school, there were poster campaigns denouncing racism and homophobia. The narrow hallway leading into East City High's theater studio was lined with posters from old productions, potted plants, and a couple of couches. In this hallway, there was also a queer and trans visibility campaign, mostly obscured by the plants, that featured photos of celebrities and asked, "Got Pansexual? Got Trans? Got Two-Spirited? Got Femme?" Scarecrow Jones, a mixed-race, nonbinary grade 9 student, abhorred this campaign. On many occasions, they ranted about the wording of this display: "What, like, I mean, have I got the disease, do you mean? Oh man, are you coming down with the bug?" Scarecrow Jones offered, "At least it's not blatant homophobia. . . . They're trying, which I guess is nice, but at the same time, it's the bare minimum form of representation that's not accurate at all." Scarecrow Jones did not see themself in these posters, but they reckoned that it was a nice attempt by East City High to recognize that trans people might exist.

Teachers, administrators, and students at the school specifically positioned East City High as representative of the east side through the school's work on diversity and inclusion. Adults elevated East City High as a liberal haven. They described east-side students as understanding the value of work, caring about progressive ideals like diversity, and rejecting convention and normativity, in contrast to students on the west side, who were framed as spoiled and entitled. For instance, one day during a lesson on political values in Mr. Harding's English 11 class, he explained how East City High was in a left-wing neighborhood and, as a result, students were "very open-minded." Mr. Harding told the class that he preferred teaching at East City High to other schools because of the progressive student body. Conversations like these were not uncommon. Teachers scoffed at west-side students, berating them for driving Mercedes Benzes while lauding how east-side students cared about equality. Though adults regularly praised students for valuing these ideals, at times these accolades seemed to serve almost as reminders to youth that these were necessary values for East City High students.

However, East City High was a unique east-side school. When the district released the list of schools slotted for closure in the area back in 2016, all but one of the schools was located on the east side of the city.[10] Unlike the underserved and poorly maintained high schools down the road, East City High was protected from closure because it offered several special programs that were not available at other east-side schools, such as French Immersion and elite science and humanities tracks. These specialized programs attracted wealthier families and thus brought additional money and resources to the school through parent advisory councils. For these families, East City High's programs served as an avenue to circumvent the underfunded neighborhood schools. As a result, there existed intense class stratification at East City High, with more resourced students concentrated in the specialized programs. Vixen, a white, low-income, and neurodivergent grade 12 student who lived with their mom in a co-op, lived within the catchment but was enrolled in French Immersion. They felt isolated in their experiences of poverty and food insecurity. During a class activity on privilege, Vixen was the only student who indicated having ever gone without food. Adults' broad-strokes pronouncements of East City High as gritty and authentic served to obfuscate the complexities of its class dynamics.

The positioning of East City High as diverse and inclusive aligns with what Sara Ahmed refers to as a "feel good" approach to diversity.[11] Teachers, administrators, and counselors did not consider the possibility that racism, classism, ableism, or cisheteronormativity existed and were endemic to schooling. Instead, they celebrated diversity as "cultural enrichment."[12] Differences added *flavor*. They did not require systemic reworking of oppressive structures within the school. As such, the school was proud to highlight *fun* diversity, such as the selection of the snake design by Ms. Man, a Vietnamese, nonbinary grade 12 student, for the grad sweatshirt (most grade 12 students were born in the year of the snake). However, these moments of visibility did not force the school to reckon with, for instance, the anti-Asian racism that informed teachers' attitudes about students.

Ms. Man's grad sweatshirt design was an artistic reference to their culture as well as a nod to the large East Asian population at East City High and in the city more generally.[13] However, despite the school's demographics, teachers at East City High did not reflect the student body. East City High staff did not stray far from general trends in schools in British Columbia, where the teachers are predominantly white women.[14] The discordance between the students and teachers exacerbated the "feel good" approach to diversity. In Senior Theater Company one afternoon, Ms. Mack, a white, straight, cisgender woman, gave the students a pep talk. She warned the class that though currently preparations felt relaxed, opening day was approaching, and she needed students to stay organized. Then she pointed at Raeyun and two East Asian girls in the class: "You are probably the most organized," she told everyone. Though she seemed unaware, Ms. Mack was drawing on the model-minority myth and perpetuating harmful stereotypes about Asian Canadian students.[15] While the students recognized this bias and appeared noticeably uncomfortable, Ms. Mack was confused by the class's strong reaction. She asked, "Is it embarrassing to be organized?" While many adults in positions of power at the school believed in the carefully presented image of East City High as diverse, marginalized students (and several marginalized teachers) found that this positioning existed in tension with their experiences of racism and oppression on campus.

Theorizing Gender Nonconformity

In North America, we are witnessing the intertwined processes of inclusion and exclusion for trans people. As I write, there is a proliferation of celebrities announcing that they are trans, alongside increased media representation in films, TV shows, and young-adult books. Award shows are removing gendered categories, and certain nations, like Canada, are making it possible to apply for licenses and passports using an X as a gender marker. However, these moves have not translated into a widespread belief in trans people's humanity. Rather, certain trans people have gained greater access to limited rights and are experiencing qualified forms of safety in mainstream North American society. These moves are occurring alongside mounting attacks on the lives of trans people with less access to privilege, notably trans and gender-nonconforming youth of color. Visibility alone does not address issues of youth homelessness, the overrepresentation of trans youth of color in the prison system, the criminalization of gender-affirming care, or the prohibition of trans women and girls in sports spaces. *Fierce, Fabulous, and Fluid* engages with scholarship from queer and trans theory, youth studies, and the field of education to question an investment in legibility and visibility as incontrovertible paths to safety and progress for trans and gender-nonconforming youth. Specifically, I interrogate how a reliance on narrow understandings of trans identity, understandings that remain mired in risk, require youth to perform significant labor to exist as gender nonconforming in schools.

From Risk to Desire

The first time I walked into East City High, I was there to discuss the possibility of conducting research at the school with a vice principal.[16] He was welcoming and almost relieved to hear about my study. He informed me that East City High was committed to creating a safe space for its trans students and then confessed that they were overwhelmed and confused by how best to support specifically nonbinary youth. He shared that the trans-inclusive policy and materials available at East City High did not always address the experiences of these youth. The vice principal was noticeably comforted by the idea of a nonbinary researcher coming to the school. He leaned forward, propping his elbows on his desk, and told me he was grateful that I would now be there to support these students and fill in the gaps. The vice principal positioned my nonnormative body as representing the solution to his concern about gender-nonconforming youth. Over the year, I would grow accustomed to attitudes like this. His anxiety over nonbinary students and relief at my arrival speak to the influence of the accommodations approach. There was a sense that adjustments to the curriculum, physical space, and other elements of schooling were only necessary in response to individual students who compelled action.[17] I rarely witnessed people at the school consider that gendered expectations affected everyone or that all students may benefit from a less cisheteronormative environment.

Accommodation approaches, which I explore in greater depth in chapter 2, arose out of aims to protect queer and trans youth, who have been consistently framed as vulnerable and "at-risk." In fact, it is challenging to find scholarship on queer and trans youth that does not position them as victims or especially at-risk in school settings.[18] Educators have predicated campaigns for inclusion and acceptance of queer and trans youth on the promotion of their vulnerability, using their struggles as arguments that they deserve protection in schools.[19] Positioning youth as at-risk is an intentional strategy to argue for their protection in schools. This type of advocacy promotes the use of research that can demonstrate the struggles of trans youth, and the gathering and then recitation of dire statistics on their lives features heavily in a plethora of current scholarship.[20] Justin Thorpe and Adam Greteman offer a warning regarding the "rhetorical deployment of quantification in order to open up space for scholarship to grapple with not only the violence of homophobia exposed by statistics but also the lived experiences of GLBTQ persons that are covered up by a 'safety in numbers' that exists in our defensive numerical citations."[21] While access to statistical research enumerating heightened levels of violence, suicidality, school leaving, depression, and drug and alcohol (mis)use, for example, can facilitate the creation of policies and garnering of support on behalf of trans youth, the overemphasis on this type of research participates in constructing queer and trans youth as inherently at-risk.

Though the framing of trans youth as uniquely vulnerable and at-risk was intended to inspire others to fight for them and care about their safety, risk is a restrictive framework for approaching their experiences in schools. It positions youth as perpetually in a state of chaos and upheaval. Protecting them from looming dangers, often understood as inherently linked to their identities, thus takes predominance over a focus on other elements of schooling.[22] While studies that document the increased harm experienced by queer and trans youth, especially queer and trans youth of color, underscore crucial ways schools can be places of violence, there is a tendency to tether queer and trans youth to risk. The ubiquity of these frameworks makes unthinkable the idea that queer and trans youth could be anyone but victims.[23]

Crucially, accommodation approaches in schools to support at-risk students rely on these students being identifiable as needing assistance.[24] Therefore, this framework for trans-inclusivity necessitates making trans youth a knowable population: if adults are going to protect students from added risk and harm, they need to know who these students are. As Susan Talburt argues, in an effort to oppose homophobia and transphobia, "educators have based appeals for inclusion and educational equity on descriptions of the characteristics, problems, and needs of gay youth. In other words, they have had to make LGBT students a knowable population to justify change in schools."[25] Educators and advocates, in attempting to protect students, rely on and reproduce categories of gender legibility. The need for knowability invests in societal expectations of transness that continue to privilege the gender binary.

In *Fierce, Fabulous, and Fluid*, I explore the relationship between understanding trans identity as risky and adults' interactions with gender-nonconforming youth by interrogating how, even as schools resolve to include and accommodate certain trans youth, schooling still aspires to socialize youth away from queerness.[26] Scholars have expanded on Eve Kosofsky Sedgwick's early theorizing in this vein to consider the myriad ways youth are disciplined toward normatively embodied adulthood.[27] At East City High, teachers, counselors, and administrators at times accepted, cared for, and were invested in the safety of the trans youth they were aware of, but rarely did an adult express desire that these youth exist in their nonconformity. Susan Stryker argues that "most people have a great difficulty recognizing the humanity of another person if they cannot recognize that person's gender."[28] As a result, Stryker asserts that trans people, especially those whose existences touch multiple forms of nonnormativity, become monstrous.[29] There is almost no space for adults to desire a child to grow up queer, trans, fat, and disabled. Further, expressing these desires approaches perilously close to the perverse. The dominance of risk discourses presumes that desiring a queer, trans, fat, and disabled future for a young person is concurrent with wishing them a lifetime of harm and struggle. Despite the mainstream forms of progress celebrated since the "transgender tipping point," people still struggle to imagine the beauty of our monstrous futures.

I join a growing contingent of school-based ethnographers as well as queer and trans scholars who consciously reject risk-based narratives in studies with queer and trans youth to consider what emerges when we stop fixating on risk, harm, and danger.[30] Several scholars have turned away from risk by documenting youth's survival strategies and queer street smarts.[31] Inspired by their work, in the next section, I turn to scholarship on labor to develop this thinking. I am likewise guided by Eve Tuck's theorizing on desire-based research.[32] In educational research, desire has never been exclusively about sex, sexuality, or romance.[33] Desire informs how we think about youth and how we understand education.[34] In a letter to education scholars, Tuck drew on the notion of desire when calling for an end to "damage-centered research."[35] Tuck offered, "Desire is about longing, about a present that is enriched by both the past and the future. It is integral to our humanness."[36] Tuck's impassioned letter called on education scholars to notice the problematic reification of damage and risk in our work and intervene in that dynamic.

Tuck unfolded desire as a framework not in opposition to damage but rather as an epistemological shift. I consider what this shift might mean in schools. How would schools operate differently if we desired queer and trans lives and futures for youth? How would infusing this queer desire necessitate an upending of the gendered standards, expectations, and language that currently structure schools and that undergird accommodation approaches? If adults desired youth to be trans, would we be able to cease knowing youth exclusively through ideas of risk and struggle? Though many of the youth I worked with were explicitly positioned as at-risk in the school, they were also brilliant, funny, creative, and caring young people. In *Fierce, Fabulous, and Fluid*, I consider their strategies for surviving and flourishing in schools by attending to the ways youth's labor practices made possible other worlds within East City High. In the absence of adults' desire for youth to be queer and trans, youth performed the labor to cultivate desire for their own monstrous lives. I theorize youth's labor as animated by desires to survive school, exist in capacious relationships with gender, and create communities of care that expanded beyond the limited gendered expectations that followed them around East City High.

On Labor and Care

The first time I went to Mr. Gallagher's grade 9 French drama class, he conducted a minilesson on French gender-neutral pronouns. Mr. Gallagher had a complex relationship to queer and trans issues. He is a queer person and was keen to have me attend his classes. However, Mr. Gallagher had also witnessed queer teachers struggle professionally when they were out about their sexuality in their school districts. It was his first year teaching at East City High, and as he established himself, he explained that he decided to be open about his queerness to specific adults but not to the students generally. Still, he did not take pains to hide his sexuality. There was a rainbow poster in his classroom, and he had a desk wedge that read, "slay the day." He figured that students who needed to know he was queer would put it together, and other students would just understand him as an accepting teacher. This strategy was successful, and I witnessed many queer students turn to Mr. Gallagher for support and advice during the year, including asking him to serve as the teacher sponsor for the musical theater club.

When I first arrived in his class in early October, Mr. Gallagher asked students if they knew about gender-neutral pronouns in English. One student excitedly popped up their hand to respond. Then, Mr. Gallagher inquired about these pronouns in French. Students had no idea, and I heard mumblings about how French is too gendered. Mr. Gallagher took out a whiteboard marker and led a quick lesson on pronouns. In French, *elle* is "she," and *il* is "he." More recently, French trans activists and scholars have begun using *iel* as a gender-neutral pronoun. Although it was a month into the school term, this was his first (and only) lesson on gender-neutral pronouns. Mr. Gallagher had not believed it necessary to broach the existence of these pronouns until compelled to do so by the presence of my androgynously gendered body. However, Scarecrow Jones was in Mr. Gallagher's class. When we spoke about this minilesson months later, Scarecrow Jones told me, "The only time anything [related to trans topics] has ever happened is when you were in Mr. Gallagher's class, and he explained the gender-neutral pronoun." Mr. Gallagher cared about queer and trans students. Throughout the year, I witnessed him intervene during lessons if students made hurtful comments, and in the spring, he invited a local nonprofit with two queer gender-nonconforming facilitators to lead a workshop on social justice advocacy. However, by waiting until I arrived to tell students about these pronouns, Mr. Gallagher indicated that this information was only pertinent if it directly affected someone at hand *and* that he would be able to tell if that were the case. This last point is crucial. Though Mr. Gallagher offered accommodations to trans students whom he knew about, he relied on his belief that he could ascertain when a student needed these supports in school. Mr. Gallagher, like the other adults at East City High, understood trans as a visible, legible identity that he would always be able to recognize. This understanding of trans identity demanded significant labor from gender-nonconforming youth. I frame youth's acts of survival and world-building as critical forms of labor they performed throughout the year to navigate and intervene in a school that did not understand or have space for their genders. In this section, I introduce this discussion by situating it within scholarship on care work as well as queer and trans theorizing about gender as work.

A major component of feminist inquiry has been the interrogation of the gendered and racialized dimensions of labor.[37] Much early feminist scholarship on labor interrogated gendered divisions of work into productive and reproductive, paid and unpaid, visible and invisible.[38] Increasingly, questions of visibility, (social) reproduction, and (un)waged labor have been explored through the lens of care and care work.[39] These have served as useful categories for apprehending various kinds of undervalued yet critically necessary work, most often done by women, particularly racialized and immigrant women. In attending to this form of labor, feminist scholars attempted to expose several mechanisms of invisibility at play across multiple facets of society. Scholars examined how care work can be positioned as informal labor and thus relegated to the private, domestic sphere. They likewise interrogated the degradation of this labor when paid. For instance, employers often take advantage of workers because of the assumption that they will be motivated by altruism to provide the best for their patients, even without overtime wages.[40] The devaluing of this labor is inseparable from the workers who perform it.[41] As the feminist scholar Evelyn Nakano Glenn argues, "To the extent that caring is devalued, invisible, underpaid, and penalized, it is relegated to those who lack economic, political, and social power and status."[42] Moreover, the association of care work with marginalized communities shapes societal perceptions of this labor. Since women of color and immigrants perform most of the paid care work in North America, care work is further devalued as unskilled, unimportant labor.

Glenn, frustrated by the degradation of care, draws on research examining the gendered and racialized mechanisms of labor to propose a perspective that respects its role in society. She issues a call for rethinking care work by "defining care as a practice that encompasses an ethic (caring about) and an activity (caring for)."[43] Within this framework, Glenn theorizes care work as a practice that creates relationships and communities. She offers a reimagining of power dynamics in addition to the valuation of care. More recently, scholars in trans studies have further extended the concept of care work, critiquing previous scholarship and inviting engagement with this thinking from a trans perspective. Hil Malatino calls for transing care in his book *Trans Care*. He invites scholars to interrogate how ideas of family "invoked in much of the feminist literature on care labor and care ethics are steeped in forms of domesticity and intimacy that are both White and Eurocentered, grounded in the colonial/modern gender system."[44] Malatino argues that trans people are forced to learn how to care for each other because we are not cared for by normative systems of nurturance and, at times, we are abandoned and rejected by the people who are expected to care for and love us. "Whatever being trans is about, it's decidedly characterized by upheaval and emergence into a social world with shifting and shifted parameters.... Surviving this process means committing to forms of healing that are unthinkable, indeed impossible, without care webs."[45] This scholarship compels a critical expansion of previous thinking on care work by acknowledging the labor involved when, to survive hostile worlds, trans people must create communities of care. In *Fierce, Fabulous, and Fluid*, I build on this thinking to consider how youth were practicing care for themselves in an environment that did not care for them in the ways they needed and desired.

Before delving into youth's care work, I first contend with the labor of gender itself. Queer and trans scholars theorize gender as not simply an individual attestation but an ongoing process that occurs through mechanisms of social recognition.[46] As the sociologist Tey Meadow argues, "Although the lexicon we have for understanding identity imagines it as fixed, as existing in some stable form, ... it makes more sense to view the assumption of a gender category as an interactional, social process, happening in concert with the others from whom we seek recognition."[47]

For gender, self-understanding is paramount, but experiences of gender are likewise informed through social interaction. As I noted, most of the youth in the study were not recognized as trans by others at East City High. This consistent misgendering did not mean that they were not trans. It did, however, affect how they engaged with their genders. For instance, despite how hard Raeyun worked to be legible as a guy, Raeyun shared how he still experienced the world, especially the world of East City High, as a gender-nonconforming person much of the time because of how others read him. Raeyun once encapsulated this complexity by saying, "I'm not like completely [gender nonconforming], but I'm also not like a cis guy, so kind of like midway. Like, I'm part of the binary, but I'm also, like, part of the binary in a weird way." This weirdness illustrates the tensions between theorizing gender solely as an identity and engaging with the importance of embodiment, enactment, and social recognition.[48] Raeyun knew he was trans. He was also deeply aware of how he was gendered by teachers and students at East City High, and this awareness shaped how he moved through the school.

Malatino contributes a necessary layer to theorizing the relationship between gender and social recognition by considering gender as labor.[49] This framework acknowledges the work that is involved in being recognized. Many of the youth had complicated relationships with recognition, simultaneously desiring it and resisting the idea that it was important. Raeyun spoke often about desiring affirmation, and he worked to become recognizable as trans at East City High. Raeyun regularly made decisions based on his understanding of what was necessary to facilitate his legibility as a trans guy. "For me in my own personal experience, I feel, like . . . transitioning is more of a thing for, like, other people—changing my name and doing that stuff and just like letting other people know," Raeyun explained. "I feel like transitioning for, like, myself was just sort of, like, knowing the switch of, like, yeah, I'm not this anymore, like, this is what feels right." For Raeyun, being a trans guy was an awareness he had of his gender, but that self-knowledge then required labor from him to become legible to others. Youth's labor practices were not linear or static, and I attend to both the work youth performed to be recognizable as trans and the labor they performed to refuse recognition. At times, these acts occurred in the same day and even the same period.

In *Trap Door*, Tourmaline, Eric Stanley, and Johanna Burton question the ways visibility and recognition have become privileged as key signs of progress for trans people. They describe our current cultural landscape, contending, "Trans people are offered many 'doors'—entrances to visibility, to resources, to recognition, and to understanding. Yet . . . these doors are almost always also 'traps'—accommodating trans bodies, histories, and culture only insofar as they can be forced to hew to hegemonic modalities."[50]

While Tourmaline, Stanley, and Burton theorize these processes within the fields of art and cultural production, I extend the concepts of *traps* and *doors* to explore these processes within schools. I am interested in the conditions that structured gender legibility and informed youth's relationships to their genders while at East City High. Youth were engaged in their labor practices within a school culture that strived to include and express care for trans youth but only when those youth were visible as trans.

Thinking with *traps* and *doors* facilitates exploring how the welcoming of recognizably trans youth into schools participates in narrowly defining a particular form of transness as the only or "right" way to be trans.

Several trans scholars have questioned the reliance on recognition in mainstream trans politics.[51] In a society that privileges palatable enactments of transness, heightened visibility is not necessarily desirable. When trans bodies are viewed as monstrous, greater visibility only benefits trans and gender-nonconforming people who aspire to and can become less monstrous according to normative ideas about gender. Furthermore, visibility assists surveillance systems and state institutions in working more effectively by making trans people increasingly knowable to power.[52] Aren Aizura offers, "Being a somebody means visibility: becoming a population, becoming a demographic, becoming (part of) a class, becoming clockable. . . . Aspiring to nobodiness, on the other hand, means being with others who are marked as nobody too, finding communality and maybe care."[53]

Those of us who live monstrous lives engage in complex labor connected to gender. This is the labor of survival that youth performed daily at East City High. I focus on three forms of labor that youth performed over the year. The first involved acts of understanding and forgiveness meant to ease their interactions with adults and others at the school who misread and misgendered them. The second was aimed at either becoming more recognizable according to others' understandings of trans identity or trusting their own sense of their genders in refusal of these gendered expectations. However, youth did not just work to survive school. They thrived and flourished. The third form of labor I attend to is world-building. Tourmaline, Stanley, and Burton explain, "in addition to *doors* that are always already *traps*, there are *trapdoors*, those clever contraptions . . . that take you someplace else, often someplace as yet unknown."[54] Over my year at East City High, I witnessed gender-nonconforming youth create trapdoors. These were places of escape and resistance that they built to have somewhere else to exist. They were both physical worlds, like Raeyun and the tech booth, and fantastical spaces like D&D campaigns and gaymances. Youth were motivated by their need and desire for spaces outside the limiting logics of East City High, and they daily performed the caring labor to build and protect their trapdoors from adult surveillance.

Thinking alongside the concept of trapdoors as well as José Muñoz's work on queer utopia, I consider the myriad forms of care work that youth engaged in not only to navigate the cisheteronormativity of East City High but to make queer and trans worlds of their own. I document the ways gender-nonconforming youth at times moved toward *somebodiness* in their interactions at East City High. They tailored their gender expression to become more legible to adults at the school, they dropped they/them pronouns because of their incomprehensibility, and they adjusted their behavior as they moved through different spaces and relationships. I likewise highlight their many complicated desires for *nobodiness*, desires that were most apparent in their acts of world-making. Through caring—for themselves and their genders, for each other and their futures—youth created and cultivated spaces outside adult surveillance that did not require recognition. These were spaces where they could exist in their genders more expansively than elsewhere at East City High.

Gender Is Never Just Gender

Shifting from a focus on risk to interrogating labor invites theorizing on the complexities of youth's experiences in schools and relationships to schooling. In the past decades, youth-focused ethnographers have expanded the fields of gender and sexuality studies by arguing that it is impossible to understand youth's genders without examining how gender intersects with sexuality, race, class, and ability.[55] In *Fierce, Fabulous, and Fluid*, I build on this legacy to consider how ideas governing gender nonconformity are likewise always mediated through systems of oppression, specifically whiteness, settler colonialism, and ability. While many of the youth in the study struggled with feeling "trans enough" and part of the trans community, the constraints youth confronted and the worlds they built were never just about gender.

Though the term "trans" has emerged to describe the experiences of any person who defies gendered expectations, there has been an unspoken whiteness underlying the word from the beginning.[56] In recent years, the growing popularity of the term has coincided with the development of a hierarchy of transnormativity.[57] Nova Bradford and Austin Johnson explain transnormativity as "a regulatory, normative ideology that holds trans people's experiences and identities accountable to a binary, medical framework."[58] This regulatory structure was created, in part, as a result of the imposition of gendered norms and standards on people attempting to access gender-affirming care in early clinical settings.[59] Crucially, this regulation is not exclusive to medical institutions. Normative ideas about legitimate and authentic trans identity exist within trans communities as well. Attending to transnormativity allows for an examination of how boundaries within the North American trans community have contributed to the formation of ideal trans identities that position adherence to medical transition as the most authentic trans experience and privilege a white, thin, andro-masculine able body as the pinnacle of gender nonconformity and gender ambiguity.

Despite these pressures, there is no one way or right way to be trans, and all trans youth navigate shared as well as unique challenges in schools. In this book, I specifically focus on trans youth who openly desired or explored gender nonconformity because these young people are rarely centered in scholarship. Youth's feelings of not being "enough," whether they were describing their experiences of transness, disability, or being mixed race, underscore the regulatory mechanisms of normativity operating at East City High that privileged only particular forms of visible, recognizable difference. Expanding on ethnographies that interrogate the intersectionality of youth's experiences of gender and sexuality, I attend to how hard trans and gender-nonconforming youth worked to navigate schooling structures that did not have space for them.

There was a sense among the youth that being gay or lesbian was increasingly accepted at East City High while gender and sexual ambiguity were still policed, misunderstood, or disregarded. For all the youth, their experiences of gender and sexuality were enmeshed since their queerness was a complicating facet of how they moved through the school as trans. Furthermore, it was impossible and unproductive to disentangle their experiences of homophobia and transphobia. In *Dude, You're a Fag*, an ethnography of high school boys and their use of the "fag" epithet, the sociologist C. J. Pascoe significantly shifted our understanding of how the policing of gender and sexuality is intertwined. Through her analysis of gendered homophobia, Pascoe interrogated how adolescent boys drew on homophobic language to demonstrate their masculine social capital. The boys did not understand their actions as homophobic and, in fact, specifically noted how they would not call known gay youth "fags." Pascoe complicated previous scholarship on masculinities by examining the performance and regulation of "proper" masculinity as entangled with homophobia. However, trans boys have a complex relationship to gendered homophobia. Pascoe observed the importance and regularity of jockeying for masculine status among adolescent cisgender boys, whose essential boyhood was never in question. They moved up and down along a hierarchy of masculinity, an unstable pecking order that affected and reflected their popularity, prowess, and privilege. Despite the jokes, at the end of the day, no one actually doubted they were boys. For Raeyun and Ostrich, queer trans boys and good friends in the study, this was not the case. As I will explore, they were consistently working to prove their boyhood to others at East City High. When they failed to perform "proper" (hetero)masculinity, this behavior not only provoked questions about their sexuality but also prompted doubts about their gender.

Queer theory examines the inextricable relationship between gender and sexuality through the concept of cisheteronormativity, which highlights how the positioning of heterosexuality as normal and dominant comes from the presumption that the most natural way to form sexual, romantic relationships is between men and women. Further, cisheteronormativity underscores the assumption that men and women are the only genders and that they exist in romantic opposition to each other. This concept facilitates an acknowledgment that heterosexuality's dominance relies on (and reproduces) a binary gender system.[60] *Fierce, Fabulous, and Fluid* continues in the legacies of queer and trans theory by attending to the ways that being able to read a person's gender is framed as integral to understanding them as human and, therefore, that many queer and trans people are imagined as outside of humanity, as monsters.[61] In *Gender Trouble* and *Bodies That Matter*, the gender studies scholar Judith Butler theorizes performativity to disrupt the dominant notion of gender as a coherent identity that remains fixed throughout a person's life, arguing instead that gender gains coherence through repetitive, constitutive acts that reproduce an illusion of naturalness. Performativity asserts that a person's legibility is achieved through adherence to socially normative gender and sexual expressions.[62]

Butler has long been critiqued for their inattention to the role of whiteness in constructing and shaping gender legibility. If, as Butler argues, "'persons' only become intelligible through becoming gendered in conformity with recognizable standards of gender intelligibility," then we need to consider the violent ideas, systems, and mechanisms that have created and continue to reify these "recognizable standards."[63] In this book, I interrogate how ideas about gender are never solely about gender. At East City High, teachers, counselors, and administrators relied on racist, colonial, and ableist assumptions and expectations about the meaning of gender (non)conformity to guide their interactions with students. Youth were positioned as trans or not according to frameworks about gender (non)conformity that adults had learned and developed. These ideas were not arbitrary, novel, or benevolent. I draw on scholarship across queer and trans theory, Indigenous studies, and critical disability studies to examine how youth's movements through the school were informed by their experiences as racialized, queer, neurodivergent, and fat students.

In Canada, whiteness cannot be understood separately from settler colonialism: Canada's construction as a white nation relies on the continued (failed) erasure of Indigenous peoples. As Leanne Betasamosake Simpson argues, heteropatriarchy and heteronormativity were part of the *"foundational dispossession force*[,] . . . a direct attack on Indigenous bodies as political orders, thought, agency, self-determination, and freedom."[64] Cisheteronormativity was enforced in Canadian residential schools, is enshrined in law through the Indian Act, is upheld through the predominance of racialized sexual violence, and is policed through settler notions of Indigeneity.[65] Education has a particularly enmeshed relationship with the colonial project, one that has historically been inextricable from the violence of assimilation.[66] Residential schools were developed with the explicit purpose of decimating Indigenous cultures by separating families and prohibiting children from growing into Indigenous adults.[67] In these schools, settlers deployed binary gender to violently discipline children out of their cultures and force them to behave according to white, colonial standards of "appropriate" masculinity and femininity. This violent approach to education reflects the racialized plasticity of how childhood is understood generally.[68] In developmental theory, the concepts of childhood and youth are framed as malleable moments, times when, with "proper" guidance and instruction, young people can be reared into (or out of) what is desired of them.[69]

The imposed white, settler criteria that dictated notions of acceptable gender and sexuality still govern notions of proper masculinity, femininity, and gender conformity in North America. These ideas regarding gender legibility influence views, for instance, on the relationship between gender and fashion, hair length, strength, facial hair, body size, and behaviors. How we read, assess, and police gender legibility, including in schools, remains mired in these paradigms. The processes informing the establishment and maintenance of the gender binary also shape ideas regarding what it means to be trans, locating idealized enactments in whitewashed visions of gender embodiments.

As a thin, white, andro-masculine person, I adhere to the conventional expectations for a gender-nonconforming person. Though I live with a chronic illness, this disability is not typically visible, and conflations of thinness with health, beauty, and success privilege the way my body looks, regardless of how it feels. Moving through East City High, I was visible as nonbinary, while most of the youth in the study were not. This dynamic became evident once while I was talking with Scarecrow Jones. They were explaining how they were consistently misgendered at school because they did not look or behave like other trans youth. "You know," they explained, "I have long hair, and I use the women's washroom." Their exasperation with being misgendered prompted Scarecrow Jones to consider that one possible solution was to express their gender nonconformity according to more recognizable parameters. Scarecrow Jones described how they could work to fit into others' expectations for what it looks like to be trans—they knew what it would take. Despite the ways Scarecrow Jones transgressed gender norms through fashion, as a chubby, Taiwanese person with long hair and not even a hint of facial hair, Scarecrow Jones did not adhere to the white, settler vision of gender ambiguity. Scarecrow Jones wanted to be unreadable to others, but, they explained, "right now the option's kind of been taken away from me, 'cause it's always assumptions, then refuting the assumption. That's how it goes every single time. . . . I think maybe having an ambiguity to [gender] or having a different kind of way to present, . . . that'd be nice." When Scarecrow Jones described their desires for gender ambiguity, I was conscious of how their gaze landed on my body. Scarecrow Jones's awareness of what it would mean for others to recognize their gender nonconformity underscored how gender is always already racialized.

Scholars in critical disability studies have likewise extended theorizing on cisheteronormativity to interrogate its interconnectedness with ableism.[70] The disability scholar Robert McRuer offers compulsory able-bodiedness as a framework for examining how systems concurrently reproduce the dominance of the able and heterosexual body.[71] There is a long history of gender and disability as conceptually entangled, and gender nonconformity specifically has been regulated through ableist practices intended to establish normative standards of embodiment.[72] The disability and Black queer feminist scholar Sami Schalk situates disability politics as "engagement with disability as a social and political rather than individual and medical concern."[73] Through her research, Schalk underscores the necessity of an intersectional approach to disability politics and justice. In particular, she highlights how white supremacy and ableism are theoretically and materially intertwined. In North America, compulsory able-bodiedness is enmeshed in the normative imaginings of the body that police ideas of the healthy, fit, productive citizen.[74] The language of disability has been (and continues to be) used to enact racist and colonial strategies of exclusion through immigration and sterilization policies.[75] To count as a contributing member of the nation (and school), a person must adhere to these standards of ability and health.

Scholars are increasingly drawing on disability studies in research with trans youth, noting the entanglement of sociopolitical impositions on bodies that do not quite fit normative conceptions.[76] In *Fierce, Fabulous, and Fluid*, I interrogate how educators at East City High responded to gender-nonconforming youth with ableist language and ideas that mired transness in discourses of risk and deficit. I concentrate on how the interconnectedness of disability and gender nonconformity exists in schools through the dominance of accommodation practices. To understand the tendrils of youth's gender (il)legibility, it is imperative to acknowledge their differential relationships to the ideas and conditions structuring gender nonconformity at East City High.

Going Back to High School

I was standing in a large, gender-neutral bathroom at a local media arts nonprofit with a video camera trained on the shower curtain. I counted down and then waited. One by one, students streamed out of the tiny shower stall that they had somehow crammed themselves into, doing their best to keep a straight face. Barry, a white, gender-nonconforming grade 12 student, was the last one to emerge. He sashayed out in his skinny jeans and faded gray Beatles T-shirt. He paused in front of my face and gingerly placed his index finger on his lips while looking directly into the camera. He winked. I stopped the tape and yelled, "All clear," and then everyone burst out laughing.

Ms. Varma, Barry's film teacher, had arranged for her classes to spend a few weeks at the nonprofit learning how to produce karaoke videos. In the first session, two facilitators demonstrated how to use a variety of equipment while introducing the students to the genre's key tropes. Then Ms. Varma instructed students to make their own versions of their favorite songs, drawing on archetypal shots and gimmicks in the process. Barry and two of his friends asked me to join their group, which is how I ended up filming students in a bathroom.

There were many ways in which my role at East City High was legible to the adults and students in the school. I was a researcher, and I behaved like a researcher. I presented my study at the first staff meeting of the year. I signed in at the office every morning. I attended classes, clubs, performances, and school events. I was always taking notes. However, there were also many ways that my nonbinary gender and my relationships with the youth eluded recognition. I often blended in while among students, leading adults and youth to regularly ask, "What grade are you in?" Over the course of the year, students, both close to the research and more distant from it, incorporated me into their school lives. As a result, I frequently wound up in situations I had not anticipated would be part of fieldwork, as I did during the karaoke video project. As a nonbinary person, I moved through the school in ways that blurred the boundaries between adulthood and youth. I understood this blurriness as critical since this study hinged on my ability to be welcomed into relationships and invited into spaces that other adults did not gain entry to and, often, were not even aware existed. My role in the school was complicated, and I discuss the myriad ethical quandaries and possibilities of being a nonbinary ethnographer in a methodological appendix. In this section, I further situate this research by considering how I approached the study and my time at East City High. I offer thoughts on ethnography as movement, attending to the methodological decisions I made in order to center accountability to the youth as well as to interrogate gender nonconformity, a fluid topic of study.

I arrived at East City High in the first week of September, and until the end of June, I was present four to five days a week. I worked with six youth at the school, spending entire days moving among their schedules. In addition to classes, I arrived early and went to Breakfast Club, accompanied students to extracurricular activities, and attended band and theater performances. Except with Ms. Man, we all also regularly met up outside of school for interviews or just to hang out. Over the year, Ms. Man and I cultivated an iteration of the study that was very different from what I shared with most of the other youth. We rarely met up outside of school because, as I will examine, Ms. Man believed they had no valuable insights about gender to contribute. With some of the youth, like Vixen and Barry, I ended up spending significantly more time outside of school just playing D&D, chatting, or being read to, rather than conducting interviews. Originally, I had thought interviews would be *the* moments when the students and I delved into the depths of their experiences at school. I quickly realized that these were just times when we could pause and have more intentional conversations to follow up on moments from school, all while eating a lot of snacks. By moving alongside the youth every day, I was constantly learning about their lives, their genders, and the complicated forms of labor they enacted as they navigated the school. Students did not save up their interesting stories or big reveals for our interviews; they told me whatever they wanted, whenever they wanted. Scarecrow Jones would rant about the latest of Mr. Tremblant's many racist, transphobic, and homophobic transgressions as they dropped their backpack into the corner of the drama classroom. Then they would disappear to their table group to entertain their friends before the bell rang. Barry would lean his head against my shoulder in the back of Mr. Hill's classroom during a lesson and scroll through photos of nail art he was considering for prom. Vixen would divulge big life moments while a teacher was momentarily turned away, which often resulted in us getting in trouble for talking in class. Though some of the young people were in classes together and a couple were friends, over time, I came to think of the project as six connected ethnographies. What each young person desired from the project was particular to them and our relationships, and we worked together to imagine each iteration.

Initially, I planned on spending roughly equal time with all students. However, since the youth each had different needs in relation to the study, I quickly gave up this plan. Some students, like Raeyun, Ostrich, Vixen, and Barry, asked that I attend as many of their classes as possible on a daily basis and wanted me to sit next to them. They invited me to their extracurricular activities, their special performances, and then increasingly into their worlds. These students will appear more heavily in the chapters that follow because of how much time we spent together. Other students, like Ms. Man and Scarecrow Jones, were apprehensive about people in the school connecting them with my research. As I noted, Ms. Man in particular maintained a cautious distance to the project, yet they were also often excitedly sliding their sketchbook across the table toward me, eyes locked on my face as I looked through all their gender-bendy and queer art. Every week, I checked in with each young person about how much time they wanted to spend together and which classes they wanted me to attend. Sometimes their needs overlapped and conflicted, and I had to make decisions about which students to accompany. I kept a list of their schedules in my fieldwork notebook and tracked my attendance to ensure that I was spreading out my time.

Though the youth are the focus of this research, schools are age-striated spaces. My days inevitably also involved interactions with many different adults. I regularly observed and engaged with teachers, staff, administrators, and counselors. Several adults at East City High were particularly keen to participate in the study, and they ended up serving as guides for me, providing background knowledge and context about the school and its history. Many adults will appear in the chapters that follow, as they were involved in youth's daily lives at the school and their interactions with the youth are central facets of my interrogation.

Since this project focuses on youth who were not regularly recognized as trans, it was imperative that I was able to move through the school alongside young people without outing them or imposing a trans identity onto them. Therefore, when I arrived at East City High in September, I moved all over the school, attending as many classes in grades 9–12 as possible. I wanted students and teachers to become used to the possibility of my presence. This made it feasible for me to attend a class without anyone knowing I was accompanying a specific student, which is how Scarecrow Jones and Ms. Man felt able and safe to participate in the study without fear of being outed.

At the start of the year, as I was normalizing my presence in classrooms across the school, I intentionally introduced the study as being about gender, believing my nonconforming body would communicate beyond those words. It did, and nonbinary, genderfluid, and trans students started to approach me in a variety of ways. Vixen announced to their entire Social Justice 12 class that they were genderfluid and then looked directly at me; while Ms. Man, who was much less extroverted, asked if I wanted to see their sketchbook and then warned me that it was "very gay." To be part of the study, students just had to identify as gender nonconforming in some way—the bounds of what that entailed and encompassed were entirely up to them.

Ethnography as Movement

The term "school-based ethnography" can give the impression of a static study that occurs entirely encased within the walls of a school. I understand ethnography as movement. In part, this understanding emerges from my fluid approach to ethnography that is both informed by and departs from a long tradition of school-based studies. Following the practice of other school-based ethnographers, I met, recruited, and connected with the youth participants at school.[77] However, given my background as a youth worker, I was likewise inspired by community-based ethnographers who centered their projects on young people instead of the institution of schooling.[78] This positioning was important to be accountable to the youth, who not only invested time and labor in the project but also built community with me as a queer and trans person. I was the only trans adult that many of the youth knew, and our relationships frequently blurred the boundaries of researcher, mentor, and friend. I intentionally aspired to challenge the parameters of school-based ethnography by thinking and researching like a community-based scholar working within a school setting. I further address the importance of this positionality in the methodological appendix.

Beyond my fluid approach to school versus community-based studies, I understand ethnography as movement because this type of inquiry required constant movement. I traveled through the school alongside the six youth, attending classes with students across four grades. The research likewise exceeded the bounds of East City High. We walked around the neighborhood, we went to cafés, we rode buses, we went shopping—basically, we were always moving around together. However, beyond the physical ways we moved, I understand this ethnography as movement because gender nonconformity moves—it is a fluid topic of inquiry. Just as our relationships with each other evolved and changed over the year, all our relationships to gender fluctuated, deepened, and shifted during the project. I grounded this study in queer methodology to enable this type of movement. Queer methodologies are not just the study of queer topics or people. Rather, a queer ethnography facilitates the interrogation of the normative ideas informing youth's experiences in schools and how they interact with and resist oppressive systems of power.[79] *Fierce, Fabulous, and Fluid* is a queer ethnography that examines a moving, ever-changing topic, and therefore, I endeavored to approach the study in a manner that invited the necessary fluidity.

Throughout the year, the youth and I reimagined and reworked the study to resist ideas about gender that would have forced them to concretize their identities and experiences. At the close of *Histories of the Transgender Child*, Jules Gill-Peterson argues, "If, in the twenty-first century, we adults really desire to learn to care for the many transgender children in our midst, we need to learn first . . . what it means to wish that there *be* trans children, that to grow trans and live a trans childhood is not merely a possibility but a happy and desirable one. And we need to come into this desire *now*, not in the future."[80]

Fierce, Fabulous, and Fluid takes this call seriously. The youth and I worked together to create a study that desired transness and gender nonconformity. Desire is methodologically complicated, especially in schools that do not desire trans youth. Cultivating desire meant resisting the ethnographic pull for a coherent narrative that could capture a singular truth about youth's genders. The refusal of certainty and rejection of a coherent narrative is a tenet of queer methodology and especially important in research with gender-nonconforming youth, who have historically and consistently had narratives imposed onto their lives and bodies.[81] Within education, medicine, law, and literature, discursive frameworks position gender-nonconforming youth as at-risk, too young to know their genders, and trapped within the "wrong body."[82] These narratives are powerful, and they participate in shaping youth's understandings of their transness and their bodies. Riki Anne Wilchins specifically denounces ethnographers for their objectification of trans people.[83] She criticizes purportedly objective scholarly approaches as immoral, lambasting how they politicize trans bodies, choices, and desires. History is replete with scholars, doctors, and others who have framed trans people as curiosities to study and understand. This discursive and material imposition likewise exists in schools.

A queer ethnography that moves with young people through their days enables the generation of layers of stories and layers of genders, as opposed to *a* story or *a* gender. I had to move with them as they navigated and reimagined their genders in response to different contexts. By rejecting the need for certainty about their genders and instead endeavoring to invite fluidity into the study, I was striving to be accountable to my community and to honor the youth as well as my trans ancestors. These intentions remained paramount when I left the field and began to grapple with analysis.

Analyzing Fluid Data

By the time I left East City High on a hot day in the third week of June, I had generated ten months of field notes, recorded hundreds of hours of interviews, and collected several folders worth of handouts and course materials. As I prepared to immerse myself in these data, I remained focused on a central tension of this work. Analyzing data is often oriented toward codifying understanding and producing knowledge. However, the gender-nonconforming youth desired unreadability. I had to approach analysis in a manner that could document their labor without attempting to stabilize or make legible their unreadability.

In the postqualitative turn, scholars critique an overreliance on coding in qualitative research, arguing against the essentialism of this analytical practice.[84] Coding solidifies data into knowable categories and concepts. However, data are not fixed nor stable. Rather, like gender, they are fluid and changing. The antiessentialist rejection of coding questions conventional understandings of data as representing "real and true knowledge."[85] Further, Eve Tuck and K. Wayne Yang reject coding because this analytical method extends from the notion that researchers can and should make knowledge claims.[86] Part of their argument is based on the overcoding of Indigenous communities. I was invested in rejecting coding because I was wary of stabilizing gender-nonconforming youth into concrete categories of knowing and because, like many other marginalized communities, these youth are overcoded. Critically, this overcoding of trans youth is part of how they become tethered to risk, vulnerability, and struggle.

As I sat at my desk, feeling overwhelmed by all the data, I wrote out my priorities: being accountable to the young people who shared their lives with me for a year, challenging a linear retelling of the research that would provide the illusion of a coherent trajectory of growth over the project, and resisting the desire to stabilize the youth into recognizable categories. I spent weeks experimenting with different approaches to analysis, searching for a practice that both honored my priorities and was practical for the amount of data I had generated. I tried and abandoned several forms of analysis before turning to mind maps. I arrived at mapping without the intention of creating a cartography of East City High or the youth. Critical geographers have used mental mapping as a method of data generation. It augments an interrogation of "where things happen and what is important about them to the place, person, and relationship between them."[87] Though much research discusses what mental mapping makes possible during fieldwork, I extend this potential to analysis. I wanted an analytical method that was mutable and visual, one that did not force me to begin in September and end in June as if our relationships, learning, and experiences were chronological and teleological. Mapping's multidimensionality highlighted the complexities and fluidity of the ways youth moved through spaces and created different relationships with their genders, teachers, and schooling as they went.

I created maps for every class I attended, for hallways and lunch hangouts, and for performances and events. I made maps for nonphysical spaces as well, like Instagram and the stories youth wrote. Working with mind maps facilitated a focus on the spaces in which I interacted with the youth. Through mapping, I could visualize and engage with how the youth reimagined and reworked their genders as they moved from space to space and relationship to relationship. Their labor was a constitutive element of the maps, filling my documents with their interventions, refusals, and world-building. The act of making and spending time with the maps underscored that certain aspects of schooling required additional labor from the youth. Importantly, the maps are not a cartography of a year in the life; they are a way to read the myriad, complicated labor that youth performed as they moved through East City High. Rather than stabilizing the gender-nonconforming youth into concrete categories by coding them, mapping the spaces we inhabited together allowed me to make the conditions of their lives knowable.

Organization of the Book

When I first arrived at East City High, I got lost all the time. I was constantly exiting a staircase, unsure of which part of a hallway I was about to enter, or frantically arriving to a class as the bell rang because I had gotten turned around. I had to become comfortable with having no idea where I was going most of the time. I eventually learned the shortcuts and established a level of familiarity with the place that surprised me. By the second term, I felt nearly at ease moving through the vast expanse of the campus. I learned East City High by moving alongside the six youth in the study. I walked with them, letting them lead me where they wanted to go. They showed me where to sit, instructed me on which teachers to be careful around, invited me into the spaces they considered special, and taught me how to navigate the school. I learned how to exist at East City High by moving alongside these youth and, as you read, you will likewise move through East City High guided by where the youth decided to lead me and the ways they interacted with the school.

In chapter 1, I return to the "feel good" diversity politics that reigned at East City High.[88] To understand youth's labor in relation to cisheteronormativity, it is imperative first to reckon with the sociocultural context that promoted a particular approach to diversity and inclusion at East City High. I begin with a discussion of Canadian multiculturalism and its role in constructing white people as tolerant and accepting of racialized others.[89] In this context, white teachers' promotion of diversity becomes an act associated with good intentions toward inclusion and equality. I think with education scholars to consider how multiculturalism is enacted within schools, attending to the ways teachers' good intentions and investment in benign diversity uphold practices of whiteness. Further, I connect this inquiry with Ahmed's research on how institutional diversity practices obscure racism.[90] I explore the many ways East City High was committed to promoting diversity that acknowledged the "right" forms of difference while simultaneously erasing hostile elements of schooling. This diversity work relied on teachers', counselors', and administrators' insistence that their niceness and good intentions could deflect the possibility of violence and harm.

In chapter 2, I focus on accommodation approaches as the dominant strategy to include trans students in schools. I consider how this framework for including trans students emerged from disability law and still follows ableist paradigms of belonging that place the onus on individuals to "fit in" to oppressive institutions. Educators at East City High attempted to open doors for trans youth by providing accommodations, such as name changes and their choice of locker room in PE. However, only certain youth could ever access these opportunities because accommodation practices remain invested in a binary gender system. In this chapter, I explore how such practices are only tenable for gender-nonconforming youth who are, intend to, or can transition to another recognizable gender identity. I highlight PE as a particularly illustrative site for this examination, given its continued reliance on gendered notions of ability. Moreover, I analyze the two main trans-inclusive documents that guided accommodation practices at East City High, focusing on youth's interactions with these materials. I am primarily interested in how these resources shaped ideas about what it meant to be trans at school.

In the already extensive research on the cisheteronormativity of schools and schooling, North American schools are positioned as dangerous spaces for trans youth, with scholars enumerating the many harms that can befall a young person in a school just because of their gender.[91] Though there were many instances of direct, intentional, and violent transphobia during my year at East City High, I am interested in the ways that a cultural context that demands tolerance only at the level of interpersonal interaction obscured the less explicit, more insidious workings of transphobia in relation to gender-nonconforming youth.[92] In the final three chapters, I explore the three forms of labor that youth performed over the year to underscore how hard they had to work to navigate and reject elements of schooling that did not serve them. In chapter 3, I build on my discussion of East City High's approach to diversity and inclusion to examine how Canadian multiculturalism and polite diversity created a context in which youth were compelled to recognize and affirm the "good" intentions of educators who consistently misgendered them, misunderstood them, and collapsed the possibilities of their genders. Youth daily interacted with educators' good intentions by putting in the work to understand and forgive adults' transphobia. Furthermore, teachers, counselors, and administrators placed the onus on gender-nonconforming youth to reframe oppressive moments as misunderstandings or even acts of care. These dynamics relied on and reproduced an understanding of trans identity as risky and undesirable.

In chapter 4, I consider how gender-nonconforming youth worked to make themselves legible (or not) within adults' narrow conceptions of trans identity. In exploring the labor that youth performed to be recognized as trans and gender nonconforming, I turn to the ways they both endeavored to trust in and desire their own knowledge of their genders and worked to facilitate others' sense of them as trans. I discuss their shifting relationships with fashion, pronouns, and scientific explanations of gender as well as the seemingly insignificant daily moments in which youth negotiated their genders in relation to schooling. In these often-mundane interactions, gender-nonconforming youth navigated unobserved complexities and made challenging decisions, often fully aware of the cisheteronormative constraints and conditions of schooling.

Finally, in chapter 5, I turn to youth's practices of world-making. Frequently unnoticed was the labor that youth performed to construct ways of existing that were unrecognizable to the adults at the school. At times alone and at times collaboratively, gender-nonconforming youth at East City High worked not just to understand and resign themselves to the circumstances and limitations of the school but to create trapdoors—spaces that did not require them to show up the same way from hour to hour or day to day.[93] These were spaces where they could be flamboyantly gay trans men who gushed about wearing halter tops or long-haired, nonbinary, mixed kids who sometimes did not know if they were having a boy day until they went to bed that night. Gender-nonconforming youth created both physical and fantastical trapdoors where they could exist in relation to their genders in ways that adults in the school either did not notice or could not understand. Their practices of world-making were often undetected because they were intentionally happening in spaces that were tucked away, peripheral, and, at times, imaginary.

I end by returning to the relationship between risk and desire. I question the ways risk continues to be associated with queer and trans youth, from both those who are interested in censoring gender and sexuality and those who are intent on building inclusive schools. In North America, we are currently witnessing a heightened conversation regarding the bodies, experiences, and lives of queer and trans youth. There is a proliferation of fearmongering about their existence, leading to district-wide book bans, the blocking of gender-affirming health care, and legislation that criminalizes discussions of gender and sexuality in schools. Often, this condemnation of queer and trans issues in schools is happening alongside the denouncing of antiracist teaching and learning. These intertwined denunciations are mired in widespread understandings of adolescence as a risky period of life and the belief that youth need adult protection to be safely guided toward adulthood. However, the six youth I spent a year moving alongside did not predominantly understand themselves and their genders through discourses of risk and harm. Rather, they worked hard to build worlds at East City High where gender nonconformity was not defined by suffering. I share their ideas on reimagining schools and schooling in ways that invite this capaciousness. Their thinking illustrates the potential of a pedagogy of trans desire in schools, and I close by calling on educators to turn away from concern and instead cultivate desire for trans and gender-nonconforming youth.

1

East City High's Diversity Culture

Toward the end of a spring day, I was having a conversation with Madame Blanchet, a French Immersion teacher. We were perched on tables in her classroom during the last few moments before the bell rang to signal that her prep period was over. After a brief pause in our chat, she walked over and leaned toward me, almost conspiratorially, to whisper that she had discovered that a group of grade 9 boys in the French Immersion cohort had been sexually assaulting the same girl for weeks. The girl took a medical leave, but the boys remained in school. None of the student's teachers were notified of the violent events surrounding her prolonged absence. Madame Blanchet explained that when teachers discovered what had happened, they wanted to write a letter to send home to parents about the situation, both so parents would be aware and to urge them to speak to their kids. When one of the teachers showed the letter to the principal, Ms. Fraser, for approval, as was policy, she was prohibited from disseminating it. Madame Blanchet told me that Ms. Fraser would not let them "because of the optics." Informing parents that this type of violent incident had occurred at school would shatter East City High's image as safe, progressive, and inclusive. During the year, I saw swastikas painted over, students tear down and burn the posters of the Gender and Sexuality Alliance (GSA), rampant anti-Black racism, and innumerable instances of oppressive language and behavior from adults and students. Individuals may have been spoken to behind closed doors, but the school carried on without reckoning with these behaviors as a part of its culture or grappling with them on a larger scale.

In the introduction, I described East City High as invested in representing itself as progressive, a stance that was associated with the school's promotion of diversity and inclusion. The school was proud to highlight acts of *fun* diversity, such as Ms. Man's snake design, for these moves bolstered this notion without forcing a conversation about oppression within the school. The incident that Madame Blanchet shared with me contradicted this vision; therefore, the administrators treated the sexual assault as an aberration to be hushed up rather than important information about problems that currently affected students. The school's image relied on the perception that its official embrace of diversity indicated it had moved past and resolved issues of injustice and violence. In this chapter, I explore East City High's "feel good" relationship to diversity.[1] Thinking alongside Ahmed, I read the school's approach as following a "cultural enrichment model" that emphasized the celebration of diversity but was unable to reckon with systemic inequities.[2] I attend to the ways diversity circulated through official channels at the school as well as how several teachers and students interacted with the tensions generated by this approach. My use of the term "diversity" is expansive in order to incorporate how "diversity" was taken up in conversations at the school, as well as the ways this idea has been engaged by other teachers in scholarship. At East City High, "diversity" was often employed as a catch-all phrase to mean acceptance of any form of deviation from the hegemonic norm. Educators in Angelina Castagno's ethnography examining teachers and the reproduction of whiteness through niceness had similar discussions and conversations about who is captured by multicultural education.[3] Castagno specifically noted educators' questions about whether these frameworks included gender and sexual diversity. Therefore, I include discussion of diversity related to Indigeneity, race, gender, and sexuality.

To understand the work that gender-nonconforming youth performed while moving through East City High, it is integral first to interrogate the frameworks structuring and demanding their labor. I examine East City High's cultural context across chapters 1 and 2, beginning with the school's approach to diversity. Probing East City High's "feel good" approach to diversity necessitates engaging with the ways niceness has come to inform this cultural context. To do so, I first situate this analysis within Canadian multiculturalism, asserting that nationalist ideologies that position Canadians as "nice" and "accommodating" contribute to the school's understanding of how to appear diverse and inclusive.[4] I continue with an examination of one-off assemblies meant to celebrate diversity in action and a staff meeting that the administrators convened in response to a rise in overt anti-Black racism. On a smaller scale, the school's understanding of and approach to diversity contributed to the imperative to accept youth whom adults recognized as trans. This dynamic was informed by the relationship between niceness and whiteness: nice educators who believed gender nonconformity to be associated with risk endeavored to include visibly trans youth in the school, even though they did not desire youth to be queer and trans.

How to Be Nice

Mr. Hill's classroom was on the fourth floor of East City High and covered in social justice posters and displays that declared, "Silence Promotes Racism" and "This Is a Homophobia Free Zone." Mr. Hill taught Social Justice 12, an elective unique to British Columbia.[5] In the middle of March, Barry and I walked into the classroom and saw Mr. Hill writing the following questions on the whiteboard: "Overall, do you think racism in the US has gotten better or worse compared to 40 years ago? In what ways has it gotten better? In what ways has it gotten worse? In what ways has racism in Canada gotten better? In what ways has racism in Canada gotten worse?"

As Barry and I took seats in the back, Mr. Hill explained that, though belated, he was beginning a unit to address racism and celebrate Black History Month. The questions on the board betrayed his approach to the topic. Throughout the year, Mr. Hill bolstered the fallacy of Canada as less violent and more benevolent than the United States by frequently locating lessons on oppression within the United States. This was a common tactic at East City High. With a few notable exceptions, when teachers discussed police brutality, anti-Black racism, rape culture, and other forms of discrimination and violence, they frequently located these issues and their historical roots in the United States. This move "is part of the foundational myth that declares Canada to be, and to always have been, a more tolerant country than the United States."[6] An integral element of this tolerance is Canada's relationship to multiculturalism, which asserts that embracing cultural diversity is fundamental to being Canadian.

Multiculturalism has been involved in Canadian educational practices and policies since before it became an official government policy in 1988.[7] Following the world wars, as Canada sought to establish an independent national identity, it created the Citizenship Act, which included the development of models to imagine and consolidate citizenship. Integral to these was the notion of cultural diversity as uniquely Canadian. As a result, the first multicultural educational programs were patriotic initiatives intended to instill these values in immigrants.[8] With the adoption of multiculturalism as an official government policy, it became further ensconced within Canadian national identity. Multiculturalism still contains this sense of instructing immigrants, who are presumed to be racialized others, on how to be Canadian. The sociologist Sunera Thobani explains that, through multiculturalism, "white subjects were constituted as tolerant and respectful of difference and diversity, while non-white people were instead constructed as perpetually and irremediably monocultural, in need of being taught the virtues of tolerance and cosmopolitanism under white supervision."[9]

Thobani credits multiculturalism with creating the notion of the visible minority in Canada because it reproduces the nation as white while simultaneously constructing Canada as defined by its acceptance of (racialized) difference. Through the widespread espousal of this ideology, it is integral to the national imaginary that difference is tolerated. However, it is likewise evident who is positioned as "different" (racialized, immigrant people) and, therefore, who needs tolerance. Canada, thus, becomes a nation of nice, tolerant white people.

As part of the Black History Month unit, Mr. Hill distributed a twenty-one-page packet to the students on the civil rights movement entirely focused on the United States. Though Canada has its own civil rights history and remains a deeply racist nation, the lesson did not touch on these topics. In the packet, Mr. Hill had reformatted a forty-two-slide presentation into a fill-in-the-blank assignment for the students. The students were instructed to read the slide and write in the correct information as he projected it on the board. When Mr. Hill arrived at the slide on Rosa Parks, a few of the students turned to each other and asked, What about Viola Desmond? Viola Desmond is known as one of the instigators of the civil rights movement in Canada. A hair stylist from Halifax, she was traveling through New Glasgow, Nova Scotia, with her husband when they were forced to pause due to car troubles. They went to see a film at the Roseland Theatre, where there was no official policy of segregation, but it was understood locally that only white people sat on the main floor. Not seeing a sign, Viola Desmond sat in a good seat and was asked to leave. She refused and was forcibly removed and arrested. Viola Desmond fought the arrest, but she was convicted of tax evasion since the seat she had paid for cost less than the seat she occupied.

Two students, Eliza and Lily, started calling to each other across the back of the classroom, checking facts about Desmond. Lily was one of the only Black students in the class, and, frustrated, she interjected, saying, "We need to talk about Canada." Mr. Hill did not hear her, but Eliza, one of Mr. Hill's most outspoken critics, loudly interrupted the lesson to demand, "What about Viola Desmond?" Mr. Hill paused the slide show, agreeing that she was important, and asked the class if anyone knew her story. Lily raised her hand and shared what she knew of Desmond's resistance. Then Mr. Hill returned to the slide show.

In predominantly focusing on the United States, Mr. Hill reinforced the myth of the United States as a nation of racism and violence in contrast to Canada, a peaceful, benevolent nation that welcomed enslaved people fleeing from the South. Though students interjected during his lessons by asking for Canadian content, they were also well versed in the language of multiculturalism. During the class discussion on whether racism was getting better or worse, several racialized students first noted that they live in a "multicultural city" and therefore "don't experience racism." However, later in that class, as well as over the course of the unit, these same students shared experiences of racism, both within the city and at East City High. Their conversations illustrated the tensions between what they were learning and living. Students were taught that multiculturalism meant a society free from racism, yet they also experienced racism. Unable to fully reconcile these realities, they lived in the uncomfortable discordance that multiculturalism produced.

The dominance of multiculturalism as integral to the Canadian national identity influences schools and their understanding of the important role diversity plays in education and school culture. Diversity is not simply a value—it is fundamental to being Canadian. However, as Thobani argues, "Multiculturalism avoided recognition of the critical intersection of institutional power and interpersonal forms of racism, demanding only tolerance at the level of interpersonal interactions."[10] This framework obscures systemic violence and harm, promoting the notion that educators can overcome institutionalized forms of injustice, such as racism, through their embrace of cultural diversity. As I will explore throughout the chapters that follow, this perspective was common at East City High. Adults relied on the presumption of their good intentions to ameliorate and excuse their oppressive actions.

Scholarship in education has previously explored the intertwined role of whiteness, niceness, and good intentions in shaping school culture.[11] Scholars document the many ways these dynamics operate in schools, notably through the enactment of policy, narratives about learning loss and the achievement gap, and the denial of the racist mechanisms that shape disciplinary decisions.[12] A focus on educators' best intentions erases the many ways racism, especially anti-Blackness and anti-Indigeneity, and ableism and cisheteronormativity are reconstituted through everyday schooling practices. In a study on the discourses people employed when discussing their experiences of supporting gender-nonconforming youth in public schools in British Columbia, Hélène Frohard-Dourlent notes, "The ways educators were invested in producing themselves as caring, open-minded adults also made it difficult for them to articulate their implication in systems of power."[13] While interacting with and advocating for gender-nonconforming students, administrators and teachers understood themselves as nice people acting with good intentions. This perspective acted to obscure the impacts of their behavior on students. East City High's nearly ubiquitous embrace of multicultural ideals shaped its particular approach to diversity. Teachers, counselors, and administrators, motivated by good intentions, trusted that their belief in East City High's commitment to diversity would remove any possibility of harm from or related to schooling. This cultural work relied on and obscured the violent conditions of East City High, including the interconnected structures of white supremacy, cisheteronormativity, ableism, and settler colonialism.

Culturally Rich, Feeling Good

There was an expectation that certain problems did not exist at East City High, especially given the school's location in a progressive neighborhood of a progressive city in multicultural Canada. This idea was connected to people's belief that transphobia, racism, and other oppressions were not "nice" and therefore had no place within such a forward-looking institution. Scarecrow Jones described this reasoning to me once when we were discussing their experiences of racism in school, and they sarcastically mentioned that racism officially did not exist at East City High because "technically" teachers were "not allowed" to be racist anymore. "They always talk like there's no problem," Scarecrow Jones told me. "They never address the problem that there are people who are homophobic, there are people who are transphobic, there are people who are racist." Scarecrow Jones paused before adding, "It's not always the students. Like, they always leave that out too. It's not always the students."

Scarecrow Jones was begrudgingly enrolled in the French Immersion program at East City High. They identified as poor, which put them at odds with many of the more privileged students in that specialized track. Scarecrow Jones loved theater and writing and almost never got through an entire sentence without swearing. I could always spot them in a crowd by their top hat. (Confuse it with a fedora at your peril: Scarecrow Jones had strong feelings about the distinction.) At the time of this conversation, Scarecrow Jones and I were sitting together in the cafeteria after school, and they were lamenting the recent loss of a secret Instagram account they had created and managed. Through this account, Scarecrow Jones had collected the racist remarks of Mr. Tremblant, their least favorite teacher. Scarecrow Jones had made the account as an anonymous venting space that allowed them to use humor to deal with and expose their teacher's racism. Scarecrow Jones, proud of their work, took out their phone to show me screenshots of old posts. When Mr. Tremblant discovered the account, he reprimanded all his classes and reported it to the administration. He was livid that any student could perceive him as racist. As Scarecrow Jones explained, there was a pervasive belief that racism did not exist at East City High because the school had taken an official stance against it. Despite the antiracist posters that lingered in a few hallways and the school's official support of diversity and inclusion, students' experiences of the school exposed a much different reality.

The pervasive belief that racism did not exist at East City High was a carefully curated stance informed by the ideology that "Canadians are a pleasant and accommodating people" and that this pleasantness necessarily involves valuing cultural diversity.[14] This position was an official part of the school's culture and approach, and was enshrined as a key tenet of its mission statement: "East City High provides a safe, nurturing and stimulating environment in which students are given the opportunity to develop their intellectual, social, ethical, aesthetic, physical and emotional intelligences; to respect the individual, embrace diversity, and participate in the human community."

Beyond this statement, administrators and other adults regularly spoke of diversity during school-sanctioned events, such as the assemblies I discuss later in this chapter. The school's persistent and official promotion of diversity reflects a "feel good" model, wherein "the very talk about diversity allows individuals to feel good, creating the impression that we have 'solved it.'"[15] Ahmed explains that the institutionalization of diversity promotes individual forms of difference as symbolic of that institution's commitment to inclusion, without investment in systemic change or acknowledgment of the way marginalized bodies are targeted for exclusion.[16] Instead, individuals come to represent and embody both difference and the promise of inclusion. Returning to Thobani's critiques of multiculturalism, this engagement of diversity reproduces a population in need of tolerance and a population in the position of celebrating and enjoying their acceptance of difference.

Though schools may devote funding, time, and staff to diversity projects, these endeavors rarely challenge the systemic forms of oppression that marginalize and police the very people meant to benefit from these projects. Rather, the promotion of diversity exists alongside the maintenance of racialized, gendered, and sexualized violence. Ahmed argues, "The use of diversity as an official description *can be* a way of maintaining rather than transforming existing organizational values."[17] In the rest of the chapter, I examine how diversity circulated as an official value at East City High through a discussion of one-off assemblies meant to celebrate marginalized communities in the school and a close look at a staff meeting held in response to escalating anti-Black racism among white teachers.

The Indigenous Awareness Week Assembly

The All Nations room was on the third floor down the same mini hallway as the gender-neutral bathroom. Sometimes when I was sitting inside, I would see Ostrich head to the bathroom. Ostrich was a white, fat, neurodivergent grade 11 student who loved superhero movies, snakes, spiders, and video games. He always poked his head into the room in case I was there. Ms. Mooseknuckle and Ms. Smith, who coordinated the space, would then invite him in for a snack and check-in.[18] Ms. Mooseknuckle taught students how to bead, make bannock, and weave cedar graduation caps. Ms. Smith helped with homework and was constantly running all over the school liaising with staff, advocating for students, and trying to help teachers integrate Indigenous content into their lessons. At lunch, Ms. Mooseknuckle and Ms. Smith played cards with the students. These games got raucous and competitive. Ms. Mooseknuckle and I had a rivalry in speed: we tallied our points on the whiteboard over the entire school year. When I lost, I had to bring in homemade baked goods for everyone.

The All Nations room, which primarily supported Indigenous students, was called the All Nations room in order to be welcoming and inclusive of *all* students. Ms. Mooseknuckle explained that they used "all" to ensure students knew that they could access the space regardless of whether they were Indigenous. There were a number of settler students who regularly came by: some to hang out with their Indigenous friends at lunch or during spares (free periods that grade 11 and 12 students had in their schedules), some nerdier younger students who preferred the quiet of the All Nations room to the rowdiness of the cafeteria, and some students who just really liked Ms. Mooseknuckle and Ms. Smith. There was a Muslim student who came between classes and used the room for prayer.

Positioning the space as welcoming to all was a "nice" move, and in accordance with Canadian multiculturalism, it aligned with East City High's general promotion of reconciliation. In Canada, the current era of reconciliation has its roots in the official inquiries established by the Truth and Reconciliation Commission, which was formed in response to the 2006 Indian Residential Schools Settlement Agreement.[19] This formal process involved listening to residential school survivors, an action that underscored the role of educational spaces in perpetuating settler colonial violence specifically onto the bodies of Indigenous children.[20] The Canadian educational system has an especially complicated relationship with the idea and practice of reconciliation. Schools have been explicitly used as sites to impose settler strategies of erasure and dispossession. Despite an individual school's uptake of the language of reconciliation, an actual reckoning would require the educational system to confront its historical and ongoing complicity in reproducing violence against Indigenous peoples. In schools, drawing on the language of reconciliation without addressing the institutionalized racism and settler structures that still organize schooling reflects a cultural enrichment model. Schools celebrate their acknowledgment of the importance of reconciliation while likewise believing that they exist in a moment that has moved past the harms of colonialism. This approach works to obscure systemic issues that reify anti-Indigeneity.

While East City High did not avoid Canada's colonial history, teaching and learning about colonialism were overwhelmingly historical. Teaching about past atrocities does not preclude the possibility of interrogating the present. However, a presumption of good intentions prohibits acknowledging the ways education and schooling remain mired in and informed by white, settler expectations about who students are and how adults should interact with youth. The education scholars Amanda Lewis and John Diamond examined how these types of expectations shape racist disciplinary processes in schools, with teachers consistently behaving with the best of intentions yet privileging whitewashed expectations for success, behavior, and expression.[21] These tensions were present at East City High, where nice teachers balked at speaking too directly about current and ongoing colonial violence in order to preserve the perception of the school as safe and inclusive for all students. As such, students learned about residential schools, but rarely did teachers examine the ongoing settler violence of the Canadian nation.

Every March, East City High hosted an Indigenous Awareness Week. This week was celebrated at most schools in the district. From conversations with students and Ms. Spensor, an Indigenous woman who taught British Columbia First Nations (BCFN), Continuing Indigenous Studies, and English, I learned about past iterations of the event. The year before I arrived, Ms. Spensor had organized the assembly that concludes the week and supported two Indigenous students from one of her classes to lead it. The assembly had been a fiasco. The organizers faced intense backlash from teachers and students who railed against the content and tone of the event. Settler students and teachers denounced the assembly for being racist against white people. While people were willing to acknowledge that Canadians had acted badly in the past, many were angered by what they perceived as the event's accusatory tone. They responded by attacking Indigenous peoples generally for attempting to access special privileges. Further, teachers and students used vitriolic language and anti-Indigenous slurs to censure Ms. Spensor and the two students for their role in perpetuating antiwhite racism.

In response, Ms. Spensor, Ms. Mooseknuckle, and Ms. Smith strategized for weeks in preparation for the next Indigenous Awareness Week. They were justifiably nervous about a repeat of the previous year's accusations, ire, and turmoil. A month before the assembly, Ms. Smith visited all of Ms. Spensor's Indigenous courses to host brainstorming sessions and enlist the help of willing students to organize the event. In the BCFN class I attended with Vixen, Ms. Spensor and Ms. Smith facilitated a conversation about the vicious backlash they had received and the challenges of hosting another assembly. The students identified framing as a primary issue: previously, the assembly focused on how much people did not know about settler colonialism, and students wanted to repackage the event. One student encapsulated their updated intention in the following terms: "To focus on education, not from the perspective of emphasizing how much people don't know but how they [in the class] didn't know things and how much they've learned [by taking Ms. Spensor's classes]." Rather than presenting material that was critical of settler colonialism, the students intended to celebrate their experience of learning. They explained their hope that emphasizing what they had learned over the year would encourage more folks to take the course.

Ms. Spensor and Ms. Smith were enthusiastic about this rebranding. During this brainstorming session, Ms. Spensor wondered out loud, "Would it be good for white students to talk so students knew [the courses] were okay for them?" This approach echoed a priority from the students: they wanted to make it clear that Ms. Spensor's classroom was a safe space for learning. The class decided that this year, primarily white settler students would lead the assembly and highlight their learning trajectory. Students would first emphasize how little they had previously understood about their relationship to settler colonialism. Then they would be able to underscore how, even though they previously thought of colonialism as past, they learned that they benefit daily from this structure. They would culminate their presentations by sharing the ways that learning about settler colonialism had inspired them to become good allies.

In this discussion, a safe learning space was defined as a classroom that is welcoming to all students. However, thinking again with Thobani's discussion of multiculturalism, this "all" was disingenuous, for the student body was presumed to be white, settler students. The material, therefore, needed to connect with their experience of learning about settler colonialism. Ms. Spensor had struggled the previous year because she centered Indigenous students during a week she had understood as a celebration of Indigeneity. In planning the current iteration, she pivoted, recognizing that this "awareness" assembly was in fact intended to enrich settler students' relationship with these topics. Hoping to avoid the vitriol of the previous year, Ms. Spensor and Ms. Smith encouraged the students to create an event that would not challenge white people's understandings of themselves as good settlers. Students discussed their plans to share uplifting stories of their learning journeys, culminating in their personal experiences of becoming "good" allies committed to reconciliation. Throughout this conversation, safety was defined from the perspective of white, settler students. The aim was to communicate to the general student population that it was safe to take Ms. Spensor's courses, even though she is an Indigenous woman who teaches about Indigenous topics. However, when the intention is to uphold the safety of all students, those students with the most access to privilege will have their safety most protected.

During the study, I came to understand Ms. Spensor's classroom as one of the safer spaces at East City High because she continuously worked to cultivate a place where students learned how to confront racism and violence. Her classroom was covered in antiracist posters and inspirational quotes from activists and writers. She had a big, framed poster above the whiteboard quoting Rosa Parks as saying, "Nah." She loved Prince and had memorabilia and multiple gender-bendy posters of him around the room. Ms. Spensor, unlike most other teachers at the school, took an active stance against East City High's discursive niceness. She did not trust in Canadian multiculturalism to keep marginalized students safe and instead worked to intervene in the normal day-to-day life at East City High, in small and significant ways. For instance, she operated a chip store out of a filing cabinet by the door in her classroom.

She kept it stocked with small bags of chips so students could pop by whenever they were hungry, drop in fifty cents, and take a bag or five, as was Vixen's favorite move. Partway through the year, during a prolonged standoff between Ms. Spensor and one of the vice principals over possible cuts to the First Nations curriculum, the administration shut down her chip operation.

On Fridays, Ms. Spensor started class with life lessons. Sometimes she approached these lessons with levity, using them as opportunities to impart practical advice, such as when she encouraged all students to get their eyebrows threaded. Other times, she attempted to prepare students for inevitable moments of pain, hardship, and grief, such as when she shared her experience of losing her father. When she relayed this story, bringing the whole class to tears, she was explicit about how racism had contributed to her father's death. Another day, Ms. Spensor acknowledged that what students learned in her course might be unsettling. She discussed how it was uncomfortable to reckon with the idea that the educational system we have all been participating in was not set up for everyone to succeed. Ms. Spensor, arms out to the class, named this lesson "difficult knowledge." She never shied away from openly discussing racism and anti-Indigeneity in her classroom, including her own experiences of racism at East City High.

This approach to pedagogy, racism, and "difficult knowledge" built trust with her students. So, in the spring, when several white teachers used the n-word in class, students went to Ms. Spensor for help. She offered refuge to Black students and provided a place for them to finish their terms, making it clear that they did not have to return to classrooms led by teachers who spewed violence against them. The administration was displeased with her approach, worried that Black students were learning to be "professional victims." This disagreement spurred one of the many standoffs between Ms. Spensor and the administrators.

When, during Indigenous Awareness Week, Ms. Spensor supported students in prioritizing the comfort of white students, I did not understand this decision as indicative of a lapse in judgment or the collapsing of her ideals. Rather, Ms. Spensor's recognition of the importance of that particular framing for this event demonstrated the ubiquity of East City High's "feel good" approach to diversity. During the classroom brainstorming session, Ms. Spensor drew a diagram on the board with three sections representing the three groups of students she expected to be present, "woke students, totally unwoke students who couldn't be reached during this presentation, and a middle group who potentially could be split in half." She recommended focusing on the top half of that latter group and trying to bump them up into the "woke" group. Ms. Spensor told the students, "Disrupting ideas is uncomfortable, learning is uncomfortable, and it has ripple effects. We have to take on that responsibility, and we will hold you, we will prepare you and be here for you through it." Ms. Spensor's decisions regarding the assembly point to her necessary understanding of how to keep herself, her students, and her courses safe at East City High. Articulating her ideas and sharing information about her courses would be easier if people at the school felt able to join with the student presenters in the celebration of diversity.

On the day of the assembly, students were called down to the auditorium by grade. The event went relatively smoothly, with only a few explicitly racist remarks from students. After the settler students presented their narratives of transformation and celebrated the importance of allyship, an Indigenous hip hop artist of the Nuxalk and Onondaga Nations entered singing from the back of the auditorium. She performed while walking up the aisle and onto the stage. At one point during her electric performance, she paused and asked how many people had heard of residential schools. Nearly the entire auditorium raised their hands. She nodded, praising their knowledge. Then she asked them how many people had heard of Idle No More, Colten Boushie, or Standing Rock. A few lone hands went up after each, but the vast majority of hands stayed in laps or clutching phones. While "the condemnation of the history of residential schooling in Canada is becoming well-rehearsed," there is not a concurrent amount of attention to the ongoing nature of settler colonialism or, importantly, Indigenous resistance.[22] Almost no students even recognized recent, important moments like the mass mobilization of land defenders at Standing Rock or the cross-Canada fight for Indigenous sovereignty during Idle No More. The silence in the auditorium while the performer listed out current resistance movements and the tragic murder of Colten Boushie illustrated that conversations on Indigenous issues were largely rooted in the past and primarily focused on residential schools. Unlike the previous year, the students were a nice, accommodating, and pleasant audience. They listened, they knew about residential schools, and they clapped loudly for the performer, appreciating cultural enrichment in action. While the altered structure of the assembly reduced the amount of violence and aggression that Ms. Spensor and Indigenous students faced, this one-day event did not intervene in the way East City High approached colonialism: as a historical event.

Color Me Diverse

When I arrived at school on the morning of February 28, Eliza and Tamar, best friends and fierce activists, were standing in the lobby frazzled and upset. It was the last day of Black History Month and the morning of the Black History Month assembly. Mr. Eaton, one of the vice principals, was supposed to meet Eliza and Tamar in the auditorium to set up the projector, but he was half an hour late. Eliza and Tamar had been working all month to set up this event on their own, but now they needed Mr. Eaton. I knew my way around the tech booth from my time with the theater company, and I offered to help. However, we were thwarted by a locked door. At Eliza and Tamar's request, I went into the office to ask after Mr. Eaton's whereabouts and overheard the administrative assistants making fun of Eliza and Tamar for being so concerned. They remarked that these students "were clearly not being taught anything about respect." Eliza and Tamar were labeled as pushy and disrespectful for being insistent.

Eliza and Tamar had organized the entire Black History Month assembly with almost no support from administrators or teachers. They had petitioned the administrators for the opportunity to lead the assembly once they discovered that there were no plans at East City High to mark Black History Month. Without their industriousness and persistence, Black History Month would have passed by largely unmarked at East City High, save for a small display of books in the front hall and a smattering of activities led by individual teachers in their classrooms. Eliza and Tamar contacted speakers and then coordinated with several teachers to ensure that there would be adequate attendance. They reached out to an organization that works to preserve the cultural, historical, societal, and economic contributions of Black people in the city, speaking back to persistent erasure following the destruction of a predominantly Black neighborhood. Two members of the organization presented at the assembly, educating students on the history of displacement and current revitalization efforts. Though Eliza and Tamar had not received administrative support in arranging the assembly, Mr. Eaton took the stage at the start to introduce the event and deliver a land acknowledgment.

Following the assembly, adults at the school lauded Eliza and Tamar's efforts. Despite the challenges they encountered in organizing, the event had been a success. Furthermore, few people were aware of the administrators' prior lack of cooperation and assistance. Instead, teachers and students, predominantly non-Black, enjoyed the experience of watching and listening to the Black speakers during the assembly. Ahmed offers, "Those who enjoy diversity have good taste.... The enjoyment of diversity is narrated as that which can take us beyond racism, which in turn is reduced to poor or bad taste."[23] Eliza and Tamar's labor benefited the school. Without their industriousness, East City High would have largely neglected Black History Month and, perhaps, had to reckon with what this erasure signified with regard to their commitment to diversity. Yet, Mr. Eaton's introduction and land acknowledgment endorsed the event and acted to maintain the school's sense of itself as a place that celebrates and respects diversity.

Just two days before the Black History Month assembly, East City High celebrated Pink Shirt Day. This event traces its origins to a moment when a group of students at a Nova Scotia high school stood up for a younger boy who was targeted with homophobic bullying for dressing in pink back in 2007. Ostrich reached back into his memory to explain Pink Shirt Day. "From what I was told since elementary, there's this kid at a different school who wore a pink shirt, and the kid was a dude, he got, like, hella bullied about wearing a pink shirt on that day." He told me, "The next day or so, I believe, like, a lot of people got together, and we're like, 'Hey, let's all wear pink shirts,' to kind of be like f-you to the bullies." Since then, schools across Canada have commodified the day, turning it into a monument to antibullying. Students are often required to wear pink to prove their stance against bullying. Schools sell T-shirts, host assemblies, and pose for photo ops all in the name of antibullying. Though the initial tale, as Ostrich recalled, involved students specifically organizing around gendered homophobia, Pink Shirt Day has come to symbolize bullying in a diffuse sense. Elizabeth Meyer argues, "by using vague terms such as bullying and name calling, scholars and educators avoid examining the underlying power dynamics that such behaviors build upon and reinforce."[24] Pink Shirt Day, in setting its sights on a generalized antibullying, does not address the systemic issues of oppression that create unsafe environments for students in school. The event is a celebration, rather than a reckoning.

At East City High, the slogan for Pink Shirt Day was "kindness is one size fits all." Some students, teachers, and staff were wearing pink shirts, though they were certainly in the minority. Beyond the donning of a pink shirt, the day went by mostly unnoticed. When I asked Scarecrow Jones if they participated in the celebration, they responded by asking me *if* it was celebrated. "I didn't hear about it on announcements," they started telling me but then added, "I think I heard about it day of? Just, 'Oh, it's Pink Shirt Day, and here's a poem' or something." Scarecrow Jones was probably referencing a statement the head counselor read on the morning announcements about the importance of standing up to bullies. I had strained to listen, but morning announcements were generally a lost cause. Students and teachers always talked over them.

Vixen was exasperated with the administration's superficial approach to bullying that was "all style, no substance." The first time I met them, Vixen was lambasting East City High's handling of bullying during a class discussion. Vixen extended their critique to Pink Shirt Day, which they declared was "bullshit." Vixen explained that Pink Shirt Day "doesn't have a purpose":

> That's the thing. Well, no, it has a purpose, but it's a forgotten purpose. . . . It's this whole thing about "Oh, yeah, for one day we'll be loving and accepting, and we'll all wear pink shirts, and we'll be tolerant and no more bullying, and we'll remember that bullying is bad. And then tomorrow we'll all go back to hating each other"—because people bully each other on Pink Shirt Day. No one cares. The message is gone. Now it's just the day where you wear pink. You know, like that's all it is now. People are like, "What is Pink Shirt Day about?" I don't know because nothing is changing. It's a movement that does nothing. It's a movement that is standing still.

Vixen desired action and intervention. They were frustrated by the empty rhetoric that denounced bullying while also supporting the power imbalances that fueled oppression within the school. "When we think about bullying, we think, 'Oh, we got to do something about that. . . . That's unjust.' But when we actually see bullying, somehow we're able to justify it every time. 'Boys will be boys.'" To Vixen, Pink Shirt Day was meaningless because it was just one day that the people in power purported to care about bullying when their actions and language every other day supported the systems and people who bullied.

* * *

At East City High, events like the Indigenous Awareness Week assembly, Black History Month assembly, and Pink Shirt Day worked to highlight acceptance of a singular facet of difference. In the process, they likewise reified who the dominant student body was expected and presumed to be. These events were opportunities for these students to enjoy diversity. In Ahmed's words, the students discovered that "diversity can be celebrated, consumed, and eaten."[25] Despite the numerous challenges that accompanied the creation and hosting of these events, by sitting in the auditorium and engaging with the speakers, students and adults at the school were able to believe that they had moved past or "solved" these injustices.

One-off events did not intervene in the dominant approach to the existence of racism, homophobia, and transphobia within the school. Instead, they were opportunities for East City High to perform inclusion and tolerance without grappling with the institutional elements that upheld and reproduced the conditions for violence. Trotting out diversity through assemblies, daylong celebrations, and awareness weeks often served to capture hearts and minds for just the length of a class period or, in the case of Pink Shirt Day, a morning announcement (if you managed to hear it!). This type of approach was never intended to critically examine, let alone challenge, the institutional structures and systems of power that created the violence or oppression put on display. These events were opportunities for "feel good" diversity, when the school could demonstrate its commitment to inclusion without having to do the work or risk upending the status quo. Ultimately, these one-off events were presented as aberrations in the school's normal functioning, and thus they worked to reproduce the institution as white, settler colonial, and cisheteronormative.

The Staff Meeting

In the spring, Ms. Stein, the district resource teacher in charge of diversity, was called in to present at a staff meeting. The region's school board had recently created her position out of what had previously been two separate roles that had each supported antihomophobia and antiracism work in the district. After the resource position's reworking, Ms. Stein, a white, cisgender lesbian, was put in charge of attending to all diversity-related issues. She represented the district's commitment to diversity by advocating for youth and against oppressive situations in schools. Ahmed explains, "Diversity is regularly referred to as a 'good' word precisely because it can be used in diverse ways. . . . [It] is an empty container."[26] This emptiness facilitated the expansiveness of Ms. Stein's role in the district. Ms. Stein attended GSA meetings to liaise with youth and hand out rainbow flag stickers with the district's logo, coordinated professional development days on numerous antioppression topics, supported students who had to leave classes or their school due to racist incidents, and created workshops on a variety of diversity-related issues.

In May, East City High administrators requested Ms. Stein's presence at a staff meeting, and they strategically utilized the expansiveness of her role to avoid directly naming the reason for her attendance. I ran into Ms. Stein in the hall the day before the meeting, and she pulled me outside to the garden to anxiously explain this tactic. Ms. Stein's assignment at the staff meeting was to lead a session addressing a recent spate of overtly racist incidents at East City High. As I mentioned earlier, several white teachers had used the n-word in their classes. Thus far, the administrators had primarily responded by outsourcing the handling of these racist events to the district's human resources department. Ms. Stein was now tasked with confronting this problematic trend in a more straightforward manner; however, both she and the administrators were apprehensive about the staff's reactions. Ms. Stein's wariness stemmed from the existence of union rules that prevented speaking ill of other teachers. As a teacher herself, Ms. Stein told me that she had to be cautious in her language and approach so as not to be perceived as crossing that nebulous line. The administrators' discomfort stemmed from their consistent safeguarding of East City High's reputation as diverse and inclusive.

To mitigate the administrators' concerns about optics and Ms. Stein's hesitations about union rules, they met ahead of time to strategize a less controversial way for her to enter the meeting. Ms. Stein's job as a diversity resource teacher included supporting the push for gender-neutral bathrooms in schools. Thus, not coincidentally, this meeting was also when the administrators finally relented and allowed Eliza and Tamar, who had been fighting for this issue for years, to present to the staff. The administrators and Ms. Stein understood the gender-neutral bathroom as less controversial than anti-Black racism and positioned it as the reason to pull Ms. Stein into the meeting. Via this decision, the administrators and Ms. Stein indicated that challenging whiteness and addressing anti-Blackness were unthinkable without a more palatable entry point.

Building a Generation beyond Prejudice

I came to school early on the day of the staff meeting, the only one I attended since my first day at East City High. I was there to witness Ms. Stein's session and to support Eliza and Tamar, whom I had grown close with over the course of the year. Eliza and Tamar had been working on the campaign for a multistall, gender-neutral bathroom in some respect for the past five years. While East City High did have a gender-neutral bathroom, it was just one, single-stall bathroom on the third floor for the entire school of nearly two thousand students. Eliza and Tamar, as representatives of a larger cohort of students, argued that not only was the current bathroom insufficient, but it contributed to a culture of othering trans and gender-nonconforming students at the school. A multistall gender-neutral bathroom, they asserted, would allow students to use the bathroom with friends and without enduring the stigma of having to wait outside for their own, separate bathroom. To even get to the point of being on the agenda at the staff meeting, Eliza and Tamar had navigated a multitude of obstacles created by the administrators. They had attended a series of frustrating, patronizing meetings with the vice principal, Ms. Walker, during which they endeavored to make the case for the importance of this bathroom. They were tasked with researching city bylaws that mandate a certain number of gender-specific bathrooms in all buildings. They also performed a scan of all the bathrooms in the school to make recommendations on possible gendered bathrooms that could be converted into a gender-neutral one. Eliza and Tamar could only perform this duty either before or after school, when there were no students in the building. I supported them in their work, joining meetings when asked and answering their questions.

Ms. Fraser, the principal, began the staff meeting with the customary land acknowledgment. As I noted in the preceding section, an important facet of diversity work at East City High rested on the good intentions of everyone toward reconciliation, reflected in a desire to move beyond a time of turmoil to an age of harmony when there is no conflict.[27] Land acknowledgments were an easy method to demonstrate these intentions. Especially in the Lower Mainland of British Columbia, land acknowledgments have become a salient way for settlers to demonstrate our intentions toward reconciliation without having to address structural racism or confront the realities of land dispossession.[28] Before every assembly, performance, and school gathering of any kind, someone would recite, seemingly by rote, the same sentence. While many land acknowledgments are meaningful, others are performed as "hollow gestures of lip service, ... quickly forgotten and brushed aside to resume business as usual, according to well-established colonial and racialized power asymmetries."[29] Land acknowledgments avoided difficult conversations about ongoing colonialism while reproducing the school's image as diverse, inclusive, and on the path toward reconciliation.

After the acknowledgment, Ms. Fraser introduced Ms. Stein by saying she was working with the school to "create a generation beyond prejudice." As had been the strategy, Ms. Fraser did not overtly reference the reason Ms. Stein had been asked to attend the meeting. Instead, her presence was couched within a general and vague interest in promoting diversity. This approach did double duty to preserve East City High's reputation: the administrators could be credited for bringing in the diversity resource teacher, and they never had to directly name the racism that necessitated her presence. Ms. Stein stood and uploaded a slide that read, "VALUE—validate, ask, listen, understand, engage." She informed the staff that she was present in part because of the "groundbreaking work" that I was doing with students and, specifically, to support the gender-neutral bathroom project. Then she added, "since I am here anyway," she wanted to discuss some mounting issues with racism at the school. Though we had spoken the day before, I was still taken aback by how she drew on my research and the bathroom issue to sneak up on racism. Ms. Stein predominantly addressed racism through her own experiences as a Jewish lesbian and refrained from speaking explicitly on anti-Black racism. She began by telling a story about hearing "Heil Hitler" and explaining what she hears in that phrase: "that I am less than human and that people want me to die, want to erase my cultural history." Ms. Stein told the staff, "I have seen swastikas, heard the n-word and 'faggot.'" Several teachers were visibly shocked when she said "faggot," and Ms. Stein explained, "I can use the word 'faggot' because I am part of the queer community." Notably, the teachers did not seem surprised to learn that educators in their district were using racist slurs in the classroom. Later, in response to a teacher's lingering discomfort, Ms. Stein added that she does not usually say the f-word, but she was making a point about the impact of this type of language.

Ms. Stein believed the best of teachers and continuously cultivated this understanding during the session by justifying the possibility of ignorant mistakes. "I have to believe that people don't know the history of those words," Ms. Stein remarked. She went on to explain that she did not learn how hateful many words were during her time as a student in the public-school system and then offered a brief history of the n-word, reminding people that Canada is not neutral in this history. "Words," Ms. Stein warned, "incite potential future violence." Throughout the session, Ms. Stein emphasized that teachers have the best intentions to support their students but, at times, can struggle if they are not sure how to help. Though Ms. Stein warned that "these words need a strong response from teachers . . . [because] minimization is a second victimization," she never directly named the racism prevalent at East City High. Instead, she drew on examples at other schools, mostly related to antisemitism and the use of the f-word, stories she felt comfortable navigating given her identities.

Ms. Stein's wariness tempered the potency of her message. Later in the day, I overheard teachers discussing the talk's goals as encouraging them to be good allies. As Mr. Hill explained to me, "Ms. Stein was instructing teachers to be good allies and stand up if they hear students use racist slurs." To say nothing of the problematics of allyship, the administrators had specifically needed to bring Ms. Stein into East City High to address anti-Blackness and teachers' use of racist slurs. She was not there to encourage allyship. By not directly addressing anti-Black racism, Ms. Stein's workshop neglected to tackle the role of systemic oppression in the school. She bolstered the perspective that teachers, working with the best intentions, could support students of color by becoming allies. This idea ultimately upholds whiteness by obscuring teachers' roles in perpetuating racism at East City High.

Quit Stalling

It matters that this staff meeting was also concerning a bathroom. There are many ways that schools communicate who belongs and who does not belong, and bathrooms are part of that messaging. Though controversy over bathroom bills appears recent, in North America there is a long history of using bathrooms as gatekeepers of people's participation in public space and access to full citizenship.[30] Bathrooms are prime examples of how ideas about gender are never just about gender. They imagine the assumed and ideal occupant and, through built environment as well as social, cultural, and legislative policing, constitute the proper citizen as white, male, heterosexual, and able-bodied.[31] More recent uproar over bathrooms in the United States coalesces around the moral panic provoked by the figure of a trans woman in public and related outcries about protecting children. These harmful myths about sexual predation echo earlier panics about integrated bathrooms. Racially segregated bathrooms relied, in part, on the notion that understanding distinctions between the genders was the mark of civilized propriety and thus only available to white people.[32] Therefore, following Toby Beauchamp, "we must also consider how today's gendered bathrooms continue to rely on racist concepts of a modern, civilized society, even if these spaces are no longer formally segregated by race."[33]

In schools, bathrooms are likewise integral to issues of access and safety. When I arrived at the school and asked where I was meant to use the bathroom, Ms. Walker was not even sure of how many gender-neutral bathrooms existed. During that conversation, she warned me against using the single-stall one on the third floor, which was in fact the only one in the school. Ms. Walker told me that it was never cleaned, and "the students vape in it." Soon after we met, Raeyun told me that he would try to make it through an entire school day without having to use the bathroom. He found the third-floor gender-neutral bathroom inaccessible because it was too far away from most of his classes and often occupied. Plus, he did not like to stand outside and wait for it, which made him feel too visible. If students do not have a bathroom, they are limited in their engagement with school.

After Ms. Stein's session, Ms. Walker invited Eliza and Tamar to present their thoughts on the multistall, gender-neutral bathroom. Though Eliza and Tamar had collided with the administrators for years on this issue, during the meeting Ms. Walker framed their work as "meaningful, necessary, and fully supported" by East City High. Ms. Walker specifically had stonewalled the students, citing bureaucratic guidelines to stall their campaign. Eliza and Tamar had been forced to perform the labor of proving the necessity of this bathroom and the logistical possibilities of creating one out of the school's current facilities. The students' experiences and labor were erased when, unbeknownst to Eliza and Tamar and without mentioning their labor, Ms. Walker and the other administrators decided to support their request while in front of the staff. This decision was a decisive and abrupt departure from every previous conversation the students had with administrators regarding the issue. Suddenly, Eliza and Tamar's carefully crafted presentation meant to convince adults of the importance of this bathroom seemed unnecessary. Visibly surprised, they moved on to a question-and-answer period, addressing teachers' concerns and curiosities. One PE teacher raised her hand and commented, "Kids find it challenging to get changed for gym. Will the washroom have taller stalls so they could get changed in there?[34] I'm not even sure where some students get changed now." Another teacher noted, "We have a problem with bathroom etiquette at this school. Obviously, I'm in favor, but is there research that shows that gender-neutral washrooms increase bathroom etiquette, that they won't make it worse?" Finally, a teacher pointed to the time and, in the interest of wrapping up the meeting, asked, "Where does this idea stand right now? What is left to do?" Ms. Walker explained that all they needed to do was change a few signs. I was stunned. If creating the gender-neutral bathroom was just a matter of a simple sign change, why did the administrators block Eliza and Tamar for years and force them to jump through so many bureaucratic hoops?

During the question-and-answer period, when the teacher raised the bathroom etiquette issue, Ms. Stein hopped up from her seat to interject.

"This is not a question of *if* this is going to happen but *how*," Ms. Stein stated. Her response was decisive, in part, because it was supported by policy. The district's trans-inclusive policy clearly stated that students have the right to access a gender-neutral bathroom. In this moment, unlike during her earlier presentation, Ms. Stein was direct, and the administrators made space for her advocacy. Ms. Stein's comments were likewise persuasive because of the staff's awareness of the trans-inclusive policy. People may have privately disagreed—and rumblings of that disagreement were audible in the room—but Ms. Stein used the policy to overrule their discontent.

The trans-inclusive policy had not previously prevented the administrators from mobilizing other policies to prevent Eliza and Tamar from moving forward with the project. As I will argue in chapter 2, it is integral to consider how policy is taken up by social actors in their contexts.[35] During the year I spent at East City High, the administrators consistently turned to city bylaws and policy on gender-segregated bathrooms in buildings to impede students' activism on this campaign. Then, with the diversity resource teacher present, the administrators uplifted policy as the reason there could be no question about supporting the gender-neutral bathroom project. Thus, policy was both the reason students had to fight for five years to even be permitted to present this idea at a staff meeting *and* the reason that the gender-neutral bathroom had to be approved without dispute.

Though the administrators and Ms. Stein had turned to policy to quash any doubts or disapproval from the staff regarding the gender-neutral bathroom, no one drew on policy to take a firm stance against anti-Black racism. Thus, while policy offered promise for Eliza and Tamar's fight for the bathroom, it was notably absent during the staff meeting as a possible form of redress against racist teachers at the school. Rather than Ms. Stein and the administrators pointing to policy or their official stance supporting diversity to declare that anti-Black racism was not permitted within the school, they approached the staff meeting with the intention of positioning East City High as moving "beyond prejudice." This indirect approach avoided actively engaging with anti-Black racism and instead promoted a vague and harmonious vision of East City High. Ms. Stein spoke to teachers with the assumption that any racist act was an aberration in an otherwise diverse, inclusive school. To bring the meeting to a timely close, Ms. Walker described the administration's position to the staff: "We believe ourselves to be a diverse and inclusive school. Let's show it." Ms. Walker's choice of phrase underscored the importance of presenting a diverse, accepting, and inclusive image, one not necessarily tethered to action and substantive change.

* * *

Ms. Stein was called into the staff meeting because both the campaign for the multistall, gender-neutral bathroom and the session regarding anti-Black racism were framed as issues of diversity and inclusion. The administrators had specifically strategized with Ms. Stein to mollify staff reactions by diluting the potential of the workshop to speak to anti-Black racism. Though Ms. Stein did discuss racism and the ways words can incite violence, her carefully crafted presentation was an attempt to address racism at East City High without admitting that racism existed or was a dire issue in the school. This strategy corresponds to a "feel good" model—Ms. Stein encouraged teachers to believe in the power of allyship but not to acknowledge themselves as complicit or potential perpetrators of harm.

The administrators' abrupt decision to support the gender-neutral bathroom project gestured at an empty form of diversity that did not address the hostile structures that shaped the school and schooling. Critically, they also did not consider there to be a relationship between the bathroom and teachers' anti-Black racism. Though treated as discrete topics during the staff meeting, both topics address which students have access to public space in the school. There was an unmarked whiteness in how trans students were imagined during the staff meeting. Approaching gender and race as distinct issues assumes that anti-Black racism was not an issue that affected the trans students in the school. By demonstrating the necessity of the gender-neutral bathroom project while simultaneously skirting the importance of addressing anti-Black racism, the administrators communicated who they presumed to be the beneficiaries of the new bathroom and what types of diversity work they saw as tenable at East City High.

For the administrators, approving the gender-neutral bathroom was an act *for* diversity and inclusion. In supporting the bathroom, the administrators and Ms. Stein were able to take an official position on the "right" side of the issue. They chose directness, ending staff questions and conversation with East City High's definitive stance on the topic, which they noted was supported by policy. Though being direct in that instance aided in establishing East City High as progressive, a direct approach against anti-Black racism would have exposed the work still needed for the school to be diverse and inclusive. Rather than pushing East City High closer to diversity and inclusion, openly acknowledging and confronting the endemic violence and institutionalized racism that fostered and protected teachers in using the n-word in their classrooms would reveal the troubling ways that East City High was not a diverse and progressive school. Therefore, to safeguard East City High's image, it was to the administration's benefit to adopt an official stance on the gender-neutral bathroom project while evading the deeper issues present during the session on anti-Black racism.

Conclusion

At East City High, teachers and administrators invested in a cultural enrichment model of diversity by engaging with it in a predominantly celebratory manner. They consistently eschewed the notion that racism, anti-Indigeneity, and other oppressions were endemic to the school and schooling by uplifting their official commitment to diversity through one-off celebrations, land acknowledgments, and strategic support for equity issues. This work was bolstered and informed by a multicultural ideology that positioned support of cultural diversity as a fundamental Canadian value and evidence of having resolved systemic oppression. This cultural context is crucial to explore because, though East City High was not an antioppressive utopia, there was a pervasive belief that the school's promotion of diversity and celebration of difference meant that these issues were not endemic. Enveloped within this understanding was the conflation of niceness, good intentions, and diversity work.

Many adults at the school subscribed to the dominant multicultural ideal that Canadians are pleasant, accepting people and that good intentions toward diversity alone fought inequities. When problems arose, such as white teachers using the n-word or students being sexually assaulted, administrators and other adults treated these as anomalies to address, discreetly, but not as pertinent information about the school's culture. Ms. Stein supported this perspective by addressing anti-Black racism among the teachers through the lens of encouraging allyship. White teachers who had used the n-word were invited to be allies to racialized students under the problematic presumption that they could offer meaningful guidance to these young people.

Though the school's preoccupation with image and optics often limited the impact of their labor, several teachers and students consistently worked to resist East City High's performative approach to diversity and inclusion by organizing events and advocating for change. For instance, Ms. Sponsor operated from the knowledge that the school was a settler, racist institution. Unlike Ms. Stein, Ms. Sponsor frequently chose a direct approach in conflicts with the administration. Ms. Sponsor was tireless in her efforts supporting students who left their classes after teachers used the n-word. She began by following the bureaucratic channels, filing grievances, and contacting human resources. However, she also refused to relent when those tactics were unsuccessful. Ms. Sponsor taught these students in her classroom for the rest of the year, despite being informally punished by the administration for this decision. Moreover, when her courses and the First Nations program more generally were threatened with cuts, Ms. Sponsor conducted research, spoke to teachers across the departments, and campaigned at consecutive staff meetings. As a result, she lost her chip store. She was verbally threatened by white, settler teachers who were angry at her activism. Still, she persisted, and the program continues to operate at East City High.

At times, teachers and students who refused East City High's optics became symbols of diversity.[36] Administrators would celebrate their efforts as indicative of East City High's commitment to inclusivity, such as when Mr. Eaton introduced the Black History Month assembly despite having zero involvement in advocating for or organizing the event. The students responsible, Eliza and Tamar, were often either held up as student representations of East City High's progressive aims or admonished for their tenacity.

East City High's "feel good" approach to diversity affected the labor that was required of gender-nonconforming youth. There was a cultural imperative to acknowledge difference and to include those bodies in the school as symbols of diversity. However, this dynamic reified who was expected to be a student at the school. While there was a "nice" desire to celebrate diversity, this framework relied on the notion that difference was visible. Furthermore, the commitment to and belief in good intentions frequently prevented teachers, counselors, and administrators from acknowledging the many forms of harm they perpetuated. I am interested in the onus that this cultural context placed on gender-nonconforming youth as they navigated East City High. In chapter 2, I continue this analysis by examining the dominance of an accommodations approach to trans-inclusivity and how this privileged an emphasis on narrow forms of trans legibility and visibility.

2

Accommodating Trans Youth

East City High's gymnasium was located in an outbuilding directly behind the main school structure. There were two entrances, one on the east side for girls and one on the west side for boys. These entrances led to gendered bathrooms and locker rooms and then flowed into the primary gymnasium, where all classes met at the start of the period to rendezvous with their teachers. At the start of the year, Mr. Gonzalez pulled Raeyun aside and gave him special permission to use the boys' locker room, but Raeyun did not feel comfortable using that space. He was worried that it would exaggerate the ways he was different from other boys. Instead, Raeyun came to school already dressed for class and sneaked in the back entrance to the gymnasium while the other students were changing. He stayed in his PE clothes all day, regardless of what they did that period and how sweaty he got. I never once witnessed a teacher talk to Raeyun about wearing his PE clothes all day or deduce that this behavior meant that he had nowhere safe to get changed.

In North America, accommodation approaches have become a dominant framework for including trans youth in schools. This application of accommodations is informed by disability law. Activists and advocates fought for years to require employers to make a "reasonable" effort to modify their institutions to be accessible.[1] This framework establishes the institution as benevolent for making space for people who had not previously been imagined as belonging. Further, the systemic marginalization of these bodies goes unaddressed once the institution expands to include them. As the legal scholar and trans activist Dean Spade argues, "we must remember that the inclusion and recognition offered by these invitations is not only disappointingly solely symbolic, but actually legitimates and expands harmful conditions."[2] By accessing accommodations in schools, gender-nonconforming students can be recognized as deserving of special attention, which then facilitates how they navigate through bureaucratic systems and gain permission for bathroom/locker-room alternatives. There are important material benefits that students can access through accommodations. However, accommodation approaches also place the onus on individual students to fit themselves into problematic institutions that never anticipated their presence. These strategies of inclusion rely on and reproduce an expectation of a normative body that can succeed and belong in a school, locating all problems within those who do not align with these expectations and perhaps do not ever desire to belong.

In this chapter, I consider accommodations as the reigning strategy of inclusion at East City High, questioning the assumptions at its foundation as well as how this framework was enacted in the school. In recent years, scholars have critiqued accommodation practices, noting their overly individualistic focus and emphasis on visibility.[3] I build on their analysis to likewise attend to how these methods rely on an understanding of trans identity as inherently risky. I examine the trans-inclusive materials guiding accommodation approaches at East City High, including how youth interacted with these resources. While this method was prevalent across all subjects, I highlight PE as a particularly illustrative example due to its continued reliance on gender as a criterion for evaluation and a form of distinction among students. I analyze this strategy of inclusion before turning in chapters 3–5 to interrogate how East City High's diversity culture promoted forms of belonging for certain trans youth while refusing to desire youth to be gender nonconforming. I am interested in the ways this dynamic structured youth's labor practices and acts of world-making.

Combating Risk with Inclusion

Decades of scholarship positioning queer and trans youth as at heightened risk of depression, bullying, substance abuse, and suicidality have contributed to the notion that being trans or gender nonconforming is inherently risky.[4] Within this framework, many adults with good intentions responded from a place of concern when interacting with gender-nonconforming youth (I will return to this notion of concern in more depth in chapter 3). This hesitant reaction reinforced the way that adults generally interacted with the presence of gender nonconformity at East City High: as undesirable, dangerous, and problematic. Because of

East City High's cultural imperative to promote diversity and inclusion, which I explored in chapter 1, educators were motivated to protect students whom they perceived as vulnerable. In practice, this commitment meant that many adults aimed to open doors for youth. Thinking alongside Tourmaline, Stanley, and Burton, these doors are "entrances to visibility, to resources, to recognition, and to understanding."[5] Adults were invested in helping gender-nonconforming youth feel included at East City High through, for instance, finding workarounds for them to participate in PE or letting them pick their pronouns in French class. However, as I explore, a focus on inclusion does not challenge the cisheteronormative operations and mechanisms of the school or schooling.

Though teachers, counselors, and administrators had good intentions to accommodate individual students into the school, finding creative solutions that did not necessitate systemic change, few educators *desired* youth to be trans or gender nonconforming. Critical disability scholars theorize how the space between these frameworks—inclusion and desire—reifies the naturalness and inevitability of cisheteronormativity, ability, and whiteness.[6] Teachers, counselors, and administrators focused their efforts on making school more habitable, hospitable, and tolerable for queer and trans students. However, few people addressed the structures that excluded and marginalized youth. Furthermore, adults were unable to desire nonnormativity among youth because nonnormativity remains mired in notions of risk and struggle, and their commitment to good intentions prohibited these types of desires. Their sense of how to grow up and live well was informed by the sociocultural privileging of white, able-bodied, gender conformity. As nice teachers, they valued cultural diversity and thus accepted visible forms of difference, but they did not want more difficult lives for their students. Therefore, when confronted with individual queer and trans students, they strategized to open doors for youth, but these moments of recognition and visibility were incapable of challenging East City High's reliance on normative aspirations for youth. Further, the good intentions to include individual trans students in the everyday practices of the school invested in the pervasive presumption that for youth to exist outside of normative expectations was an unnecessary burden and, if possible, to be avoided. This perspective compelled accommodation approaches and shaped interactions between teachers and students as well as the forms of labor required from youth.

In a recent *Teachers College Record* special issue focused on the experiences of trans and gender-nonconforming students in the education system, including trans-inclusive policies and practices, the education scholar Wayne Martino outlines the various attempts to support trans youth in schools. He offers that these strategies "have tended to focus on a more individualized approach that relies on trans students being visible and declaring themselves as a catalyst for intervention and accommodation."[7] Similar to disability-specific accommodation approaches that ask disabled students to make themselves known in order to qualify for legal protections, the trans-inclusive initiatives at East City High forced students to self-identify as trans to teachers and staff if they wanted any form of support or concessions. These policies made possible the offering of accommodations only for individual students who were recognizably trans and thus deemed in need of special attention. As a result, these approaches relied on and reproduced trans as a visible identity. I explore accommodations as forms of doors—they are pathways to belonging in schools. At East City High, accommodations (doors) were often also traps, for they were only available if students performed their genders in recognizable ways. The reliance on a narrow understanding of gender nonconformity meant that accommodation approaches were limited in their ability to disrupt binary thinking and language.

At East City High, accommodation approaches were primarily guided by the district's hard-fought "Policy on Sexual Orientation and Gender Identity," which garnered significant media attention during its revision process back in 2014. A small yet vocal population of parents and conservative organizations opposed the expansion of the policy, rooting their argument in a rejection of trans identities, an investment in a transmisogynistic rape myth, and a perceived attack on parental rights.[8] Advocates for the policy used their time during the public meetings to recount the numerous challenges and dangers faced by trans students in schools.[9] Despite the protests, the policy passed by a majority of the school board trustees. In its codification, the policy was then positioned as a solution to the heightened risks faced by trans students and a primary method for ensuring their safety.

The education scholars Wayne Martino, Jenny Kassen, and Kenan Omercajic highlight the limitations of relying on policy as a form of emancipation in schools.[10] They assert that this approach only supports individual, visible trans students and is unable to address institutionalized cisheteronormativity. Likewise, the sociologist Travers points out in their book *The Trans Generation*, "schools typically do not adopt measures for trans inclusion until a visible transgender kid shows up."[11] The reliance on visibility as a catalyst for action means that schools are always responding to trans youth instead of working to address and change school structures that exclude, target, and marginalize gender-nonconforming youth. Travers argues, drawing on their ethnography with trans kids and their parents, "This attitude is inadequate for the well-being of all of the kids at the school and is limiting for the trans kids who feel safe enough to become visible and in the identities they feel comfortable exploring and asserting."[12] As I explore in this chapter, when the school is in a position of reacting to visible trans youth, it reproduces narrow ideas of trans identity. This dynamic fails to acknowledge the breadth of harm cisheteronormativity causes in schools, including the fact that it is not only trans youth who are affected by these structures.

In East City High's policy, trans youth (their bodies, their genders, and their movements through the school) represented problems in need of specific solutions.[13] Policy is often framed as a solution to a problem and even as "a substitute for action."[14] However, I theorize policies as enacted and attend to "the importance of focusing not so much on what documents say but what they do: how they circulate and move around."[15] East City High's trans-inclusive policy sought to remedy what its creators and advocates understood as the harmful and challenging situations that individual and recognizable trans youth confronted in schools. Specifically, the policy aimed to clearly identify the situations in which to expect trans students and the types of needs trans students will have as they move through school. To open doors for youth, it addressed a student's right to access the bathroom or locker room that matched their gender identity, to be addressed by the name and pronoun they "preferred," to dress in clothing that aligned with their gender expression, and to join athletic activities that corresponded with their gender identity. The policy locates any problems, such as a student not having a place to change for PE, within the young person who does not align with the normative student ideal and then offers suggestions for how to fit them back into the school as seamlessly as possible. As I noted at the beginning of this chapter, this model emerges from disability law and constructs the institution as functional and benevolent. The flaw in these provisions (doors) is that once concessions have been provided, the burden is on the individual young person to adapt back into the school.

In listing out the anticipated spaces and moments in which trans youth collide with the cisheteronormative culture of the school and then providing "fixes," the policy assumed that by adhering to these new rules, trans youth can be accommodated without any trouble. This framework neglects to interrogate the systemic role of schools and schooling in creating environments that have no space for nonnormative bodies, either because schools are literally built without considering the possibility of disabled, trans, and racialized youth or because schooling continues to privilege an ableist, cisheteronormative, white experience.[16] This approach places the onus on individual students to do the work of fitting into schools, which assumes that youth desire to belong in the first place. Furthermore, as with Ms. Stein's presentation confronting anti-Black racism, this perspective assumes that teachers serve as protectors and facilitators instead of potential points of harm and violence.[17] Following the guidance of other school-based ethnographers and education researchers who have interrogated schooling as structured through settler colonialism, anti-Blackness, white supremacy, cisheteronormativity, capitalism, and violence, I query the assumption that including youth into schooling practices and routines is a benign endeavor.[18]

Trans students appear as a monolith in East City High's materials. For instance, an appended glossary explains the policy's use of "trans*" as an expansive umbrella term to include gender-nonconforming and nonbinary students. As I examined in the introduction, though the use of "trans" as an umbrella term has a long history in the community, it fails to address mounting internal divisions over membership and inclusion.[19] The policy likewise neglects to consider a diversity of trans experiences and instead presumes that all trans students experience similar challenges in school. The assumption is that trans is a stable, concrete, and knowable identity and that educators will be able to recognize trans students by their need to use a different bathroom, play on the other sports team, and change their name. This articulation, which intended to ameliorate the challenges experienced by students in these moments, participated in defining what it meant to be trans in school. Do you still count as trans if you never wish to change your name? What if there is no locker room that aligns with your gender identity because your gender identity does not exist in the boy/girl options provided by your school?

The policy at East City High predominantly centered on the experiences of transnormative students. While gender-nonconforming and transnormative youth may navigate similar schooling conditions, they also diverge in the particularities of their experiences. As Travers points out, "The majority of transgender kids... are invisible.... This invisibility masks the harm that a binary and heteronormative social culture causes in school settings."[20] Initiatives and programs that exclusively focus on transnormativity elide the possibility of gender nonconformity by not acknowledging fluidity and ambiguity *as* trans. Instead, these policies and resources make possible individualized experiences of belonging while maintaining the conditions that create gendered exclusion. As trans-inclusive undertakings grow, it is integral to attend to the ways they both expand protections for certain students and participate in narrowing conceptions of what counts as gender nonconformity.

The creation and implementation of trans-inclusive policies does not simply cultivate safer schools for trans students. Youth who relate to their genders in ways that are not legible within the parameters specifically laid out by the policy will be further excluded. Policies create "a kind of 'script' that further defines and restricts the legibility of gender, creating restrictions and unanticipated barriers for non-binary students, and others whose identities and forms of self-expression do not fit neatly into a dichotomous male/female gender binary."[21] Policies are enacted by people and through daily interactions that are mired in the cultural contexts of the school. East City High's trans-inclusive policy and resources made possible the offering of accommodations (doors) only for individual students who were recognizably trans and thus deemed in need of special attention. The policy's reliance on a narrow understanding of gender nonconformity meant that these materials were limited in their ability to disrupt gendered thinking and language, a trap.

Since being recognizable as trans guys was important to Raeyun and Ostrich, they both took on the responsibility of seeking out workarounds from teachers who did not initially understand them as trans. Through talking about their transness with teachers, Raeyun and Ostrich distinguished themselves as students requiring accommodations—they became visible. However, most of the other youth in the project did not want to announce themselves as trans and, as a result, were not identified as students being excluded by gendered activities, standards, and language. Adults in the school frequently struggled to recognize them as trans because their movements through the school and gender performances were not detailed by the policy. Teachers, counselors, and administrators shared the predominant belief that the structures of binary gender only affected visible or known trans and gender-nonconforming youth.

Trans-Inclusive Policies as Easy as (SOGI) 123

Vixen changed their name in grade 8, shortly after figuring out that they were genderfluid. When I met them in grade 12, most people knew them as Vixen. However, whenever there was a substitute teacher, that person would call out their deadname during attendance. Classmates would then look around confused. Later, some would refer to Vixen by their deadname, now unsure what their "real" name was. Why had their teachers never just crossed out their name and rewritten it? Or better yet, why hadn't any of Vixen's teachers changed their name in the school's system? In January, Mr. Hill pulled Vixen aside during a library block in Social Justice 12 and asked them if they knew that they could officially change their name. Vixen had no idea that was possible. Later that day, they went to the counseling suite to talk to Mr. Adams, who was their favorite counselor. Vixen told me that the name change was quick and easy (although in chapter 3, we will encounter how this was not the case for all youth). This process was one of several trans-inclusive protections enumerated by the district's policy.

Trans-inclusive policies have many important benefits for students, and I do not intend to deny the very real, material impact they can have on youth's lives.[22] Yet, none of the youth I worked with had ever heard of the policy or any of the other resources meant to protect and include them at East City High. When I read through the various documents with them, they were generally surprised at the detail, and some were amazed at its relevance to their lives. Raeyun asked, "Did this change at some point?" When his parents found out that he changed his name at school, they threatened to sue. He was terrified and had no idea there was a policy supporting his decision. Knowing that a policy existed that protected his transition at school would have been comforting and helpful.

I am particularly interested in how gender-nonconforming youth at East City High related to the materials meant to support their experiences at school. In the rest of this chapter, I consider how the dominance of an accommodations framework permeated interactions around gender in the school and explore how the youth came into contact (or not) with elements of these policies and ideas, often without knowing. First, I document youth's awareness of the schools' trans-inclusive policy and of a province-wide program created to support teaching, learning, and policy development related to sexual orientation and gender identity, which has been abbreviated to "SOGI" in British Columbia. Then I turn to PE with a particular focus on how teachers and youth navigated the gender-segregated elements of the curriculum.

At East City High, adults' good intentions in cultivating safe and inclusive classrooms were directed and bolstered by the trans-inclusive policy as well as the province's funding and support of the SOGI (sexual orientation and gender identity) 123 initiative, a vast network that connects educators to explanations of policies and curricular initiatives with the aim of creating inclusive schools. This program was created through a partnership among the provincial Ministry of Education, a private foundation, the teacher's union, and numerous other stakeholders and collaborators. It initially launched in 2016 as a pilot program and has since expanded to all school districts. Its uptake has been extensive to the point where many people in the province colloquially refer to queer and trans issues by using "SOGI" as a shorthand.

Through participating in SOGI 123, educators gain access to learning modules, inclusive lesson plans, workshops for training staff at meetings and professional development days, and other resources to support schools in creating queer- and trans-inclusive teaching and learning. Furthermore, each school (ideally) has a lead teacher who oversees disseminating materials and connecting staff with the larger SOGI network. According to SOGI 123's mission statement, it fosters the opportunity for teachers and administrators to collaborate across the province and share inclusive policies, strategies, and lessons.

None of my participants were aware of either the district's trans-inclusive policy or SOGI 123. Raeyun astutely pointed out the absurdity of this unfamiliarity, remarking, "[SOGI 123] was never brought to my attention, which is funny because I'm trans." Since SOGI 123, in part, was intended to cultivate inclusive schools through integrating topics and issues into the curriculum, students' unawareness of the actual program is not necessarily meaningful. It could be silently operating in the background as teachers challenged cisheteronormativity in their classrooms. Raeyun, who generously presumed the best of intentions in most situations, determined that not hearing about SOGI 123 was indicative of its success. The first time I asked him about it, he ruminated for a while before telling me it was "sneaky." Raeyun explained that since he had no idea it was happening, then his teachers must be integrating the content extraordinarily well. Other students were not quite as generous. They were enthusiastic about the possibility of this type of program existing at East City High and then shocked to hear that it already did. Ostrich, for instance, was skeptical that it was real, immediately telling me how he had experienced the exact opposite during high school. He recounted the almost complete absence of queer and trans people and issues in his sex education classes, sharing with me that he felt entirely unprepared besides what he had managed to look up on the internet. In Ostrich's experience, teachers were not integrating materials about queer sexuality and trans identities into the curriculum, and he was discouraged by that lack.

Scarecrow Jones felt similarly frustrated by how nonnormative genders and sexualities never came up in any of their classes. The exception to this absence was when a student initiated the conversation, which, they argued, was entirely different than if a teacher were to broach the subject. I asked them to explain how it would differ if a teacher were to bring up the topic, and in responding, they also gave specific examples for how a teacher could integrate queer and trans material into a theater or PE class. They suggested,

> Well, because then it acknowledges that they're aware and are trying and . . . that they're doing a part. It's such a big deal on its own when a student comes up with it, like, and then it's normal, but if a teacher were to be, like, "All right, let's do a scene, and two girls, Ashley, Kate, and they're in love, go," and then picked two random people—doesn't matter

what gender they were—and just picked them and up onstage, and there you go, like, that would be so different than, "All right, this girl goes up, and that guy goes up, and you're in love, go." And okay, especially when they're teaching dance in gym. Just split the class in half. This group is going to lead, this group is going to follow. Put on pinnies leaders, there you go. Doesn't have to be like, "Girls go to this side, guys go to this side."

In pointing to how teachers could open space for queerness to exist by asking for a romance scene between two girls or shifting their language choices when teaching dance, Scarecrow Jones was describing an ideal enactment of the stated intentions of SOGI 123. The program's website explains, "Sexual orientation and gender identity (SOGI) is not its own curriculum; it is one aspect of diversity that is embedded across a range of grades and subject areas."[23] However, this type of integration requires training and labor on the part of teachers and schools, which in turn necessitates funding and time. The teaching and networking resources compiled on the SOGI 123 website can be helpful, but they do not, on their own, compel changes in schools. Every year, there is a training for district leads, who then provide training for one lead teacher at each school. These leads are responsible for translating inclusive materials into their school context. This task can vary greatly from location to location. For instance, East City High had nearly two thousand students and one lead teacher, making that position a considerable challenge. Even though a funded training network exists, without attention to the institutional obstacles that either prevent teachers from integrating inclusive content or make them wary of the idea, these types of initiatives will be more successful at promoting the idea of schools as diverse than affecting any real change.[24] To return to the discussion of Ahmed's interrogation of systemic racism and diversity work from chapter 1, institutional practices that promote inclusion without addressing foundational issues can actually participate in masking racism, ableism, cisheteronormativity, and other underlying inequities.

Scarecrow Jones noted and was frustrated by the reactive nature of trans-inclusivity. Rather than cultivating desire for queer and trans youth to exist in schools, adults would incorporate trans-inclusion into their classrooms only in response to the presence of a visible trans student.[25] This reflects the scholarship on accommodations, which highlights the reliance on visible trans youth prior to any changes being made in schools. This approach, as I have argued, emerges from and reifies the idea that there is something risky about gender nonconformity. Adults at the school were willing to accept and support transness in the classroom once they were aware of it, but their inability to pedagogically desire gender nonconformity betrays their belief that wanting youth to be trans is akin to wishing them struggle and hardship.

The Trouble with Fitting In

The first time I met Mr. Gonzalez, he was relieved to see me. He suggested we sit off to the side of the outdoor basketball courts while students shot hoops. He wanted to ask a litany of questions about how to handle trans students in PE class. Where should they change? What teams should they play on? How can he find out if a student was trans? "There are only two change rooms," he pointed out. "Would a solution be to just give trans kids more time to change?" Mr. Gonzalez was invested in guaranteeing a fair and safe environment for all students in his class, though at times he viewed fairness and safety in tension. "There are different three-point lines for girls and boys, and girls get very upset when I say this, but also it's not fair for them to use the same one because they're not as strong," he told me, looking out at the basketball courts and the students running around. Mr. Gonzalez had no idea how to guarantee Raeyun's safety, and this uncertainty worried him. He wanted concrete answers on how to protect Raeyun.

Throughout the year, Mr. Gonzalez confided in me about the predicaments that Raeyun provoked for him. He explained that he knows Raeyun "identifies as a . . . boy," but it is difficult and not really fair to put him in the same group as the other boys because he was not like them. "I have to split up the class and need to make sure teams are fair. If I count Raeyun as a boy, it doesn't work." He told me that the distinctions in PE were not actually about gender; they were about ability. Mr. Gonzalez recognized that Raeyun "saw himself" as a boy, but he argued that there were just some realities about bodies that he had to consider, even though he did not want to offend anyone.

During one of our conversations, I asked Mr. Gonzalez if the teachers in the PE department ever discussed these topics in their meetings. He told me that they never had. Though Mr. Gonzalez had been accruing a long list of concerns and queries, he chose to save them for the first nonbinary person he met in the school. Mr. Gonzalez never sought out external resources to help support Raeyun or raised his questions with the other members of the department who encountered similar situations. Instead, Mr. Gonzalez viewed my nonnormative body as holding the answers to his anxieties. He believed that I was the solution to his problem *because* I am nonbinary. As I noted with one of the vice principals, this dynamic was not uncommon during my time at East City High.

Beyond forcing students to funnel into the gymnasium on the basis of their genders, PE class relied on white, ableist, and cisheteronormative assumptions as the foundation for defining physical health.[26] In Canada, physical education has been historically shaped and entangled in heteromasculinity, nationalism, militarism, and settler colonialism.[27] Settlers used physical education and sport as methods to "civilize" Indigenous youth and children, and these violent strategies relied on gendered segregation in addition to the imposition of Euro-Canadian norms of movement and discipline onto Indigenous bodies.[28] Settlers weaponized ideas of productivity and ability to "justify" both the removal of Indigenous peoples from their lands and the sending of Indigenous children to residential schools. Health, therefore, became entangled with settlers' conceptions of capitalist production and fitness in service of the nation. Moreover, the Canadian government adopted similar discourses to restrict immigration, constructing a rigid understanding of the "right" type of newcomer on the basis of these intertwined perspectives of health, productivity, and ability.[29]

During the year, students participated in conventionally North American sports, like hockey, basketball, and golf. Many students in the class with access to certain privileges, such as wealth, already possessed athletic skills in these areas, probably as the result of participation outside of school. Other students were never passed the ball or picked for teams because of their immediately apparent inferior level of play. Therefore, PE class was frequently dominated by the same small group of cisgender, able-bodied, heterosexual boys whose refusal to share space was rarely challenged by the teachers. In fact, the only time I ever witnessed a teacher reprimand a student for hogging the ball was when Mr. Gonzalez and another grade 10 teacher combined their classes to conduct basketball scrimmages. The other teacher, Ms. Murphy, spent the entire period following one of the only Black students around with a whistle, scolding him for not passing enough. Several times she halted the game entirely to reproach him in front of the rest of the class. She did not admonish any of the white or East Asian boys who behaved similarly.

The colonial and ableist origins of physical education endure. Through the elevation of uniform measurements, testing, and standards in physical education, the "healthy," "productive," and "fit" citizen has been constructed as a white, settler, able-bodied, cisheteronormative man. Normatively fit bodies are celebrated and rewarded, while racialized, gender-nonconforming, disabled, and fat youth are more likely to encounter a variety of challenges in PE classes. At times, students who struggled to fit in during PE class were offered workarounds in the form of accommodations. Teachers gave certain students special permission to rework an activity, sit out a class, or participate in the space differently to facilitate their inclusion, as when Mr. Gonzalez told Raeyun that he could use the boys' locker room. These individualized modifications did not disrupt the Euro-Canadian standards of normativity, ability, and fitness that dominated in the space. Rather, teachers recognized that some students would never be able to fit in or perform at the expected level and then provided alternatives that permitted the standards to remain unquestioned. The regulatory practices and constrained parameters that govern PE courses have contributed to the trend of trans students dropping out of these classes and divesting from sports and fitness programs generally.[30]

There's a Test for That

Each term, Mr. Gonzalez guided the class through a seemingly neverending slew of fitness testing. In North America, these types of tests were originally established in response to national anxieties over creating cohorts of men who were masculine and strong, and they have been entangled in militarism and nationalism since their foundation.[31] Fitness tests, which have been widely discredited as invalid and ineffective, rely on normative standards of movement and ideas about health that reproduce gendered, colonial, and ableist views of the body.

Fitness testing is no longer required by the province of British Columbia, and not all PE teachers at East City High incorporated this activity as part of their repertoire. However, Mr. Gonzalez spoke about fitness testing *as if* it were compulsory. Every term, the students did sit-ups, push-ups, and timed runs; held their chins above bars; jumped toward taped-out markings on the floor; and stretched their arms across a board. The fitness testing took so long that it felt as if the class had barely finished by the time Mr. Gonzalez warned students that they were but a couple of weeks away from fitness testing ramping back up. Mr. Gonzalez instructed students that, to pass a fitness test, they had to perform according to an index of gendered standards that he maintained at the front of his binder. These standards functioned as a mandate in Mr. Gonzalez's class. He was not officially required to utilize these tests or any gendered criteria for assessment; however, the tests dominated his curriculum and were the salient form of evaluation each term. Though Mr. Gonzalez had selected to implement these tests in his classes, he still worried about how they excluded Raeyun. "What am I supposed to do with my trans students?" Mr. Gonzalez once asked while pushing his binder toward me and pointing at the page of gendered standards. He wanted to open a door for Raeyun, but he was unclear of the process.

When individualized and approached on a case-by-case basis, accommodations reproduce normative expectations for students and reproduce a certain type of student that is allowed to be included.[32] For instance, the existence of trans students did not disrupt Mr. Gonzalez's faith in biological essentialism. Rather than addressing the underlying cisheteronormativity that characterized PE class in general, Mr. Gonzalez worked to create modifications for Raeyun's "unique" situation. As Martino, Kassen, and Omercajic argue, "an individualist approach . . . does not lead necessarily to addressing the cis(sys)temic barriers preventing trans recognisability and intelligibility, . . . not to mention the prevalence of transphobic microaggressions that are enacted against gender diverse youth in schools on a daily basis."[33] Reworking the curriculum to accommodate Raeyun as an individual trans student permitted the cisheteronormativity of PE to remain intact. The assumption was that Raeyun, as a *known* gender-nonconforming student, was the only one who would benefit from a less binary alternative in class. However, many of the youth in the study were never recognized by their teachers, counselors, or the administrators as gender nonconforming and thus were never presented with any options for workarounds at school.

Preying on the Weak and Chubby

Almost no one read Scarecrow Jones as gender nonconforming. "In terms of other people, no, I think that they probably do not see me [as gender nonconforming]," Scarecrow Jones explained. "Since I'm not out to many people, I don't want to give anyone any reason to think that I am not what I appear to be." Since Scarecrow Jones's gender nonconformity did not align with others' expectations, they were not offered any special permissions. To others, Scarecrow Jones did not *look* as if they needed them. Therefore, Scarecrow Jones got ready for PE in the girls' locker room, was counted as a girl during activities, and was judged based on the assessment standards for girls. Scarecrow Jones described PE as "this weird heteronormative culture, like, heteronormative, cisgender ingrained into everyone's brain that's just making it so much more difficult and so much weirder for everyone every day." Scarecrow Jones understood the prevailing cisheteronormativity of PE class as affecting "everyone every day," not just recognizably trans students. Furthermore, teachers' strategies of offering individualized alternatives for visibly nonconforming students did not address, let alone disrupt, the cisheteronormative culture and curriculum of PE class that Scarecrow Jones found so difficult and weird.

Scarecrow Jones's disdain for PE was not limited to the transphobia of that space. One day after Junior Theater Company, Scarecrow Jones lingered by the doorway to delay their departure for PE class. They explained that they did not want to attend because PE class "preys on the weak and chubby." Discourses on fatness are entangled in ideas about the "right" way to exist in a body. Following the feminist scholar Alison Kafer, "Fat bodies and disabled bodies . . . neither [are] permitted to exist as part of a desired present or a desirable future."[34] Schooling struggles to acknowledge youth in their nonnormative bodies and cannot fathom the possibility that youth desire their fatness, disability, and gender nonconformity.

The disparagement of fat bodies in PE likewise fostered Raeyun's ambivalent relationship to the class. On the one hand, Raeyun regularly struggled with the cisheteronormativity of the space. In response, he frequently enacted small forms of refusal, such as opting to be the first person out during group games on purpose, so he could sit on the sidelines and chat with friends or me rather than participate. On the other hand, Raeyun also spoke at length about his desire to sculpt himself into the gay male ideal of slender litheness.[35] He believed that assuming a particular form of masculine musculature would facilitate his legibility as a gay trans guy. Therefore, he was eager to perform certain activities that he thought might help him lose weight and address his body dysphoria.

* * *

Uncertain how to evaluate Raeyun's performance but adamant on using gendered standards for the class, Mr. Gonzalez finally just asked Raeyun how he wanted to be judged. Raeyun looked at the list and decided on a middle ground between the criteria for girls and boys, in the hopes of getting a passing grade in his least favorite class. Though Mr. Gonzalez's willingness to follow Raeyun's guidance demonstrates that he had some understanding of the ways these systems did not work, he remained tethered to the promise of their overall efficacy. Mr. Gonzalez refused to question the cisheteronormative foundations informing fitness testing and the prevailing notions of physical ability and health. Raeyun merely represented an anomaly, and Mr. Gonzalez was committed to finding a way to accommodate his unique situation. In the context of PE class, Raeyun was tasked with understanding that his way of being a boy was distinct and, at least in PE, less than others. Rather than learning from Raeyun's presence that fitness testing was flawed and that notions of physical ability and health that relied on rigid, normative conceptions of bodies enacted violence, Mr. Gonzalez found a way to still include Raeyun in the class and in fitness testing. Raeyun's inclusion was a sign of the institution adapting to make space for a particular form of gender nonconformity without having to abandon any of its ingrained cisheteronormativity.

Conclusion

Accommodations have become the dominant approach to trans-inclusivity in North American schools. Scholarship assessing accommodation strategies depicts these policies as vital protective factors for trans youth.[36] Researchers likewise underscore the constraints of these approaches, summarized well by Martino, Kassen, and

Omercajic, who highlight "the limits of an individualist approach to supporting transgender affirmative education and policy mobilisation in schools that required the embodied presence and visibility of the transgender student as a basis for ensuring their recognisability."[37] While the particular facets of the policies differ across schools, in districts that have adopted this model, individual trans students become responsible for making themselves known as requiring concessions. These students must first become visible and recognizable as trans, often through aligning themselves with the school's expectations for trans identity. Frequently, youth are also responsible for approaching educators to request concessions. Students were forced to pursue these tactics on a regular basis, for an accommodation in one class or even the accommodation of an individual trans young person did not engender any larger change at the school. At East City High, the existence of gender-nonconforming youth did not compel educators to question the underlying cisheteronormativity of the school or schooling. Rather, each student represented a singular exception who required their own accommodations to fit back into an otherwise functioning system. Instead of creating space for gender-nonconforming youth to exist as they desired, the aim of accommodations was to minimize the ways these students were different and as seamlessly as possible to incorporate them into the mainstream operations of the school. Through this approach, the school was imagined as a benevolent institution that could be safe for these students.

While trans-inclusive policies that employ accommodation models are poised to ameliorate school settings in response to visible, known trans youth, these approaches do not address institutional cisheteronormativity or transphobia. They struggle to acknowledge, let alone consider the needs and desires of, gender-nonconforming youth, whose experiences and genders are rarely encapsulated within the policy's language and expectations. Further, given the reactive nature of these policies, they are not working to change school cultures. Rather, they are *responding* to the presence of individual students and then endeavoring to fit those students back into the existing cisheteronormative culture. This framework presumes that schools are fundamentally operating in a safe manner, and, with minor adjustments, that all young people can belong within these institutions. This premise is flawed and dangerous, for it ignores and erases the cisheteronormative violence endemic to schooling.

Beyond these substantive critiques, I remain concerned about accommodations as a model to include youth in schools for the ways they rely on and reproduce a narrow understanding of trans identity that is mired in risk and harm. The lack of attention to systemic forces depicts youth as a problem to be fixed in schools. Furthermore, the individualist orientation of this framework positions trans youth as in need of protection and safeguarding in schools *because* they are trans. Instead of addressing the ways cisheteronormativity functions in the school, these approaches intend to alert adults to youth who may need extra attention and protection. As a result, educators with good intentions express concern and worry for these youth because they understand part of their job as keeping vulnerable young people safe. The idea that trans youth require extra support then further tethers them to risk and struggle. In this context, it becomes even more challenging for educators to consider the possibility of desiring gender nonconformity. Instead, adults concentrate on cultivating protective factors. These types of programs and the policies they engender hinge on the notion that to keep young people safe, we need to know their genders. The assumption is that by knowing students' genders and therefore identifying students with "different" genders, educators can quickly determine who needs protection in schools.

Educators aim to open doors for visibly trans and gender-nonconforming students by finding pathways of accommodation for individual students whose lives, bodies, and genders do not make sense or fit easily within schools. However, only certain trans youth will ever be able to become knowable in ways that align with the school's understanding of gender and thus be approached by teachers for accommodations. Youth whose genders do not adhere to the school's expectations of transness—racialized youth, disabled youth, and youth whose genders resist stable knowing—will continue to elude legibility and, therefore, the school's safeguarding.

To further think through these questions, I turn in chapters 3–5 to the ways students interacted with the expectations for how gender nonconformity would show up at East City High. I focus on the labor this context required of youth as they navigated others' constrained ideas about legibility and created their own spaces to exist.

3

The Labor of Understanding and Forgiveness

Christmas was a notable event at East City High. In the weeks approaching winter break, students, teachers, and staff decked out the school in decorations. As a Jewish person, I found this clash between official secularism and holiday decorations in a public school confusing and, to be honest, irritating. Students covered their lockers in festive wrapping paper, and teachers did the same with their doors. There was a huge lit-up tree in the main entrance to the school, and someone had strung lights up along the grad hall. There was no mistaking what holiday we were taking a break to celebrate in a few weeks.

Most mornings, I arrived at the school and went directly to a small room just to the left of the main entrance to find Ostrich at the Breakfast Club. I doubt East City High's Breakfast Club program would have run without him. Teachers told me this fact all the time, praising how indispensable Ostrich was to the early-morning space. Ostrich's family life was complicated and often challenging. He lived with his father and two sisters. His abusive mother had left the previous spring, and the family was still recalibrating. Ostrich preferred to spend his spare time at school. Since grade 8, instead of being at home, he had opted to come to school at least an hour early every day to lead Breakfast Club. Most days I arrived early as well, so we could hang out and chat. Not generally loquacious, Ostrich more often communicated through sharing memes and videos. In between his tasks, like restocking the yogurt and milk, slicing banana bread, and toasting bagels, we spent a lot of time hunched over his phone, scrolling through content, and laughing.

When the bell rang on Day Ones (East City High was on a two-day schedule, and students attended different classes on Day Ones and Twos), we left Breakfast Club to navigate our way to the west staircase through the throngs of students bustling to class. We then walked down to the basement for Science and Tech first period. Ms. Conway's science classroom contained several rows of black-topped lab tables. Ostrich and I always sat in the front on the left side at the table closest to the door. Ms. Conway taught Biology as well as Science and Tech. She had a reputation as both quirky and strict. There was a wooden shelving unit behind her desk for student work, and once a deadline had passed, she would use masking tape to create a giant "X" across the shelves. This move prevented students from turning in late assignments. Technically, this practice was against school rules. Still, Ms. Conway was a beloved teacher at East City High, mostly for her creativity in the classroom and obvious passion for science, perhaps also because Ms. Conway was a taxidermist, and her classroom was covered in her handiwork. Students found it weird and oddly compelling.

On this day in December, Ostrich and I slid into our usual seats, and he then immediately took out his phone to scroll through his recent artwork: bee pun drawings. Ostrich was currently obsessed with bee puns. Every morning at Breakfast Club, Ostrich created new bee puns and drew them on the white board. At the end of the club, he took a photo and posted it to an online account that Scarecrow Jones, Raeyun, and I followed.

Since it was first period, students were slow to trickle in, so Ms. Conway decided to begin with a bonus-points activity. The class was studying forensics and learning how to identify handwriting and font type. Ms. Conway handed out a worksheet with examples of different fonts at the top. At the bottom were ten David Letterman jokes written in the various fonts. Ms. Conway instructed the students to match the jokes with the correct font. Ostrich and I chatted while he worked through the examples.

After a couple of minutes, Ms. Conway interrupted and asked if she could show me something in the instructor-only room off the side of the classroom, a staff space I had never seen. I followed her, and when Ms. Conway closed the door, I noticed that she was distraught. She instantly started explaining that she received the handout from a colleague who taught forensics at another school and that she had not read through it until after she distributed it. Flustered, she showed me the handout and pointed to one of the sentences, which read, "I'm your teacher, Mrs. Weston. Last year you knew me as Mr. Weston." She was appalled because she knew the statement was transphobic, but she was also afraid. She looked at me, pleadingly. She did not know what to do, and she wanted my help. She confessed that she would rather be able to reverse the situation, to have never handed out the worksheet to begin with, than to have to address it now with the class.

I was struck most by her fear. By December, I had witnessed casual and not-so-casual acts of transphobia at East City, most often from teachers. However, Ms. Conway displayed a genuine sense of fear at having disseminated transphobic material to her class. Ms. Conway understood herself as a nice teacher with good intentions, and this type of teacher would not use a transphobic example on an activity, especially when they knew they had a trans student present. Though Ms. Conway was appalled and sorry, she was uncertain how to resolve the issue because she had not intended any harm. For Ms. Conway, this incident represented an anomaly in her classroom, not the possibility that cisheteronormativity and transphobia were part of schooling. She was concerned that by directly addressing the transphobic "joke," she would exacerbate her mistake and hurt Ostrich's feelings. She wanted to pretend that nothing had happened. However, she did not. She walked back into the classroom and asked for the students' attention. She apologized. Then she went through each joke on the worksheet and explained why they were not funny. When she finished, she looked at me and mouthed, "I think I'm going to throw up."

Many adults at East City High would surely rankle at the notion that transphobia existed within the school walls. As I interrogated when considering the school's "feel good" approach to diversity and inclusion, a multicultural imperative to be nice and accepting permeated East City High, informing the work of teachers, counselors, and administrators as well as fueling policy related to gender-nonconforming students. In this chapter, I examine the ways adults opened doors for gender-nonconforming youth through their good intentions to support and care about their well-being. Building on the cultural context I explored in chapters 1 and 2, I turn to the assumption that since educators were motivated by good intentions, transphobic incidents were not anyone's fault but rather the result of misunderstandings. If adults in the school had good intentions, then how could the school not be a safe space for all students? However, safety was a qualified concept for trans youth. East City High prided itself on being safe for all, yet an accommodations framework encourages adults to position trans youth as in need of protection. The reactive manner of trans-inclusivity promoted by this perspective reflected educators' awareness that it was vital to accept recognizable, visible trans students. Yet, as I discuss, the doors that adults opened were always already traps, for their acceptance of youth relied on an understanding of trans identity that was situated in risk and struggle. When adults accommodated gender-nonconforming youth, they were often concurrently positioning these youth as vulnerable. Therefore, their acceptance belied their inability to approach teaching and learning with the desire that youth be and grow up trans. In this chapter, I attend to the way adults' "good intentions" and notions of "care" often required youth to be legible through at-risk discourses.

In particular, I am interested in the ways East City High's understanding of trans identity and approach to diversity culture demanded labor from youth as they navigated how to survive the various microaggressions and transphobic incidents that populated their days. As I turn in chapters 3–5 to a focus on youth's labor practices, I begin with their acts of survival. I consider the forms of care work that youth engaged in as they interacted with adults' good intentions to be accepting and supportive. In this chapter, I attend to the ways youth were compelled to reframe transphobic moments, such as the one in Ms. Conway's class, and erase their violence. To care for themselves and their genders as well as facilitate their movements through the school, gender-nonconforming youth performed the labor of understanding and forgiveness. This is work they enacted to survive and engender care but also labor that was required of them by educators who were unable or unwilling to acknowledge the harms they caused. In a context where the prevailing assumption was that students are safe and transphobia does not exist, students became responsible for making sense of the marginalization they experienced. They worked to appreciate adults' concern for their gender transgressions or to recognize the effort teachers put into remembering their names and pronouns. I am fascinated by the largely invisible labor that this cultural context demanded from students.

Language of Concern

At East City High, good intentions were often enveloped in what I have come to think of as the "language of concern." Many teachers, counselors, and administrators deployed the language of concern, often unconsciously, to displace their transphobia by imposing worry onto youth who were not actually in danger. Adults at the school expressed concern over the well-being of students whom they perceived as not fitting in or conforming to gender expectations. For instance, in the winter, a grade 9 Indigenous student started wearing short skirts, platform shoes, and low-cut tops. Several teachers stopped me in the hall to talk about him. Ms. Varma, the film and art teacher, approached me because she had overheard teachers talking. She told me, "I am worried, not about him but about how some teachers are responding to him, because he doesn't do well with authority." She spoke quietly, not to be overheard. "I am worried that teachers are conflating his gender presentation with that behavior. I want to make sure he is getting support." Ms. Varma was wary of the way teachers were drawing on caring language to speak about this student while concurrently pathologizing his gender nonconformity. This student was already framed as vulnerable *because* of his Indigeneity. As an Indigenous student in an overwhelmingly settler institution, this student was frequently labeled as at-risk, and thus gender nonconformity became an additional concern. This reading challenged his ability to create and express his own relationship to his gender by imposing settler notions of legibility onto his embodiment and dress. Adults at the school positioned their concern as nice and supportive, for they were looking out for him. Furthermore, teachers anticipated that this student would be thankful for their intervention because niceness asks people to be grateful. This relationship reflects a multicultural understanding of tolerance and illustrates one way that Canadian pleasantness upholds settler colonialism.[1] In the era of reconciliation, settlers expect appreciation for niceties like land acknowledgments while hedging on questions of land, clean water, overpolicing, and child welfare services. Settlers want Indigenous peoples to acknowledge and laud our good intentions. It was not incidental that educators drew on a language of concern to protect a gender-nonconforming young person whom *they* had positioned as vulnerable and at-risk.

In the fall, I was walking through the counseling suite when Ms. O'Connor, the grade 11 counselor, called out to me. She wheeled her desk chair into the doorway and asked me if I was in touch with Ostrich, reminding me of his deadname. I nodded, and she beckoned me closer.

Ms. O'Connor told me that she had some "concerns" and wanted to chat. I stepped into her office hesitantly, because many adults at the school assumed that I was happy to pass along information about students when they were curious.

Ms. O'Connor told me a story I already knew about how Ostrich had come to see her, requesting that she change his name and pronouns in the system and update his teachers. I thought back to Ostrich's telling of this story. When he excitedly relayed it to me, it had been a seamless narrative: he told Ms. O'Connor about the changes, she updated his file, and then she spread the word. Ostrich believed she followed through on their conversation. However, Ms. O'Connor informed me that she had not done it. She continued, "of course I will because East City is really good about that stuff, but I have some concerns." Ms. O'Connor laid out her concerns for me: namely, that Ostrich was "super vulnerable." He had been on her radar since before high school as an at-risk student, mostly because of his family situation and how his neurodivergence put him at odds with mainstream notions of school success. "I am just worried about him," Ms. O'Connor told me, "because this is a big change and a lot for someone who is already so vulnerable." Ms. O'Connor did not expand on what it meant to be "so vulnerable" because the assumption was that I could make the necessary connections, piecing together who Ostrich was from the stories that were told most often about him by adults in the school. Ms. O'Connor let me know that she had set him up with a counselor outside East City High. "Can you ask him how counseling is going?" She wanted me to regularly report back to her. I did not agree to this arrangement. Ms. O'Connor leaned forward, hands clasped, and smiled at me, believing us to be on the same team. In this conversation, she positioned herself as a counselor going above and beyond. She was not just nice; she was compelled by her good intentions to seek additional supports for a vulnerable youth. Ms. O'Connor suggested that she was attempting to protect Ostrich. However, her concerns were rooted in an understanding of Ostrich as disabled and therefore vulnerable, which she believed made him unable to know and articulate his own gender. The door, Ms. O'Connor's concern, was also a trap that required Ostrich to relent to others' positioning of him as in need of protection. Those concerns made permissible the upholding of an ableist, cisheteronormative order within the school.

Though explicitly displaying unease or discomfort about gender nonconformity would be blatantly transphobic and thus not pleasant and nice, expressing concern for a student functioned differently. Concern has become an avenue for adults who are invested in protecting youth from the hardships and struggles that are deemed inseparable from being gender nonconforming. Ms. O'Connor understood Ostrich's gender nonconformity as intensifying his vulnerability because transness was largely not desired at East City High.

For a student like Ostrich, who was positioned as always already struggling, being trans was deemed an unnecessary burden. I was asked multiple times by support staff if I thought he was faking it or just looking for ways to garner attention. Some adults wondered if Ostrich thought of transitioning as a way to deal with his fatness, extending their concern to the multiple ways his body touched nonnormativity in the school.[2] By framing these inquiries within the language of concern, adults obscured their transphobia, ableism, and fatphobia. Moreover, they pulled Ostrich into this dynamic with them, forcing him to recognize the interaction as one motivated by good intentions rather than by oppression and violence. Ostrich became responsible for understanding the nature of their concerns, a trap that denied his access to feelings of anger and violation. I noticed Ostrich performing this labor. Ostrich increasingly articulated an idea of transness that was tethered to danger and risk. He wanted to medically transition, but he mediated these desires within his growing awareness that a person cannot understand themselves as trans until they have proved that they are stable in their identity. This framework reflected ideas he heard from Ms. O'Connor as well as his father. In sifting through people's reactions to his intentions to transition, Ostrich explained to me others' reasoning through a lens of caring. He listed safety concerns, which he framed as understandable given that no one wanted him to be harmed in any way by taking "irreparable" steps toward transitioning when he was "too young."

Months after my conversation with Ms. O'Connor in the counseling suite, on a day when Ostrich was absent from school, Ms. O'Connor contacted his mother, who was not his primary guardian and was known to the school as abusive. In the process, Ms. O'Connor communicated his name and pronoun change to her. While Ostrich had explicitly given Ms. O'Connor permission to share his name and pronoun change with his teachers, he was decisive that this information should not go to his mother. If Ms. O'Connor's actual concern in withholding Ostrich's name and pronoun change from his teachers had been one of protection, why had she, without consent, divulged this information to his abuser? Ms. O'Connor's decision was an act of violence that impeded Ostrich's safety.

Ostrich ultimately had to perform the labor of both updating his teachers *and* handling the fallout of Ms. O'Connor's exchange with his mother. Thinking alongside Hil Malatino, Ostrich was forced to perform his own care work, to "cultivate arts of living that make [trans people] possible in a culture that is alternatingly . . . either thinly accommodating or devastatingly hostile."[3] Though, as Ms. O'Connor had articulated to me, "East City High is really good about that stuff," the dominance of an accommodation model at the school had not shifted adults' understanding of or engagement with trans identity. Ms. O'Connor still believed gender nonconformity to be risky, and this perception framed how she approached her responsibilities to Ostrich. In urging caution around transition, she understood herself as ensuring his safety. However, after her unprompted disclosure, Ostrich was forced to explain his gender to his mother, a discussion he had previously avoided. While Ostrich was gradually sharing more about his gender with his father and sisters, he had been steadfast that his mother have no role in that part of his life. Despite Ms. O'Connor's many concerns for Ostrich, she was the one who placed him in danger by giving information to his abuser that she had no right to give.

Nice Spaces Are Safe Spaces

Raeyun and I left the theater studio, walked through the cafeteria, and slowly climbed the back staircase to sneak in the ulterior entrance to the gymnasium. We found an empty bench against the wall and huddled together. Raeyun munched on a muffin, and we looked through his doodle-covered planner to find the classroom number for a meeting he had later in the day. East City High was on a block rotation, meaning that the order of students' courses shifted every term. The first couple of days in a new rotation were always a mess, with students frequently walking into the wrong classroom. There was a nutrition break that separated first and second period, and in the new rotation, Raeyun and

I were now stuck in the gymnasium for an extra twenty minutes before PE class started.

Many students chose to spend their breaks in the gymnasium, shooting hoops and tossing frisbees. On this day, like most days, the energy was aggressive and overwhelming. A group of boys yelled and pushed each other, shouting, "fucking homo" and "I'll fucking jerk you off right now," while gesticulating grabbing each other's penises in violent manners. Raeyun and I commiserated. He recounted the other day, when I was out of town for a conference and the school handed out the annual demographics survey. There was a question on it about how safe you feel. He put a seven out of ten, but he told me that if he had to respond right now, he would be a three. Raeyun explained that he had kind of just answered without thinking about it, but he does not actually feel that safe at East City High.

In this section, I examine the assumption that the school was a safe space and how this perception then demanded labor from youth to care for themselves. As I have explored, East City High promoted and reinforced this vision of itself through its mission statement, ways of speaking about the school (think back to Ms. Walker's pronouncement at the staff meeting), and the visuals that were plastered throughout the hallways. However, the school's understanding of itself as safe for all students at times clashed with youth's experiences. Moreover, there were tensions within even the school's self-promotion. East City High positioned itself as safe for all students, but it also framed certain students, like trans and gender-nonconforming students, as at-risk. For both to be true, the risks that trans youth confronted at East City High could not be framed as endemic to the school or schooling. Rather, the harms they experienced had to be positioned as aberrations to the standard functioning of East City High. This framework forced trans youth to perform the labor to understand these transphobic incidents as anomalous, forgive those who had hurt them, and learn how to care for themselves as a result.

As Safe as a Rainbow

"Safe space" stickers were ubiquitous at East City High. Every single classroom door had a "safe space" sticker adorning the window, although some stickers looked as if they were replaced every year while some were mostly faded and almost entirely peeled off. Scarecrow Jones blasted these supposed signs of support. "'Safe space' stickers don't mean anything, come on. It's, like, the district is, like, put these up, and the teachers are, like, 'Pay me more,' you know." They continued their rant: "The stickers, people will say that they're accepting, and they're all for it, and whatever, but for a lot of people, when it actually comes down to it, they're not." Scarecrow Jones would not be fooled by peeling-off pieces of plastic and paper. "They will, like—I mean, don't get me wrong—a lot of people are very accepting of it and will respect it. But then there's some people, they won't outright say it's wrong." Scarecrow Jones then affected a high-pitched adult voice to demonstrate the berating approach of teachers they knew: "But they'll be like, 'Hmm, what does that mean for you? What—how do you know? Are you sure, but you're a child?' Maybe not in those words, but, like, just, like, that kind of feeling, and then they treat you differently." The easy presence of a symbol of acceptance offended Scarecrow Jones, who had no tolerance for hypocrisy. Scarecrow Jones saw traps in the rainbow stickers on doors. In their experience, people might not "outright say it's wrong," but their attitude and behavior toward queerness and gender nonconformity betrayed their discomfort. If people knew you were gender nonconforming, they would treat you differently. Scarecrow Jones pointed out the typical questions that teachers might ask to undercut the legitimacy of gender nonconformity. In these questions, there were echoes of the way Ms. O'Connor denied Ostrich the possibility of articulating his own gender. Ms. O'Connor, drawing on adultist and ableist notions of knowing better, believed she was acting in Ostrich's best interests.[4] Travers argues, "The assumption that children's and young people's identities are static and that their exploration of gendered identities, trying on of names, and so on are not to be taken seriously speaks to the disabling effects of binary gender and age subordination as key organizing principles of mainstream schools."[5] Scarecrow Jones experienced this ableist paternalism, noting how their teachers' line of thinking ("Are you sure, but you're a child?") undermined their sense of their gender.

East City High was constructed as a safe space in part through visuals, like the rainbow stickers and posters in the school that denounced bullying, racism, and homophobia.[6] Scarecrow Jones refused this superficial rendering of the school as safe, listing several alternatives for their teachers that would be more generative and positive in their life. Scarecrow Jones explained, "I just kind of wish they understood at least what the terms mean because I'm, like, a kid, and I know what all these terms mean. I bet half the teachers don't even know what the word 'pansexual' means." Scarecrow Jones was full of ideas on how to improve East City High: "Maybe put some proper grammar on the posters that you put up in the classrooms. . . . You can't learn every single thing you need to know in the course of one session, so . . . like, you can't get it done in one professional development day." They feared the level of commitment was the biggest obstacle because it "means the teachers have to be willing to put in the time. . . . Everything seems to be stacked against it."

Scarecrow Jones was consistently frustrated by East City High's official stance toward queer and trans students and how that formal narrative contrasted with their daily experience. What difference did it make if a teacher had a "safe space" sticker on their door when Scarecrow Jones was aware of the underlying cisheteronormativity that shaped their life at East City High? Despite the pervasive "safe space" stickers in the school, Scarecrow Jones did not use "they/them" pronouns in school because they did not trust teachers to understand. As they pointed out to me, "If the school is such a safe space, why aren't more teachers actually out?" For Scarecrow Jones, safety would never be encapsulated in a rainbow sticker but instead had to be demonstrated by the everyday acknowledgment that queerness existed. In their frustration, Scarecrow Jones exposed the many tensions within East City High's approach to safe spaces, highlighting the doors and traps that educators provided for gender-nonconforming youth in the name of safety.

I Am Concerned about Safe Spaces

In English 11, I sat in the back row behind Raeyun. One day in March, Mr. Harding, his English teacher, finished the lesson unexpectedly early and gave the class free time until the period ended. Most students hung out on their phones. A few industrious boys pushed their desks together and set up a Nintendo Switch to play *Super Smash Brothers*. After a few moments, Raeyun turned sideways in his seat and placed one arm on my desk. It was a Day One, which meant that Raeyun was in his standard non-PE-day outfit: jeans, a T-shirt, and a hoodie jacket that he had bought at Old Navy. His sketchbook was propped on his knees, and he was mapping out his future with doodles. He imagined different pathways toward his currently preferred careers: cook, forensics detective, or musician. He plotted short- and long-term goals, like getting his driver's license and his food safe certificate and studying criminology at a local university. Raeyun filled the page with his characteristic illustrations of nonhuman creatures. He thought there was more possibility when you did not get stuck drawing human figures.

Leaning against my desk, Raeyun recounted what happened last period in his French class: "People were doing speeches, and one student did a speech about 'transgender washrooms.'" Each student had to present opinion pieces in the form of three-minute speeches. This student "said he was uncomfortable with the idea [of sharing bathrooms with trans people] and worried about safety." Raeyun generously relayed his classmate's concerns to me. The student viewed it as a matter of his safety, and Raeyun was quick to acknowledge this student's fears and anxieties. Furthermore, he empathized, noting unironically, "I am not always comfortable using the washroom with cis people, so I get how that could work." Raeyun and I went back and forth a bit, grappling with these ideas of fear and safety. He described to me how last summer, at a camp for queer and trans youth, "all the washrooms were gender neutral, and it wasn't a big deal." He paused and then commented, "It's not like you are going to go into the washroom to stare at someone taking a shit." I laughed, adding, "Yeah, washrooms aren't sexy places." Raeyun agreed, "Yeah, they're just washrooms. What's the big deal?" He momentarily left behind the multiple justifications he had generously been creating for his classmate and instead started ranting about how "trans people were using bathrooms years ago, and no one cared; why now?" Still leaning on my desk, Raeyun concluded, "I thought it was an interesting thing to come up in class." Then he turned back around and continued sketching for the remainder of class.

After English, I swung by the classroom of Raeyun's French teacher. Madame Blanchet and I had an amiable, easygoing relationship, and I hoped to inspire her to tell me the story as well. I poked my head into the classroom, and she smiled, welcoming me in. After a few minutes of casual conversation, I asked if I could chat to her a bit about one of her earlier classes. She did not hesitate for a moment. She knew what class I wanted to talk about, which was not all that surprising given my role in the school. She had a prep block and was keen to talk about the event. I spent most of the next period with her. She leaned in and said straight away, referring to the boy who made the speech, "Isn't it interesting? He has two moms!" In locating this student within, or at least adjacent to, the queer community, Madame Blanchet was signaling *something* to me. Perhaps she thought that this student could not possibly be transphobic because of his queer or lesbian parents?

Madame Blanchet enthusiastically described the activity and throughout our conversation stressed that the boy's work was "neutral" and "not aggressive." Madame Blanchet explained that she had reviewed all the opinion pieces before students presented them. "I had read it ahead of time, and there was nothing that flagged to me." She continued, "It was an opinion piece, and there weren't any slurs, and it was actually more neutral and benign than a lot of other things that people have talked about in class." She was particularly impressed by this student's perspective. "He talked about his discomfort and his concerns about safety. . . . Wasn't it interesting? Because he wasn't thinking about trans people's safety." Madame Blanchet went on to explain how when most people discussed this topic, they focus on the safety concerns for trans people, but this student took an entirely different approach. For Madame Blanchet, this perspective signaled creativity. "But," she continued, "many people prickled once he gave the title of his talk, and they didn't listen all the way through to his logic, to his discussion of separate bathrooms. There were parts that were very empowering." As a result of not listening all the way through, students could not grasp the empowering parts of his presentation. I nodded and asked her to tell me more about those elements. For me, her response was vague and difficult to follow. Mostly she explained that the student thought both sides needed a solution, and she stressed, "He didn't say any myths." Then she paused for a moment, staring at me. "I am concerned about safe spaces," she underscored to me, "but also that was his opinion, and I didn't rebut any of the other students who spoke on similarly tough issues like abortion and vaccines." She kept looking at me, compassionately, and explained, "I know Raeyun is trans. I hope he still feels safe to come to class." After an uncomfortable moment, she asked, "Does he?"

The assumption is that schools are safe, and safe spaces are places where there is no trouble.[7] This lack of trouble can mean the avoidance of challenging topics and a hesitancy to confront issues that would disturb the dominant perception of the school as diverse, inclusive, and safe.[8] Though the move toward safe school policies in British Columbia originated to protect queer youth from bullying and harassment, the concept of safety in schools "has evolved into a catch phrase to encompass all of the policy intended to create diverse climates within schools, encourage inclusive environments, recognize the potential for violent incidences, and limit bullying, harassment, and intimidation within the school environment."[9] Within a neoliberal framework, "bullying" has become a diffuse buzzword unconnected to challenging systemic oppression. Scholars in education have critiqued several dimensions of safe-space rhetoric, from the ways safe-space programming fails to address the underlying need for safety to the ways youth are differentially positioned in relation to notions of safety.[10] Furthermore, there has been a growing call in queer scholarship to move beyond bullying as the capstone of safety.[11] These appeals are grounded in the awareness that continuously and exclusively theorizing queer and trans youth in connection to risk and harm tethers young people to these notions of hardship and danger.

There is also, as I mentioned, an underlying tension in East City High's relationship to the notion of safety for gender-nonconforming youth. On the one hand, the school prides itself on inclusivity and presents itself as safe for all. Yet, on the other hand, educators regularly positioned gender-nonconforming students as unsafe or, at least, less safe than their peers with access to cisheteronormative privilege. East City High's particular diversity culture complicated gender-nonconforming youths' relationship with safety: they were not exclusively victims or considered free from danger. The expectation of safety for all students existed in a tense duality with the recognition that gender-nonconforming youth confronted unique challenges at East City High. At times, this awareness that gender-nonconforming youth might be less safe than other students provoked an impetus to advocate on their behalf, as with Ms. O'Connor. Even when advocacy was not the result, educators' good intentions to accommodate gender-nonconforming youth relied on the recognition that they were less safe than other students.

However, the pervasive assumption that East City High was a safe school prevented the interrogation of the underlying power structures that contributed to the cisheteronormativity that gender-nonconforming youth daily navigated. This framework aligns with Ms. Stein's workshop at the staff meeting. She presented the racist incidents as misunderstandings instead of evidence of structural violence, advocating allyship as a solution. This move positioned teachers as protectors rather than participants in violence. Reflecting educational scholarship, the sense at East City High was that teachers were present to safeguard youth.[12] Thus, when students confronted unsafe incidents, these moments were labeled as aberrations, divergences from the school's proper functioning. These were mere slipups, like Ms. Conway not prereading the handout and accidentally distributing transphobic material to her class. The reigning belief was that no one was intentionally transphobic.

A young person's disparate experience of the school as safe could potentially disrupt that careful positioning. However, if all actors had good intentions, then no one *deliberately* caused harm. As Castagno explains, "Within a frame of niceness, oppressive actions are not actually oppressive; they are just hurtful. They are assumed to be the result of individuals who have made bad choices or who just do not know any better. This framing diverts attention away from patterned inequity, structural oppression, and institutional dominance."[13]

In this framework, acts of violence, such as transphobia, racism, or anti-Indigeneity, are not anyone's fault; instead, they become the result of misunderstandings. This framework does not work without students' (even reluctant) participation. When the pervasive framework positions adults as acting with good intentions, it becomes the students' responsibility to *understand* and *forgive*, to recognize the terms of the misunderstanding and engage in the process of reconciliation. Furthermore, since the "protection" and "safety" that youth are receiving from the school is, at best, inadequate and, at worst, violent, if trans and gender-nonconforming youth desire communities of care, they need to create them on their own. Raeyun did this work when he retold the story of that French class. He worked to understand and empathize with a student who stood in front of the class and argued against his right to access public space. Raeyun listened to this diatribe against his right to exist while in a school that repeatedly positioned itself as safe, inclusive, and welcoming. Critically, in reaching out to share this story with me, the only trans adult he knew, Raeyun was cultivating trans care. He processed his feelings, found laughter and humor, and reimagined his relationship to the transphobia he endured.

Raeyun had previously explained to me how he experienced whiteness at school as white boys taking up space. During the queer and trans camp he attended, he had participated in a workshop on race and space-taking that revolutionized how he understood racism at East City High. He described his "huge takeaway" as "just being aware of how much space you have, how much you are taking, and how much you can give and how much people can take from you." When his teacher did not interject or debrief the white, cisgender, straight boy's speech, that student's views were allowed to dominate the classroom space. Madame Blanchet explained to me that there just would not have been enough time to debrief each topic. However, by not intervening during the discussion, Madame Blanchet failed to foster care for Raeyun and for transness. Instead, she signaled that this white boy's opportunity to express an opinion was as important as, if not more than, Raeyun's safety in the school, ability to access a bathroom without fear, and right to sit in class without being policed. As I discussed in chapter 1, the social policing of bathrooms is never just a gendered regulation. Bathrooms are contested spaces that heighten normative expectations of bodies regarding gender, sexuality, race, and ability.[14] Not thinking about bathroom access is a privilege. Madame Blanchet's decision not to interject reproduced normative power dynamics in the classroom and at East City High, constructing a limited version of safety at the expense of Raeyun. In this context, it became Raeyun's responsibility to reframe what he heard as not oppressive.

Raeyun and I were at McDonald's after school one month later, discussing why the proposal for a multistall, gender-neutral bathroom kept getting blocked by the administration at East City High. Raeyun, who tried to make it through the entire school day without using the bathroom, had previously supported the proposal for the bathroom. Our conversation began in a similar vein as others on the subject. Raeyun blamed the school's stinginess, complaining that administrators just did not want to spend money on improving the school for trans students. He told me, "Not a lot of people say much [about the bathroom] 'cause if people say something, like, they could always just be like, 'We already have a nongendered washroom.' But . . . is that really enough though? It's one washroom on the third floor." Raeyun explained how this one bathroom was not enough for him and infrequently felt helpful. "I could be in Ms. Mack's room [in an outbuilding] and walk all the way there, and it would be occupied, and I would be pissed."

However, as Raeyun kept talking, he remembered risk and safety issues that had recently been brought to his attention. He explained how a space that all genders can access could be dangerous. "I think a lot of people might not be comfortable themselves with going because a nongendered washroom means that both genders can go at the same time, right? So that might cause a lot of risk for people." While attempting to recall what made such a space dangerous, Raeyun shared where he learned about this possibility in the first place: Madame Blanchet's class. "This was just brought to my attention, but, like, people could, like, try to kill themselves in there because it's locked, right? There's also the whole problem with sexual harassment. . . . There's a lot to consider." Ever the good student, Raeyun performed the necessary labor to understand the event in Madame Blanchet's classroom. "I feel like I used to say, 'Oh yeah, it's easy,' but now that I'm thinking about it, . . . I feel like it's either a cost issue, a plumbing issue, or a safety issue." By leaving the student's diatribe against "transgender bathrooms" unchallenged, Madame Blanchet fostered a nice classroom environment that avoided controversy. This evasion, however, occurred through a privileging of dominant voices. Though Raeyun was at first uncomfortable with the gap between his experience and the viewpoint left unquestioned in class, he worked to bring the two sides closer together. He recalled examples of danger and harm from the class discussion and let this new knowledge affect his previously steadfast belief in his right to public space. No one was asked to care about Raeyun and his right to access a bathroom safely and easily. However, Raeyun was tasked with being responsible for caring about the potential risks of this space. Since Raeyun cared about safety, now that he knew there was something dangerous and risky about a gender-neutral bathroom, he worked to incorporate that understanding into his perspective.

Theater Company by Any Other Name

There was an intimacy among the students in theater that I did not witness in other classes. They held hands while sitting together and teased each other about their sexuality in an affectionate rather than hurtful manner. At the end of the year, Campbell, a white, femme, gay boy was cast as a big man on campus in a student-directed play. The whole group joked lovingly with Campbell as they tried to help him figure out how to lean against the lockers in a sexy, masculine way during a scene. Everyone, including Campbell, was laughing so hard that they had to keep pausing rehearsal. Then the student in charge decided just to switch the stage directions to whatever position Campbell felt more comfortable enacting. In media (think *Glee*) and scholarship, theater and arts classes are often considered an encouraging space for queer and trans students.[15] Four participants in the study were involved with East City High's theater program, and all of them struggled with Ms. Mack, the unpredictable, demanding director. Students complained about Ms. Mack's propensity to take her stress out on them. Scarecrow Jones summed up this issue, saying, "I don't think she copes with stress well, ... As soon as she gets a little bit stressed, it's immediately—bam!—world is ending. She's yelling, 'You're not doing this,' and ahhh!" Still, all four participants loved the art of theater, tech, and acting. They worked hard to understand and forgive Ms. Mack's transphobia to enable their continued participation in that space.

Opening a Can of Worms

The first time I went to Ms. Mack's theater studio, she was delighted and asked me to accompany her to the tech booth for a chat. The booth was up a flight of stairs and looked out over the rest of the studio. There was a lighting and sound board and then huge windows so that whoever was working tech could have an unobstructed view of the stage. Ms. Mack perched on a stool and explained that ever since I presented my research at the staff meeting in the beginning of the year, she had planned to find me and invite me to her theater classes. Then she leaned forward, tipping the stool onto two legs, and asked if I had arrived with any specific students. Before I could deflect her question, she waved her hands excitedly and asked if she could guess which students I was working with in her class. She believed gender nonconformity to be visible and knowable, an identity she could easily see in her students. I wiggled out of the question, informing her that my participants would remain in confidence. She reluctantly dropped the topic.

Over the course of the year, Ms. Mack incorporated me into her theater company. She tried to cast me in every play the Senior Theater Company produced. When I demurred, unwilling to take a role that should belong to a student, she enlisted me as a production assistant. I helped to build sets, ran her errands, sat through auditions, learned how to work the lights and sound in the tech booth, and assisted in creative decisions. I have a bit of a background in theater, and Ms. Mack glommed onto that experience, believing it meant we had a special connection. Though Ms. Mack knew, on some level, that I was present in the school to work with students and that I attended a variety of classes in all subject areas, she operated as if I were *really* at East City High because of the theater program.

The theater studio was in one of the outbuildings at East City High. To get there, you left the main building through the back doors, walked across a small courtyard, entered through the far doors (the ones that led to the cafeteria, not the gymnasium), and went down the stairs. The theater studio was directly under the old gymnasium. When PE classes used that space, we would hear lots of stamping feet and balls bouncing above our heads. Originally, the theater studio was going to be a pool, so it had very high windows that Ms. Mack had entirely blacked out. Actually, everything in the theater studio was black: black painted floors, black painted block bleacher seats, black curtains surrounding the stage and the tall windows. When you entered the studio, you lost all sense of time and weather.

Occasionally Ms. Mack started class with a check-in circle. These check-ins were inconsistent. When Ms. Mack had an issue to raise with the class or tensions seemed particularly high, she instructed everyone to grab a chair from behind the black curtains and circle up. Everyone went around and shared how they were feeling and then said "check" to indicate the end of their turn. Often students would lament their workload, lack of sleep, and conflicts with teachers. Sometimes a student shared a more serious story, telling the class that they had not eaten in days, for instance. Then they would say "check," and we would just move on to the next person's story. I never witnessed Ms. Mack follow up with a student after these circles, though it was certainly possible that she did.

Toward the end of September, Ms. Mack breezed into class her customary few minutes after the bell and told students to form a circle. Ms. Mack wanted to "open a can of worms." In the script they were considering for the main production, there was a character whose name was "Slut." The play hinged on stereotypes and, ideally, would provide commentary on these terms through exaggerated performances. Ms. Mack facilitated a conversation about the word "slut" before asking different students to read the part. She asked Campbell to read the role, wondering out loud how having a "male" read the part might shift the meaning of the term. Then Ms. Mack looked directly at me. She turned back to Campbell and announced, to raucous laughter, "Actually, I don't know how you identify." Ms. Mack informed the class, "I don't want to assume pronouns or gender." She then initiated a pronoun share. Three of my participants were students in this class, and now, three weeks into the term, they had the opportunity to tell everyone their pronouns. Ostrich told the class "he or they," Vixen said "anything," and Raeyun asked for "any pronoun except 'she.'" Ms. Mack ended by telling the class that absolutely any pronoun was fine. This comment betrayed Ms. Mack's lack of awareness of her access to cisgender privilege. Would Ms. Mack truly be fine if the students referred to her with *any* pronoun? If so, why did she never encourage the students to use different pronouns?

At the end of the period, Raeyun was gathering his bag when Ms. Mack stopped him and said that now that she had heard about his pronouns, she was going to have trouble using anything but "she" for him. Ms. Mack did struggle with Raeyun's pronouns. She was a nice teacher with good intentions, but she was new to trans issues. Throughout the year, Ms. Mack regularly misgendered Raeyun, sometimes catching herself and apologizing, other times just blazing ahead. She consistently relied on Raeyun to understand and forgive this behavior that she had prepared him for in September. Ms. Mack told him she was trying and depended on her good intentions of one day getting his pronouns right to avoid the possibility of transphobia. By positioning herself as working toward getting it right, Ms. Mack attempted to erase the potential of harm. She was not transphobic because she was not *intending* to harm

Raeyun; she was simply in the process of learning. She believed her commitment to doing better absolved her transphobia and compelled Raeyun to forgive her or else risk being seen as unsympathetic and overly demanding.

Raeyun had a hard time interjecting to correct Ms. Mack and instead settled into a routine of understanding and forgiveness. "I'm kind of awkward about it," Raeyun admitted, "'cause I feel like Ms. Mack, for her specifically, I feel like she speaks too fast, so then I just can't correct her." Raeyun consistently felt thwarted by Ms. Mack. "She just speaks too fast. I can't stop and be like, 'Hold on a second. It's actually "man."'" Raeyun was at times exasperated by this dynamic, but he was likewise forgiving. "And to be honest, I feel like she knows. She just kind of forgets sometimes. And to me, that's fine. If you forget, we all do. I forgot to do my homework one time, that's fine." Though Raeyun was hurt by Ms. Mack's behavior, he trivialized it. In the same breath, Raeyun informed me that he believed Ms. Mack knew she was misgendering him while also excusing this behavior. In classic Raeyun fashion, he approached this hurtful experience with tremendous generosity, likening her constant misgendering of him (which he explained as forgetting) to him forgetting to do his homework one time. He took responsibility, and Ms. Mack never did.

For Raeyun, forgiving Ms. Mack was a form of care work. By choosing to understand her behavior and frame her misgendering as forgetting, Raeyun showed himself care. Malatino explains how trans people rely on each other for survival because of "the affective and practical disinvestment of the people and institutions" that should be upholding our lives. He argues, "We have learned to care for one another in the aftermath of these refusals."[16] Raeyun learned to understand and forgive Ms. Mack as a method of survival in a school and a class where his gender was consistently denied. Over the year, I likewise witnessed Raeyun and Ostrich develop a friendship forged in the care that they demonstrated for each other's queerness and gender nonconformity. In chapter 5, I explore how, in the absence of trans recognition and the school's multitude of affective refusals, Raeyun and Ostrich cultivated their own community of care.

Though Ms. Mack had not warned Ostrich, she similarly misgendered and deadnamed him throughout the year. Initially, Ostrich had wanted significant distance between us during the project, but he quickly changed his mind and often attached himself to my side during classes. Since we were frequently together, I was standing with him when he informed Ms. Mack that he had changed his name, a process he took responsibility for because Ms. O'Connor was dilatory on her end. Ms. Mack responded enthusiastically, letting him know that now that he had a more conventionally masculine name, she was much more likely to remember his pronouns. This perspective was not uncommon at East City High and is reflected in research, which states that "educators are more likely to use correct pronouns when students reinforce the gender binary."[17] In an interview a few weeks after Ostrich updated Ms. Mack about his name change, he described to me the importance of helping people understand your gender. "If something helps, then it'll help. Like, with pronouns, having a name that's kind of associated with more feminine is kind of more hard to think of more masculine pronouns for a name that tends to be more feminine." Ostrich agreed that it was necessary to match your name and pronouns so that both are coded as either masculine or feminine and indicated that he had a role to play in preventing people from misgendering him. "Having a name that's kind of more masculine, it helps . . . put your mind-set to the more masculine side." Selecting a name that helped people understand him as a man was a way that Ostrich performed care work, endeavoring to safeguard his experience and prevent himself from being misgendered.

Still, even after Ostrich chose a masculine-coded name, Ms. Mack struggled to remember his pronouns and would often revert to his deadname. Because Ostrich did not present as people expected a guy to look, many people could not reconcile his gender with their assumptions. Ostrich told me, "When it happens, it's, like, I just feel so uncomfortable. And sometimes I would rather stab myself in the shoulder than be called that." Ostrich had done everything possible under his control to facilitate a better experience for himself in theater class. Despite his labor, he was still misgendered, and that was extremely painful for him.

Ms. Mack's persistent misgendering of Raeyun, Ostrich, and Vixen also made permissible their classmates' inattention to their names and pronouns. At the start of the year, students interjected and corrected Ms. Mack, predominantly on behalf of Raeyun and Ostrich. Students in the class tended to struggle in recognizing Vixen's complicated relationship with gender, and classmates had an easier time supporting Raeyun and Ostrich. However, ultimately even this encouraging behavior waned, perhaps in response to its inefficacy. By the spring, many students in Senior Theater Company not only had ceased to advocate on behalf of Raeyun and Ostrich by reminding Ms. Mack about their pronouns and names but had forgotten themselves. The expansion of Ms. Mack's misgendering into a classroom dynamic intensified the labor required of Raeyun, Ostrich, and Vixen. There were now more people to forgive and more incidents to reframe as misunderstandings.

Keep It Confusing

Over the year, Ms. Mack referred to me by every pronoun in quick succession, as if she wanted to make sure to cover her bases. Students would laugh at this frenetic display of confused gendering, but I found it exhausting. Vixen, however, would have loved it if Ms. Mack cycled through multiple pronouns for them. Vixen used every pronoun, though people rarely acknowledged this important aspect of their gender. When Vixen first came out as genderfluid, they created an elaborate system with differently colored bracelets to signal which pronoun they wanted their friends to use for them that day. However, Vixen found that system quickly became overwhelming and overly complicated. Plus, they realized they were not always sure what pronoun felt best, so having to stabilize their decision by choosing a bracelet did not work for their fluid relationship to gender. Instead, Vixen switched to all pronouns. Vixen believed gender should not be boring, so they wanted to "keep it confusing."

Vixen was an actor in Senior Theater Company as well as in a social-justice-oriented youth theater program in the city. But beyond that, they exuded theatricality. Vixen was a writer, and we often met up to discuss their novels. When Vixen read out loud, they did not just read the words off their phone. They performed. Everything Vixen did, they did with flourish. They embodied their characters and brought the story to life, gesticulating and doing the voices to curate the dramatics. Despite their deep love of theater, Vixen loathed Senior Theater Company. They regularly clashed with Ms. Mack and, on multiple occasions, ended up kicked out of rehearsals. During the winter, when Vixen was struggling to attend school regularly, Ms. Mack took away their role in the main production. When they found out, Vixen, ever the actor, did a nearly convincing job of feigning dispassion, but I saw their eyes slowly fill with tears. They quickly concealed it with cutting critiques of Ms. Mack's leadership, but there was a small sliver of disappointment underneath their tough exterior of aloofness.

Since Vixen's gender nonconformity did not align with adults' expectations for what it means and looks like to be gender nonconforming, they were infrequently recognized as such at East City High. Instead, people defaulted to the pronouns that seemed most obvious to them and did not hear Vixen when they communicated about their gender. Vixen described it this way:

> I've definitely noticed, like, I notice the irony of that, like, when I say, "You can use any pronouns," I mean any pronouns—like, it really does mean just use anything. But I know that saying that is basically futile because as soon as I say I'm fine with any pronoun, people are, like, "Oh, then I can call you 'she.' Great," you know, and that's all they really care about, because that's what they would have called me anyway. So, just to hear it's, like, "Oh, it doesn't offend you. Great," which is kind of annoying, in some ways, because it's, like, I say, "any pronoun," I mean anything: switch it up, make it confusing, you know. But I think it's, like, it doesn't, like—I say it doesn't offend me, so it's, like, fine if people want to use "she/her" pronouns because I respond to that and that works just as well. And it's just, like, I would appreciate someone switching it up from time to time, you know, because that's what I asked for, you know, anything.

Though Vixen was frustrated by people's tendency to take the easiest and least disruptive approach to addressing them, they were not offended by this behavior, so they did not view it as transphobic. Vixen, who was often quick to call out oppression around them, frequently performed the labor of understanding why people struggled to use their pronouns. "I don't take offense to it, and I know that people are not trying to be hurtful by just using basic pronouns," Vixen told me. "They're not trying to harm anyone or anything. Like, whatever is most comfortable for them or whatever is easiest for them that—that's also fine by me because I get it." Because Vixen knew that people were not being intentionally hurtful, they decided not to be hurt when people misgendered them. Instead, Vixen worked to understand and forgive people's inability to see the complexities of their gender and use their pronouns. Their labor participated in protecting others from having to confront the existence of genderfluidity. Their teachers and classmates did not understand shifting, messy pronouns, and having to interact with that reality would have upended the positioning of gender as tidy, stable, and coherent. Vixen's gender could not be framed in those ways; it exceeded the bounds of legibility.

Deciding to understand and forgive was also a method of care for Vixen themself. Vixen was consistently misgendered, and approaching these experiences with understanding protected them from the idea that there was intention, malice, or transphobia involved. Though Vixen would have preferred that people notice, others' inability to understand their genderfluidity did not deter them from using all pronouns. While teachers and classmates may have been confused, Vixen explained, "naming myself as genderfluid was like a freedom from constant confusion." They did not need their gender to make sense to other people; they just needed it to make sense to them. Vixen worked hard to care about themself and their genderfluidity despite others' persistent refusal to recognize and appreciate their gender.

Conclusion

The cultural imperative to be nice and accepting of diversity directed attitudes of acceptance toward queer and trans youth, for, as Canadian society increasingly recognizes these students' rights, schools must endeavor at least to appear inclusive. However, a commitment to diversity is a door that is always already a trap because it does not interrogate the power structures that create challenging school environments for queer and trans students. Rather, educators at East City High endeavored to support students whom they recognized as trans while concurrently believing gender nonconformity to be risky. When trans identity is understood through discourses of risk and harm, adults may tolerate and accept youth, but it is impossible for them to desire young people to be or grow up trans. Since normative ideas of childhood configure "successful" and protected growing up as directed toward stable cisgender, heterosexual adulthood, desiring transness would contradict educators' good intentions for youth to grow up free from harm and struggle.[18]

For educators who work within accommodation models, desiring gender nonconformity for a young person is akin to wishing them more challenging lives. Instead, these approaches encourage adults to regard gender nonconformity as a catalyst for worry. This dynamic was present when Ms. O'Connor cited Ostrich's wish to change his name and pronouns at school as a signal of increased vulnerability. Ms. O'Connor, like other adults at the school, understood herself as wanting the best for Ostrich and working to keep him safe. As a result, she made decisions on his behalf that contradicted his own desires about his gender and how to express it at school. Through disregarding his capacity to know himself, she likewise put him in danger.

The tensions of this approach were exacerbated by a "feel good" diversity culture that erased systemic oppression and positioned adults as uncomplicated protectors of youth. East City High's rendering of itself as diverse, inclusive, and progressive obscured the fundamental and endemic violence of schooling. It is not nice to acknowledge that schools, in upholding certain systems of power, may actually be functioning as intended, for these are not good intentions.[19] At East City High, good intentions manifested themselves in a variety of forms, from attempts to safeguard gender-nonconforming youth from perceived harm to finding accommodations for individual students. Rather than reckoning with structural inequities, this belief in good intentions helped teachers reframe instances of violence and oppression. Transphobic incidents and interactions, such as misgendering or the distribution of harmful material, thus had to be aberrations and not indicative of institutional cisheteronormativity. Youth were pulled into this dynamic, performing the labor of recognizing transphobic violence as instead misunderstandings or even acts of care.

Since the school was deemed a safe space and everyone was positioned as operating with the best of intentions to accommodate trans youth, adults were bolstered in depicting themselves as on the path toward greater acceptance. This stance facilitated adults' sense of entitlement to youth's understanding and forgiveness. Ultimately, this situation demanded significant labor from youth: the labor to make sense of this dynamic and the transphobia they experienced as well as the labor to cultivate care for themselves in the absence of care from their teachers and the school.

I witnessed youth perform this labor throughout the year, in sometimes small and sometimes momentous ways. Attending to their labor—how it was required of them and how they performed it not just to survive but also to care for themselves—is necessary to recognize how challenging of an environment East City High was for them. While accommodation approaches are helpful for many trans youth, they are not adequate to care for youth in the complex, fluid ways they desire. In the absence of that care, the gender-nonconforming youth I moved through the school with over the year performed labor to care for themselves. This was their survival work, and reframing the transphobia they daily encountered was a small facet of this labor.

Though it is possible to read these youths' labor as resignation, for instance Raeyun's, Ostrich's, and Vixen's decisions to understand and forgive Ms. Mack, these were also forms of triage and work they performed to survive a hostile school environment. In Senior Theater Company, all three had started out the year engaging with Ms. Mack and articulating their names, pronouns, and genders. However, confronting Ms. Mack was exhausting and ineffective. Regularly explaining their identities and working to be recognized by her involved significant labor that was not sustainable. Therefore, when they were continuously misgendered and deadnamed, they chose to divest from their relationship with her and, in the case of Vixen, from the class entirely. The youth practiced care for themselves by being discerning and determining when it made sense and was worthwhile to make themselves legible to their teachers. In chapter 4, I turn to this question of recognizability and visibility, focusing on students' complex and ongoing relationship with trans legibility.

4

The Labor of Gender Legibility

In the first week of November, East City High hosted a clubs day during lunch. All interested student groups were invited to set up tables in the cafeteria to introduce themselves and recruit new members. Members of the GSA draped a gay pride and trans pride flag over a table on the west side of the cavernous room. They fanned out stickers and buttons for indicating pronouns and declaring oneself an ally next to their sign-up sheet. At the start of the year, the GSA had a few packed meetings, but then their numbers quickly dwindled. By early spring, there were only five to six regular members. Several of the youth in the project began the year attending the GSA's Friday lunch meetings, but they all stopped at different points, picking other spaces they preferred. Reflecting scholarship in the field, most of the students who did attend the meetings were white, cisgender girls, and many identified as allies.[1]

I was walking around the cafeteria, looking at the clubs' displays, when I ran into Ms. Man. We had first met at a GSA meeting back in September when they arrived a couple of minutes late and slid quietly into a seat next to me. During the check-in circle, I noticed that they were one of a handful of students present who used "they/them" pronouns. We chatted and joked around at the meeting, finding easy conversation in *RuPaul's Drag Race*. When I brought up the project, Ms. Man was interested but unsure they had anything to offer. Whenever we saw each other, we had variants of that discussion. Clubs day was the latest iteration. Ms. Man came over to chat, and we ended up walking around the cafeteria together, poking around the different tables. They had been thinking about the study, Ms. Man told me, and though they were interested in participating, they thought I should talk to their friend instead because "they are smarter and can articulate this stuff better."

Soon after that conversation, Ms. Man asked to join the study, but throughout they maintained their view that there was always someone better and smarter whom I could speak to about gender. During the year, no one ever guessed that I was working with Ms. Man, even when I showed up to their classes and sat next to them. They did not talk to people about their gender, decided against sharing their pronouns with most folks, and generally moved around East City High without people knowing they were trans. They had an ambivalent relationship to the study. When we spent time together, they qualified their participation with comments like the one about their smarter friend, telling me how incapable they were of saying anything of import about gender. However, if something queer or gender-bendy happened in school, they immediately found me. They wanted to talk about it and tell me their feelings. Likewise, when we met up outside school, they would first make sure to lay out all their usual caveats, but then they would speak without abandon about the queerness of gender and excitedly ask questions about my experiences as a trans person.

Ms. Man was well aware of what was considered gender nonconformity at East City High and in Canada more generally. Despite what they knew about themself and their gender, they did not think they counted as trans because they did not fit the dominant mold or the popular narrative. Their experience was not captured by the language in the "Policy on Sexual Orientation and Gender Identity"; their gender was not easily categorized by what Barry, a participant in the study and their close friend in the music program, referred to as the "bureaucracy of gender." Barry explained, "The more specifically something is defined, the more specifically it's thought about. And with specificity comes a kind of bureaucracy. And the bureaucracy of gender is something I try to avoid." The expectations for where and how gender nonconformity exists in schools are grounded in ideas about what it means to be gendered as well as what it means to be trans. Following Ahmed, "That the arrival of some bodies is more noticeable than others reveals an expectation of who will show up."[2] As I have been unfolding, these expectations are not arbitrary, benevolent, or recent. Rather, they are predicated on the relationship of gender policing to forms of disciplinary power that regulate bodies. Logics of whiteness, ability, and settler colonialism inform these expectations, as they all participate in structuring what "counts" as a proper body and therefore what it means to be gender (non)conforming.[3] Normative ideas about gender extend to the "correct" ways to identify as trans, go through transition, and relate to your trans body and experience. Despite early uses of trans as a way to disrupt discourses of medicalization, pathologization, and categorization, there remains a privileging of stability and coherence in trans communities.[4] Gender-nonconforming youth interacted with these notions of what it means to be trans when working to understand their own genders, especially when colliding with adults' inability to see them as gender nonconforming.

During my year at East City High, I witnessed youth work to make their genders legible (or not) according to others' understandings of gender nonconformity. Their often-unobserved labor entailed daily decisions about, for instance, when and with whom to share pronouns or what to wear to school. As I have discussed, like Ms. Man, most of the youth in the study were never recognized as gender nonconforming because they performed their genders in ways that did not align with dominant expectations of transness. The youth who were read as trans more regularly, like Raeyun, worked to secure those readings, often in response to others' understandings of trans identity. In the preceding chapters, I explored the interconnectedness of gendered structures and ideas in Canadian society and schooling. In this chapter, I highlight one pervasive perspective that influenced youth's relationships to gender nonconformity: the idea that nonbinary genders were less "real" and "valid" than transnormative ones. These ideas informed youth's internal and external labor involving gender legibility. They worked both to believe in their own knowledge of their genders *and* to prove to others that their genders were legitimate. These forms of labor were not mutually exclusive. They overlapped and fluctuated within a conversation, a class period, and a day. I first document how youth engaged in internal labor by considering their anxieties over not being "trans enough" and how they turned to scientific explanations of transness for validation. I explore their external labor through their work navigating pronouns and grappling with fashion choices. Confronting dominant views of gender legibility at East City High was exhausting and, at times, demoralizing work for many of the youth. I end the chapter by turning to the toll that this labor took on youth as they explored their relationships with their genders. Throughout, I consider how they worked to care—for themselves, their genders, and their trans community—as they negotiated ideas of legibility and visibility.

Trans Enough?

Significant work, energy, and scholarship have gone into documenting trans lives to make them more visible and legible.[5] In Canada, visibility has provided several doors for trans people, such as access to legal rights, formal inclusion in schools, and greater media representation. Yet, as I have been examining, visibility is likewise a trap. The privileging of visibility occludes the expansiveness of trans genders and winnows transness into a monolithic identity. Following Aren Aizura, aspiring toward visibility means aiming to become a "somebody" and therefore to become known as trans by the state and other institutions.[6] At East City High, being a trans somebody required that youth perform their genders in a way that was legibly gender nonconforming to others in the school. Pervasive expectations informing what it meant to be gender (non)conforming, what Barry labeled the bureaucracy of gender, constrained the possibilities for gender nonconformity by only recognizing it when it showed up in predictable, knowable forms.

Though the youth in the study all continuously cultivated their own constructions of their gender identities, they also performed the work of mediating others' perceptions of their genders and navigating the tensions of the spaces between those understandings. This labor was illustrated in their pervasive concerns over not being "trans enough." In *Women without Class*, the sociologist Julie Bettie challenged scholarship on girlhood by observing the importance of girls defining themselves in relation to other girls and women, not just to boys. In this chapter, I am inspired by that work as I consider how trans youth defined themselves in relation to other trans youth and adults, predominantly through their fears of being "enough." Anxieties over being trans enough were common for all the youth in the project and were linked to their perception that nonbinary gender identities were considered less "real" or "valid" than transnormative ones.

Chase Catalano, a trans scholar, argues that "'trans enough' means crossing the binary, not living between two genders."[7] Several youth shared this definition of "trans enough" and worked to become increasingly legible in order to count as enough. For these youth, like Raeyun and Ostrich, being perceived as guys was paramount to being trans enough. Ostrich described his desire to one day move through the world as just a guy: "I hope that it's, like, 'Oh, that person was born as a guy.' I hope as soon as possible." Over the course of the project, both Raeyun and Ostrich embodied myriad desires from their transness. They lived the reality that there was no one way to be trans enough. Yet, they also struggled to believe that they were enough and that their transness was real. In chapter 5, I explore how they supported each other in this process, performing vital acts of care work that built queerer worlds within East City High where they could exist as trans without explanation.

Other youth extended the meaning of "trans enough" to consider their feelings on being read as gender nonconforming enough. These youth desired their genders to be confusing and fluid but frequently felt unrecognized in those aspirations. At times, different forms of labor were required and enacted by these youth. However, for all the youth, being trans enough required other people to acknowledge their transness.

The Tensions in Being Trans Enough

Though performing a transnormative gender does not translate into an easy, charmed life or uncomplicated passage through school, there was a sense among many youth that aligning with expectations of trans legibility would ameliorate their struggles. When students' experiences of their genders did not easily align with societal narratives about transness, they felt they had to work harder to trust their own understanding of their genders. Returning to Hil Malatino's theorizing on the importance of social recognition to gender, I consider youth's acts of trusting as a form of care work. Since gender is socially entangled and the structures that inform trans recognition privilege white, able-bodied people, many trans people have complicated relationships with legibility. Malatino argues, "This means that we all recognize gender as a morally loaded laborious *process*. It is *work*."[8] When youth were anxious about being enough, this was work. Their responses to these anxieties were also forms of work, often forms of care work that they engaged in to facilitate their own relationships with their gender nonconformity and their ability to move through East City High with the least amount of trouble.

In the middle of November, while Raeyun and I were eating an after-school snack during an interview at a funky neighborhood café, we discussed his fears about not being trans enough:

> LJ: Is that something that you worry about, that you're not trans enough?
> RAEYUN: I feel like it just depends on the day. I feel like some days, I would worry about, like, "Is this really considered to be, like, trans?" or kind of like, "Is this kind of a phase thing?" But then some days, I'm like, "Yeah, this is it."
> LJ: What does it feel like when you're worried that you're not trans enough?
> RAEYUN: Um, I guess it feels like—so I feel like a lot of the input that I get from my gender is, like, kind of, like, from outside. So, like, I feel like I've always had this constant knowing that I'm trans, kind of thing. But I feel, like, um, it was kind of, like, this revelation my friend had, like an epiphany, like—she always feels like she needs that reassurance, or else she's always indecisive. I feel like that's me with my own gender—like, I already know what I am, but I just need that reassurance, and it depends on whether or not I'm getting that reassurance.

Raeyun referenced a constant knowing that he was trans alongside an awareness that this self-knowledge had its limitations. Raeyun was consistently misgendered at East City High by adults and other students, and that outside input had an impact on his relationship to his gender. If trans is a knowable, visible identity that others can recognize in us, are we really trans if people do not see us as trans? Raeyun's experiences of misgendering did not alter his understanding of his gender, but, as I discuss later in this chapter, it did take a toll and motivated him to make choices that would cultivate the reassurances he desired. Raeyun had to perform different types of labor to be trans at school because of the constrained ways trans identity was understood. He worked hard to make himself visible, which was not always effective. When not read as trans, Raeyun resolved to put in the work to approach teachers and tell them, which was uncomfortable for him since he was introverted and not interested in being generally that visible at school.

In my conversations with youth about not being trans enough there was an underlying awareness that nonbinary genders were considered less real than other trans identities. There are important tensions here that I flagged in the introduction. If trans is a knowable identity, then if you are trans enough, others should be able to recognize you as trans. This idea is already complicated by the concepts of "passing" and "living stealth." While many of the youth desired to be recognized and understood *as trans* because of the ways they transgressed gender norms, others believed being "trans enough" to mean no longer being knowable as trans. This perspective was explained by Ostrich earlier when he commented, "I hope that it's, like, 'Oh, that person was born as a guy.'" However, youth also connected with gender nonconformity and nonbinary genders because they viewed them as ambiguous and unplaceable gender identities. Youth specifically desired gender nonconformity because of its unrecognizability. These tensions are important, and I am not interested in resolving them. I am highlighting them to suggest that knowability is a fraught intention and that, rather than invest in policies, initiatives, and curricular programs that rely on gender being knowable, we disrupt that desire and question its foundations. Do we need to know a student's gender to teach them? Do we need to know a young person's gender to care about them? Cultivating desire for youth to be and grow up trans moves away from ideas of "enoughness." No longer would adults be in the position of assessing and evaluating who is trans in order to determine who needs protection or who qualifies for accommodations. Instead of responding and reacting to trans youth, educators could approach teaching and learning with the pedagogical, political, and ethical intentions of inviting queerness and transness into the classroom and into the school. This shift would free youth from having to prove that they are trans or to align themselves within the societal parameters of gender (non)conformity to be recognized.

Regardless of the strength of youth's self-knowledge, resisting the pervasive delegitimization of nonbinary genders at East City High required substantial work. Some youth endeavored to become more recognizable according to the bureaucracy of gender (to become somebodies), while others predominantly focused on valuing their own self-knowledge (on caring for themselves as nobodies). Judith Butler's work is again instructive here: "'persons' only become intelligible through becoming gendered in conformity with recognizable standards of gender intelligibility."[9] Though Butler emphasizes gender as salient in establishing and maintaining structures of legibility, we have been exploring how understandings of gender (non)conformity are likewise constructed and policed by norms of whiteness, settler colonialism, and ability. Over the course of the study, I witnessed all the youth I was working with make decisions regarding how much information about themselves and their genders to share and who they thought was likely to understand. The youth with less access to other privileges had to work even harder, confronting racist and ableist ideas about transness that prevented people from recognizing their genders. This labor was ongoing and messy.

Trans: It Is Science

Faced with qualms about legitimacy and enoughness, some of the youth turned to science to provide evidence that they existed and were valid. This move is reflected in scholarship. In a study with the parents of trans and nonbinary children, Elizabeth Rahily observed that parents found comfort in medicalized language. Further, through medicalizing their children's transness, the parents situated gender nonconformity within a disability framework. This move affirmed parents' belief that no child would *choose* to be trans and that, therefore, it must be an unavoidable "defect."[10] This perspective positions both transness and disability as signs that something has gone "wrong" and further tethers gender nonconformity and disability together as undesirable futures for youth. I am fascinated with the way the hesitancy and unwillingness to desire nonnormative presents and futures for youth inform the ideas they can access about gender nonconformity.

Ostrich began the year identifying as nonbinary. Over the course of the study, he distanced himself from nonbinary gender and increasingly embraced a biological explanation for his transness that located gender identity in brain development. It is not possible to know all the reasons that Ostrich made these decisions, nor do I think it is important to know. I am interested, however, in the ways Ostrich moved from understanding nonbinary gender as possible to positioning it as impossible. He explained, "Trans is more accepted than, like, nonbinary. I've seen it's kind of a gray area because, like, I've seen people be, like, 'Oh, yes, nonbinary people are great,' while other people are, like, 'Yeah, they're just transtrenders.'" I asked him to define "transtrenders," and he continued, "I'm not 100% sure, but from my understanding, it's just people who claim to be trans just for the sake of claiming to be trans—trying to get, uh, like, more minority points." Ostrich's perception of trans identities as more authentic was bolstered by scientific arguments, learned both in school and on the internet.

In the winter, Ms. Conway led a unit on genetics in Science and Tech. During one of the lessons, she explained that all people have forty-six chromosomes and that males have one Y and one X, while females have two Xs. Ostrich and I met at a café after that class for an interview. That day, for the first time, he explained his gender in biological terms, telling me that he was "more related to people who have XY chromosomes, who identify as male." He had never used this type of heavily scientific language before. I was intrigued, and I asked him more about it. Ostrich told me, "When I was born, my brain ended up developing more as a male than a female even though I have XX chromosomes." I heard this type of essentialist language from teachers at other points during the year, mostly when they referenced gendered behavior as hardwired in the brain by explaining that girls were inherently better at communicating and boys were naturally skilled at sports. Ostrich said that he primarily learned about the brain-development aspects of trans identities on the internet. Ostrich was a frequent gamer and liked to stream YouTube videos while he played. He followed several trans guys who shared their thoughts on transitioning, the psychology of being trans, and other trans topics. Malatino analyzed this genre of recordings, noting how they are almost exclusively informed by the perspectives of wealthy, white, straight, and transnormative subjects.[11]

Ostrich wanted to medically transition like the guys in those videos, and he consistently located this desire within the "wrong body" narrative. Ostrich described how he came to understand this idea and gender dysphoria generally through watching YouTube. "I was watching a lot of trans-related videos," he told me, "and it helped me in a way where I am able to understand, like, more why I'm like this." The trans men whom Ostrich followed online offered him a scientific framework and language for making sense of his relationship with his body. "Like, dysphoria and why a lot of trans people experience dysphoria . . . I have a chest where

I want it to be, like, completely flat. I have female genitalia where I wish it wasn't there. I wish that it was, like, more masculine, and I feel, like, really shitty that I don't have it." However, the videos did not provide a path toward resolution. While scholars note a paradigm shift in how health-care professionals and parents respond to gender-nonconforming youth, not all young people have access to the support or resources to transition if they want.[12] The narratives that these videos provide offered a trajectory toward a legible trans existence, one that Ostrich desired but, as a poor, neurodivergent, fat, and queer nonconforming trans guy without access to gender-affirming health care, he could not reach.

Though Ostrich's father was supportive of him being happy, he approached Ostrich's gender with fear and concern. Ostrich found a way to make sense of this dynamic by couching it in the language of concern. "I'm most likely too young to go through at least the surgeries," he began. "Anyways, so, I was kind of asking my dad, 'Can I have a packer? Can I have a binder?'" Ostrich recounted a conversation that he had recently had with his father: "He was, like—he was saying, 'Yeah, but I just want to make sure that I—that it won't psychologically or physically or just in general harm you in any way, shape, or form,' which is understandable." Ostrich was accustomed to people policing his decisions for his own good. He continued, "You, like, don't want your child to be hurt. So, I just think he's kind of waiting for, like, a doctor to give the okay before he does it." Ostrich worked hard to understand other people's views about his gender. Though at times he expressed frustration with his father's dilatory approach to providing consent for his transition, Ostrich was overwhelmingly compassionate and patient. He agreed that there were risks involved. Ostrich interacted with many service providers and youth workers. As a result, he regularly navigated gatekeeping. Framing their prohibitions, such as his father's refusal to let him get a binder, as safekeeping was also a way that Ostrich could interpret these actions as a form of care. In adhering to their protocols for him, Ostrich could likewise care for himself.

Raeyun felt similarly blocked from accessing gender-affirming health care. However, he had no plans of even attempting to medically transition until he was able to leave home and live alone. The previous summer, at the queer and trans camp he attended, Raeyun had shared space with other trans kids for the first time. He described how some of the white trans guys there were already on puberty blockers. "They [white kids] can start HRT [hormone replacement therapy] early and get all that stuff, and they never have to worry about paying for it on their own and MSP [Medical Services Plan]."[13] Raeyun paused. "I mean, I feel like even—'cause my parents aren't supportive really—but, like, I feel like at the end of the day, at some point, I'm still going to get those things. It's just that I have to wait a little bit." Raeyun knew that his situation was different as a Filipino trans guy navigating conversations about gender with unsupportive parents. While this current generation of trans youth is positioned as distinct in part because of established pathways to living stealth (or the possibility of passing posttransition without maintaining a connection to transness), access to gender-affirming health care is inequitably distributed.[14] Increasingly, there are distinctions among which youth benefit from early medical interventions. These disparities have become even more pronounced in the United States as certain regions criminalize this health care. Families with means will always find a way to circumvent these restrictions, while more marginalized youth will bear the brunt of the enforcement. Ultimately, the youth with the most privilege are poised to become the youth with the access to the best gender-affirming care.

Even youth who were not personally interested in being stealth or invested in positioning trans as a legitimate identity struggled with the devaluing of nonbinary genders and at times turned to science for reassurance. Vixen, who consistently rejected desires for legibility, preferring to confuse people, still felt pulled to assert the validity of gender nonconformity. Once when we were hanging out at a café near the school, our usual meet-up spot to listen to K-pop and read their novels, Vixen told me a story of a conversation they overheard in class one day. Two students had been discussing queer and trans issues, so they perked up, ready to be offended and to interject. Vixen was surprised at how open-minded and knowledgeable the students were, especially about trans topics. They leaned forward to tell me the story:

And then they got to the topic of nonbinary, and they went, "Oh, but that's not real." They were like, "That can't be real because they proved that with, like, chemicals in your brain, that's what makes you trans. If your brain chemicals are different from what your actual body is, that's what makes you trans. But that doesn't really apply to nonbinary, so it can't be real." And they were basically, like—they completely switched the script, and I just felt closed off. It's, like, literally listening to two people deny my existence, telling me I don't exist. And it's, like, okay. It's, like, 'cause it's, like—I don't know how to refute that because I have no argument. So they say there's no scientific explanation for it. You're right, there's not. And I can't even think of one if I tried. And if they were to ask, "Oh, explain how can you prove that you are genderfluid?" I can't. I can't prove that, and I can't even describe what genderfluid is like well enough for people to find it believable, just because I can't put it into words. So if people are telling me that I don't exist, I basically just have to sit there and take it. There's nothing I can do. But it's, like—the only argument that I have is that I know I exist because here I am. You know, because me existing right here in my own head, nonbinary and genderfluid has to exist because otherwise what is this, what's happening here? There has to be something behind it because you can't tell me it doesn't exist and have all these people feeling the same way if it's not real. Because I'm not the only genderfluid person on this planet. I'm one of very many. It just rubs me the wrong way.

In Vixen's story, two students drew on the same scientific argument that bolstered Ostrich's sense of validity and legitimacy as a trans guy to discount the existence of nonbinary genders. For these students, trans identities were real because it was possible to know them. Rahily also observed parents make these types of distinctions between trans and nonbinary identities in her interviews. The parents distinguished between "truly trans" and other forms of gender nonconformity while concurrently expressing their belief that transnormative genders were "easier" because of their legibility to others.[15] In the conversation that Vixen overheard, scientific evidence concretized the ambiguity of trans identities by providing tangible proof, a way to know that trans people's claims about their genders were real. Since nonbinary genders were scientifically unknowable, they became unreal.

Most of the time, Vixen disregarded desires for legibility. In general, they approached their gender and being misgendered with nonchalance. "I think I've always been relaxed about most things," they told me. However, even this carefully crafted casualness had its limits. Vixen wanted people to care that nonbinary genders existed. They wished that there was a scientific explanation for nonbinary gender, research they could trot out and point to so they could prove that their gender was legitimate. Without the science to back them up, Vixen could only rely on themself. However, Vixen was not defeated by the lack of scientific evidence. Vixen knew that genderfluidity was real because they knew they existed. This form of knowing did not require their gender to be stable, coherent, or permanent. Rather, this form of knowing was an opening that created possibilities that had previously been unimaginable. Vixen once described what it was like to learn about the existence of nonbinary genders. "I came to understand that there are all kinds of different types and that not everybody fits into those little box standards. And I think I was totally fine learning that." We were at our usual café, hunched close together. Vixen had a spare that period, and they had texted me earlier in the day to see if I wanted to hang out. "A lot of people are put off by the idea," they explained. "Like, 'Wait, wait, what? You can't generalize a person? What do you mean there are unique people?' You know, for some people, yeah, for some reason, they cannot compute, but for me, I was pretty happy learning that." Vixen leaned back before adding, "I didn't know you could be anything else, so it was nice to learn because it meant that the world was so much bigger." Vixen worked every day to affirm their own understanding of themself as genderfluid and to assert genderfluidity as not just real and valid but also beautiful, complicated, and brilliantly confusing.

External Labor

Barry dabbled in bringing little bits of flamboyance into his life, but he was careful about the unconventionality of his dress at school. He played saxophone in the senior band, and while backstage before the first concert of the year that fall, he watched his friend Taylor do her makeup with envy. Though Barry painted his nails, he had never worn makeup to school. The pushback he got just for his nails was enough to persuade Barry that makeup was going too far. However, that night he decided "fuck it" to what other people thought, and he asked Taylor to do his makeup. In this section, I turn to the external labor that youth performed as they worked to demonstrate their gender legibility to the people around them at East City High. I focus on how they negotiated pronoun usage and fashion decisions, since these were two common issues the youth confronted over the year.

I Like Looking Pretty

Several weeks after the concert, Barry and I met up after school to walk to his favorite café. The cast list for East City High's first student-directed musical, *Into the Woods*, had just been posted, and Barry ranted about his part as we weaved through side streets to the neighborhood's main drag. He had wanted to be the Baker, but he was cast as Cinderella's Prince. The student-director cast himself as the Baker, and Barry was irked. He was also nervous. He was worried that he did not have the vocal range for the role of the prince.

When we got to the café, Barry found a table, and we got tea and treats. Barry and I often met up after school. These hangouts were part interview and part meandering conversations during which we each took turns leading. Barry always came with his own topics and questions. Sometimes we met up to discuss D&D, and sometimes I just listened to Barry pontificate or work through facets of his life. A while into our conversation on this day, I asked him about his decision to wear makeup at the band concert. Barry explained, "Around then, I was feeling real rough. I was kind of crying backstage before the concert while all the things were being set up, and I was like, 'Not again. I'm going to have fun.'" So, he asked himself, "What do I want to do?" That is when Barry found Taylor and asked her about doing his makeup. Wearing makeup, he figured, would lift his spirits and help pull him out of his funk. Often Barry worked hard to move through East City High without being noticed for his femme flair. Easing his experience of the school was one way that he showed care for himself. However, that night at the concert, Barry desired recognition of his gender. Instead of working to be the easiest version of a high school student, Barry performed the care work of asking his friend to do his makeup, despite how he knew this would disrupt his cis-legibility. "And she was like, 'A just—a simple mascara?' And I was like, 'Hmm, eyeshadow? Eyeliner?' And then I just did it, and I was like, 'I feel great!'" Barry had felt beautiful. He had a photo of that night that he regularly took out to show me when we were sitting together in class.

Though Barry delighted in his evening of makeup at the band concert, he did not decide to start wearing makeup to school. Barry told me, "I would like to [wear makeup to school], and it would definitely be, like, closer to the end of the year, when, like, I'm never going to see these people again." Barry felt that wearing makeup around folks in the music program was entirely distinct from showing up to math class or walking down the halls at East City High in eye shadow and lipstick. Barry worked hard to balance his desires for femininity with his anxieties over gender policing. "I've definitely said to myself, 'I'm going to do this every concert because I like looking pretty, . . . and why the heck can only super-female-presenting people do that?' Why the heck, I ask you?" Barry daily made decisions about how to present his gender to others and who was likely to understand the complexities of his fluidity.

Every subsequent band concert, Barry did ask Taylor to do his makeup, getting a bit more adventurous each time. The night of the final concert in June, I ran into Barry in the lobby. He rushed toward me and scooped me up in hug. Barry was wearing a paisley bow tie, eyeliner, and blush. He looked beautiful. Filtering his presentation from one space to the next permitted Barry to legibly move through the school as a guy if he needed to, only reveling in his femme flamboyance while among people who would understand, or at least not police, his gender.

Reflecting Malatino's theorizing on gender as labor, it was not uncommon for youth to frame decisions they made regarding their gender expressions and presentations as work they did more for others' sake than for their own. Think back to when Ostrich changed his name and discussed the importance of picking one that would signal to others that he was a guy. He took on the responsibility of presenting a coherent gender with pronouns and a name that all aligned with people's conventional expectations. Similarly, Raeyun noted that he understood transitioning as more of a process he undertook for other people. He already knew that he was trans, but that knowing required certain actions on his part in order to be understandable to the people around him. At times, this type of gender work was more visible than the labor of internal validation, for it focused on proving to the rest of the East City High community that youth were trans and gender nonconforming. Other times, this gender work was less visible because it meant that youth were refraining from dressing how they wanted or otherwise engaging with their genders in ways they desired for fear of how those performances would undercut their legitimacy. All these forms of labor required acknowledging the elements that maintained the bureaucracy of gender and then aligning their genders with them.

Pronouns

Raeyun worked hard to become recognizable as a trans guy at East City High. When I first met him, he used both "they/them" and "he/him" pronouns. However, just a couple of months into the study, I noticed that Raeyun had dropped "they/them" from his lexicon. When I asked about it, he expressed reservations about using "they" with teachers, despite wanting to, citing a time when Mr. Harding, his English teacher, facilitated a grammar activity and highlighted the singular "they" pronoun as grammatically incorrect. "It was super, like, I guess culture shock," Raeyun told me. Overall, he figured it was just easier to use "he."

Ostrich had been similarly wary about using "they" pronouns from the start, uncertain how teachers would respond to the idea. Like Raeyun, Ostrich decided to stop using "they/them" pronouns partway through the year. He explained, "It's just quicker to say 'he/him' instead of having, like, 'he/him' and 'they/them.' So, it's just, like, gradually narrowing it down." Ostrich added, "I don't mind people referring to me as a 'they,' but at the same time, like, I don't want to say both, because, like, yeah, I kind of just narrowed it down to 'he' when introducing myself to people." Ostrich was not against the pronouns themselves, but, he explained to me, he was apprehensive about the work involved in communicating those pronouns every time he had to introduce himself as different than people expected. Though the district's policy stated that students were entitled to use the pronoun that matched their gender identity, most adults in the school were unfamiliar with "they" pronouns. This lack of awareness meant that youth were responsible for educating their teachers on correct usage and navigating often awkward phrasings and interactions. Ostrich, who experienced social anxiety, was unlikely to view using "they" as worth the trouble.

Most of my participants included the "they" pronoun in their repertoire at some point. Ms. Man and Scarecrow Jones only used "they/them" pronouns with me and a couple of close friends. Scarecrow Jones believed that they were already navigating enough challenges in school as a mixed-race, queer person taking classes in a second language. They did not want to make their life more difficult. Plus, like Ostrich and Raeyun, Scarecrow Jones did not trust their teachers with this information. "I feel like because partially I don't want to let all my classmates know, and if teachers suddenly go—calls me that, people are going to go, 'Wait, what? What did you say?'" Scarecrow Jones and I were at the Tim Horton's by the school, eating donuts and drinking hot chocolate. It had snowed the day before, and they were wearing huge red and black lace-up snow boots that went up nearly to their knees. They had picked the place, but they kept surreptitiously looking around to see if they recognized anyone and leaning in close to me to speak quietly. "Then there's some teachers that I just, like, you know, some teachers I am not fond of them and then even teachers that I think are great and would totally accept it. It's just a whole other level of complications to, like, an already—an already complicated school life that I would then have to figure—refigure out and deal with." Scarecrow Jones explained what that figuring out would entail. "You know, what if that teacher doesn't understand what that means, right? What if that teacher doesn't accept that, and then I tell them this, and then it just is this whole debacle that I would rather avoid." Scarecrow Jones determined that using their pronouns with teachers and classmates was not worth the risk. However, they created little interventions, forms of care and resistance that worked to disrupt the cisheteronormativity imposed on them daily. They had a close friend who sat in front of them in several classes and would turn around whenever a teacher referred to Scarecrow Jones as "mademoiselle" to instead mutter "m'theysie." For Scarecrow Jones, this private nickname served as a reminder that someone understood them. Scarecrow Jones did not want large-scale recognition of their nonbinary gender because they did not believe that their teachers and other students grasped the complexities of their gender. They were apprehensive about being held to others' standards and expectations for being gender nonconforming. They did not desire to be a trans somebody at East City High. I understand their small subversions during class as space for them to exist differently as a nobody within a community of care.

What Not to Wear

Ostrich and Raeyun became close friends during the year. I watched as they bonded over their experiences as queer trans guys and tech kids in theater. In chapter 5, I consider their dynamic more closely, exploring their unnoticed acts of world-making in Senior Theater Company. Their friendship invited conversations around genderfluidity and trans flamboyance that I rarely observed either of them have with others.

One day after theater class, Raeyun, Ostrich, and I left as a crew to eat lunch. First, however, Ostrich needed to put his backpack away and head to the third-floor gender-neutral bathroom. Raeyun wanted us to stick together, so we wended through the school guided by Ostrich. As we walked, Raeyun excitedly unfolded his fashion plans for the NCT concert he was attending that weekend. He had plans to bleach his hair and get it styled after one of his favorite K-pop idols. Raeyun took out his phone to show me a photo of the idol. He also shared his worry that the stylist would think he was a girl and then do a more feminine cut than he wanted. Raeyun had a plan: he was going to lower his voice as much as he could for the entire haircut to help him be read as a guy.

K-pop idols are famous for androgynous presentations that "are considered neither an absence of masculinity nor homosexuality."[16] As Raeyun explained, "They're so pretty, and they're all so—they're strangely feminine but still masculine.... It's so weird. It's not weird, it's impressive, because honestly, I wish." Raeyun looked to K-pop idols as men who were able to be both men and femme, who could wear makeup, crop tops, heels, and extravagant outfits without having their manhood questioned. However, Raeyun feared the policing of his gender and sexuality that he understood as concurrent with presenting as femme. To understand the tensions that Raeyun experienced, I return to C. J. Pascoe's analysis of adolescent masculinity. Pascoe's study focused on straight, adolescent boys and their policing of heterosexual masculinity through the deployment of the "fag" epithet, a process that was always racialized. I noted in the introduction how the surveillance of masculinity is more complicated for trans and gender-nonconforming youth, who must work harder to prove that they are boys. Unlike the straight, cisgender boys in Pascoe's study, Raeyun and Ostrich did not have the shared understanding that they were boys to fall back on if they strayed from conventional expectations at East City High. While the boys in Pascoe's study could embody and then deflect the specter of "fag" throughout a class period, trusting that others knew that they were boys, Raeyun and Ostrich had to consistently construct their gender legibility just to be read as boys. This labor limited how flexible they could be in their relationships to masculinity.

One day Raeyun and I were leaving East City High together, and he recounted a story from PE class earlier that day. He and a friend had been on the same team and physically close to each other for most of the period. A couple of guys came over and started asking Raeyun questions about being gay. "After that, they just started asking, like, a bunch of questions about, like, my sexuality and my gender. Well, it was kind of interesting because their views of it were kind of like—I mean, to put it nicely, they were very politically incorrect." When he told them that he was gay and trans, they asked, "Isn't that just being straight?" They could not understand why Raeyun would be a gay trans guy instead of a straight woman. "Then they said, 'So you're trans and gay. Aren't you just gay squared?' I thought that was pretty funny." Raeyun could not tell if the boys were intentionally bullying him or genuinely curious about queer and trans issues. He felt uncomfortable, though. In relaying the story to me, he traced it all back to his behavior with his friend. "I was just being extra touchy with, like, my friend. And I guess they just picked up on it." The boys in Raeyun's PE class believed that he had transgressed acceptable masculine behavior by displaying affection toward another boy. Furthermore, Raeyun's transness was confusing to them. The boys were at a loss as to why anyone would choose a queer trans existence over cisheterosexuality. Therefore, they began to question his gender and his sexuality. Though both Ostrich and Raeyun navigated this labor, Raeyun's experience was distinct because of the racialized structures of masculine legibility that already position Asian men as more feminine than white men.[17]

Therefore, even though Raeyun strongly identified as flamboyantly gay and wanted to dress like the K-pop idols he admired, he decided against it. While he longed to embody the seemingly easy balance of femme flamboyance and masculinity that circulated in the world of K-pop, Raeyun did not believe it to be possible at East City High. Instead, he tempered his clothing choices to facilitate his legibility as a guy. Thus, importantly, sometimes the work of being legible as trans actually required the absence of action. In school, Raeyun daily chose legibility as a trans guy over expressing the complicated layers of his gender.

The Messiness of Gender

Many of the youth in the study expressed a deep understanding of their genders as fluid, illegible, and, at times, bewildering. While they desired this ambiguity, at times they struggled to maintain their confidence and trust in themselves and their genders. Both Barry and Scarecrow Jones came to our conversations wanting space and camaraderie to work through these complex thoughts. Scarecrow Jones described this aspect as one impetus for participating in the study: "I can talk about [gender nonconformity], which is already a huge thing. . . . I don't think I really have anyone else to talk about it with. . . . I don't have any friends who are trans." While at East City High, Scarecrow Jones often exercised a careful caution about their gender, but when we were together, they were able to relax and think through their feelings and questions. "It's nice to be able to talk about things, . . . share things that I can't really share anywhere else." This chapter primarily concentrates on the internal and external labor that youth performed to make their genders legible at East City High. However, frequently the dominance of legibility threatened to detract from the more complex, gender-affirming work that youth desired to engage in as they explored the beauty of being trans. Before closing this chapter, I consider the messy work that happened alongside and in response to the labor of legibility. This labor emerged when youth directly acknowledged the parameters of gender legibility and responded with questions, curiosities, and uncertainties. Rather than contorting themselves into trans somebodies to receive adults' support and accommodations, this was the labor of being a trans nobody. Youth performed the challenging work required to survive and flourish in a school environment that did not desire or understand how to care for them.

Living in Confusion

For Scarecrow Jones, since most people did not know that they were trans, they did not have many people to talk to about their questions, curiosities, and desires. Scarecrow Jones often worried about not being trans enough, and we had long discussions about the many varied ways we can exist as trans people. They understood, on an intellectual level, that nonbinary genders were real. "Some days I know logically there's nothing that is invalid, and, like, if someone told me 'Hey, I'm nonbinary,' I would accept that right away." Still, they struggled to maintain that understanding in the cisheteronormative context of East City High, which had little space for such fluidity and ambiguity. "It's just, like, the dumb intrusive stuff in my own head that you're faking it." Scarecrow Jones had to work to believe in their existence in the face of others' delegitimization of their gender and refusal to recognize its complexities.

During one of our conversations, Scarecrow Jones laid out their quandary for me. "This is a little weird and convoluted, so just a heads-up. Here's the thing. I am pretty sure that I'm not female, but I don't know if I am nonbinary, some kind of that—there in the spectrum. I don't know if I'm a guy, and that changes from time to time." They were leaning toward me, arms on the small table we were sharing. "Of course, if it changes, I'm like, 'Oh, my god, what if I'm a trender?' 'Cause it changes, so what if I'm a trender, and I'm actually just convincing myself of this and that." As they spoke, they laid out all the facets of this dilemma. "But then at the same time, this is really impacting sexuality as well because pansexual, bisexual, whichever, I think that I am more attracted to masculine guys, that kind of thing—of course, not just them, obviously, but I don't like the idea of being someone's 'girlfriend.'" They used scare quotes and laughed. "So, am I a guy and I'm gay? Or am I nonbinary and something else? Or am I actually just a girl? Am I just cis, and I'm convincing myself that I'm all these things, and I'm just a straight girl?" They leaned back in their chair. "And, of course, there's no answers 'cause it varies all the time, and no one has any idea about all the people. So, I just kind of have to live in this confusion."

Scarecrow Jones described feeling trapped by the idea of permanence, stability, and adhering to others' expectations that you remain one way forever or risk being labeled dishonest or unable to understand yourself. They expressed their frustration by pushing back against the popular application of "phases," a concept that has been used to delegitimize trans youth's self-knowledge.[18] Scarecrow Jones explained, "Well, a phase is an interesting word in the way it's been used. Technically there's nothing wrong with [gender nonconformity] being a phase as long as you're not doing it to, like, look cool, as long as it's something that you honestly believe and then it changes later—I think there's nothing wrong with that." Scarecrow Jones considered this idea. "If it does change, then I'm not going to look back on what I'm feeling right now and think that wasn't valid, 'cause it was valid." They explained, "That's how I was feeling, and I know that it can change from day to day, so why not from year to year? And, so, I can respect that about myself. I just am unsure if other people will." Scarecrow Jones did not need to know that their gender would be the same from one day to the next to trust that it was real. However, they were aware that the fluid and ambiguous ways they expressed their gender nonconformity undercut their validity as trans at East City High. No one recognized Scarecrow Jones as gender nonconforming, so no one believed that cisheteronormativity affected them. Furthermore, Scarecrow Jones noted that others' attempts to fix their gender into place had an impact on their sexuality because being nonbinary was integral to their pansexuality. Scarecrow Jones was able to travel along the spectrums of their genders and sexualities without needing specific, lasting answers. They worked to lean into their ambiguity, choosing to "live in this confusion" even though others were only ever able to understand them as singular, stable, and fixed. This work was ongoing and largely unnoticed.

Just a Pause

Barry admired genderfluidity. "It's part of what it means to be human, being in a constant state of flux," he told me. However, Barry struggled with this dynamic in himself. He celebrated others' transness but balked at his own uncertainties. Barry regularly spoke about gender nonconformity as distant and removed from himself. His perception of the normative expectations for being trans and gender nonconforming prevented him from identifying as such because he knew that he did not adhere to others' ideas. Once when I asked Barry how he would describe his gender, he simply paused. After a long moment, he answered, "That's it, just a pause." I assured him that a pause was a perfectly reasonable response. Then he added, "You know, I don't know. That's interesting. It's not even like I'm thinking things; it's that things are ticking away below the surface but not something that I can put into words, you know?" This exchange was illustrative of Barry's relationship with his gender. He was thinking about his gender but also hesitant, anxious, and uncertain about attaching concrete language to those thoughts. Barry frequently identified as "male" because he understood that identity as easiest and most honest with regard to the privileged ways he moved through the world. Still, he had lingering questions about his gender, questions that he rarely felt entitled to discuss or that he had the space to explore.

Another time, Barry and I were sitting outside at his favorite café, discussing the walls he constructed when we talked about gender nonconformity. I asked him if he felt that his gender was encapsulated in the words "cis male." Barry paused before responding, "I don't really know, in short. I feel like I can simply say that, and it's a conveniently simple way of going about it." He continued, "But then, it's really—you want to talk about what masculinity is and what being a cis male has to mean, and in a very traditional sense, like, maybe not fully?" For Barry, working to comprehend his gender was not possible without contending with the specter of masculinity. His experiences are also reflected in Pascoe's study, where the adolescent boys policed each other's gender transgressions using homophobic language. Pascoe observed how mobile and fluid this form of policing was among the boys and how easy it was to become a target. Barry regularly dressed and behaved outside of "proper" (hetero) masculinity. He worried about being visible because of this behavior. Yet, he likewise worked to reject these ideas—this bureaucracy of gender. "Like, um, but in a more, broader, modern view of what a man can be. I don't think anything I do makes me less or more of a man, because I think that's very limiting to a lot of people." Barry was not interested in categorizing his gender according to a bureaucracy that he did not agree with and metrics that made little sense to him. "There's always a bit of a yes and no because there's a bunch of different ways—a bunch of different ways that anything can be looked at like that." Why should Barry accept other people's definitions of "man" and "masculinity"?

Still, Barry collided with these limiting definitions while at East City High, and they affected how he expressed his gender. Barry always had perfectly polished nails. He painted them himself, left and right. It was a skill he took pride in, but at East City High, boys did not paint their nails. Barry told me a story about colliding with this tension. "One day I had my nails painted, and someone—I don't even know him very well—he said, 'What's that on your nails?'" Barry was taken aback. "I said, 'Nail polish,' and he just—he didn't—he just said, 'Why?' And then I just peeled off all my nail polish because that's not a fun thing to deal with." Ultimately, Barry's nail painting was not thwarted by this interaction. He still daily came to school with freshly painted nails, and he spent months meticulously planning his nail art for prom. However, painting his nails was one thing. He could easily pull down his sleeves and hide them—and he did. As I discussed, Barry felt pretty when he put on makeup but would never wear it to school. "I'm terrified of breaking out of the status code," he once told me. "I would love to dye my hair, change the way I dress, but I don't feel like I'm able to do that and not be judged by people for anything I do." Barry's awareness of the possibility of gender policing followed him around the school.

Though Barry was increasingly comfortable expressing his queerness, he imposed strict boundaries with himself about gender. No one understood him as gender nonconforming; therefore, he believed that it was appropriative if he identified that way. However, Barry shared with me a desire to distance himself from this distance he had imposed on himself about gender. He explained, "There's so much precedence, and that's a good thing, 'cause when [gender transgression] was never talked about or when it was punished, then that was bad. But there's such a level of fear that comes with that precedence, so much of it irrational, but irrational fears are the ones that are hardest to get rid of." In this conversation, Barry described the ideas that circulate about being trans and gender nonconforming in the school through the idea of precedent, which he described as the language that has developed to envelope trans students. Barry was afraid that he did not have a legitimate right to his questions about gender or to his feelings of nonconformity. I asked Barry about this fear. He explained:

BARRY: Um, like talking about gender and not knowing about validity in yourself. And not knowing about validity through, like, through this space and, uh, yeah, so. You're—you've well noticed, yeah.
LJ: I'm not trying to push you.
BARRY: No, I absolutely know. It's like a point of—not, like, contusion—but a point of anxiety in my brain of not wanting to. I

never want to be the person taking away from what someone else has to say, and I'm the first to preach to someone else that that's not the case, but you know, practice and preach don't always go together.

Barry and I had developed an intimacy that allowed for this conversation. I pushed him far more than any other participant because I knew he came to our conversations wanting a space to think. In this moment, I experienced a sadness tinged with frustration. I spent a lot of time with Barry, and I heard him push away his thoughts about gender, eschewing the very idea that he could even have a relationship with his gender. It was disheartening to watch him do this again and again. He theorized a space for himself as a gender-nonconforming guy and then kicked himself out of it by questioning his own validity. We had variants of this discussion several times over the course of the project. This version was one of the most direct. Then, in our last interview, Barry created a little bit of space for his own iteration of gender nonconformity. He shared, "Even if I don't myself prescribe of—not the binary of male/female—I think I have found expressions of that, that are, if not—they're not atypical, they're just not typical. To what degree? I don't really know." Barry decided that it did not matter how he identified. "It doesn't matter to me right now to explore the far reaches of myself, but I think, in a sense, in a very real sense, not trying to be dismissive of anyone, including myself." Barry was exploring his gender and did not understand that process as oriented toward a decisive conclusion. For Barry, not knowing his gender was not the same as not caring or being dismissive of its importance. Other people did not have to recognize the complexities of his relationship to gender, as long as he did.

Conclusion

The youth in this study were aware of the dominant understandings of trans identity at East City High. In response, they worked both to become legible as trans by adhering to societal expectations of gender nonconformity and to trust their own genders regardless of others' capacities to recognize them. The youth performed this labor to ease their days and avoid transphobic interactions as well as to cultivate care for themselves and their genders.

Since gender-nonconforming youth cannot be stabilized into concrete identity categories, they can elude recognition and legibility within schools. When youth in the study worked to become legible according to others' expectations, they often adhered to transnormative parameters. For instance, they dropped "they/them" pronouns and resisted dressing in the flamboyant attire they desired. These decisions illustrated their awareness of East City High's bureaucracy of gender and how important it was for them to have their gender recognized. Furthermore, their labor highlighted the contortions necessary to move through their days. Many of the youth articulated complex, fluid relationships with their genders. Yet, they did not understand the school or people within its walls as capable of engaging with them in their complexity. When legibility was important to the youth, they privileged dressing, behaving, and interacting in ways that would facilitate others' recognition of them as trans rather than what being trans meant to them.

As I have been exploring, drawing on the work of Tourmaline, Stanley, and Burton, performing that type of legibility is always a trap. Ideas informing what it "means" and "looks" like to be trans are not arbitrary. They are mired in cisheteronormativity, whiteness, and ability. The youths' ability to be read as trans and gender nonconforming was mediated by these structures that privileged specific expressions and embodiments. They were more likely to be recognized as trans if their way of being trans aligned with what was societally expected. Therefore, even though Raeyun worked hard to become legible as trans, his labor was rarely finished. He was compelled to continuously prove his transness or articulate it to his teachers and peers. Despite the many ways Raeyun contorted himself for the aim of recognizability, including by neglecting his femme desires, his trans identity did not adhere to expectations, and, thus, he was forced to announce it.

Even for the gender-nonconforming youth who did not desire recognizability, being illegible and ambiguous required work. This labor was largely internal work that youth did to acknowledge their existence despite consistent delegitimization from others. In this chapter, I returned to Malatino's work on gender as labor and the impossibility of untethering gender from social recognition. Malatino notes, "when such recognition is withheld, we intimately sense that we are being relegated to the position of the monstrous, simultaneously both more and less human."[19] Youth who were regularly misgendered focused on believing themselves to be valid. They worked to care for themselves, trust their genders, and refuse the primacy of others' recognition. For all the youth, expectations about what it meant and looked like to be gender (non)conforming informed their relationships with their genders. These ideas did not cause them to stop being trans or gender nonconforming, but adults' expectations did require them to work hard to trust themselves and, at times, motivated them to censor aspects of their genders while in school. However, what if youth did not have to respond to adults' ideas about trans identity and their constraining expectations for the way gender shows up in schools? A pedagogy for trans desire abolishes anxieties about being "enough" or who is "valid" or "real." There is an important distance and difference between responding to a known, recognizable trans youth with acceptance and creating schools that do not require adults to know if a young person is trans as a first step for action. If educators desire youth to be and grow up trans, then we can move away from litmus tests that demand youth to be "trans enough" to qualify for accommodations or as a catalyst for the development of less cisheteronormative learning environments. Instead, schools can become places that actively make possible queerness and transness, not as a risk factor but as a beautiful way to grow up. In chapter 5, I turn to the way youth are already doing this work of desiring transness in schools.

5

The Labor of World-Making

One day in the spring, I popped by the All Nations room to find Ms. Mooseknuckle wanting to commiserate about a frustrating meeting that she and Ms. Smith had recently attended with the principal. In their meeting, Ms. Mooseknuckle and Ms. Smith attempted to connect the problem of Indigenous students leaving the school in record numbers with their support of students fighting against anti-Black racism. While Ms. Fraser, the principal, claimed that she would address these issues as intertwined, Ms. Mooseknuckle was not convinced. "We should smudge," she told me, standing up and gathering her supplies.[1]

Outside in the garden, Ms. Mooseknuckle and I smudged. The smoke billowed up into the sky. Ms. Mooseknuckle explained that the smoke knew we needed to smudge the whole school and that was why there was so much of it. We stayed outside together until the smudge went out.

As Ms. Mooseknuckle and I walked back into the building, she recounted a story she had told me the first time I went to the All Nations room back in September. They used to smudge often with the youth, she recalled; however, teachers started to complain. Then teachers began calling the office to report smoke whenever they smudged. Now if they wanted to smudge inside the All Nations room, Ms. Mooseknuckle or Ms. Smith had to first alert the administrators or the office staff. Calling down to the office for permission was not just a hassle; it affected their experience of the smudge. When we had climbed the three flights of stairs to arrive back at the room, a teacher poked her head out into the hall and asked us if we smelled burning. Ms. Mooseknuckle shook her head, walked back into the room, and then just laughed at the timing.

Ms. Mooseknuckle, Ms. Smith, and the youth who accessed the All Nations room constructed and protected it as place of escape that refused East City High's status quo. Students regularly chose the All Nations room instead of their classes to work on assignments and take tests, to spend their spare periods beading and weaving, to meet with friends for lunch, and to just swing by for a conversation, snack, or pause in their day. Over the year, I observed youth who confronted challenges at East City High connect with each other in the All Nations room more expansively than elsewhere in the school. They made TikTok videos, shared personal and vulnerable stories, and forged relationships. The All Nations room was a place to step outside the ways East City High functioned, especially for the many youth who collided with the normative expectations underlying the school and schooling.

The All Nations room was partially established to promote a commitment to diversity and inclusion. However, unlike East City High's other diversity strategies, this space did not reify whiteness and settler structures. Rather, it was an important space of intervention, a place where it was possible to escape and resist oppressive forces at the school. I draw on the concept of *trapdoors* to consider how this type of space offers not only escape but possibility. Tourmaline, Stanley, and Burton suggest that "in addition to *doors* that are always already *traps*, there are *trapdoors*, those clever contraptions that are not entrances nor exits but secret passageways that take you someplace else, often someplace as yet unknown."[2] Following their work, I turn to trapdoors to theorize youth's practices of world-making. I am interested in how the gender-nonconforming youth in the study found and created spaces to both reimagine their lives and engage with their genders more expansively while in school. At times, adults, like Ms. Mooseknuckle and Ms. Smith, participated in this world-making by supporting youth in their need for an escape. However, trapdoors were important for youth because they were often ways to evade adult surveillance. Given the book's focus on youth labor, in this chapter, I concentrate on this form of trapdoors, "secret passageways" that youth built themselves to imagine other ways to exist in school in part by existing differently in other worlds first.[3]

As I have argued, gender never exists on its own. Though I concentrate on spaces that prioritized capacious gender expression, world-making was a way that youth could resist the interlocking conditions that shaped their movements through the school. Throughout the year, it is probable that youth were constructing trapdoors to refuse the many ways they felt constrained or unnoticed at East City High, beyond the transphobia they escaped while with me. The focus of the study as well as my whiteness may have contributed to which worlds the youth decided to invite me into with them. Since I was one of the only nonbinary, queer adults that the youth knew, I believe they chose to invite me into spaces in which their refusal of gender legibility was salient.

The youths' world-making was animated by their desires for an escape from the everyday functioning of East City High. In that sense, their world-making was queer, trans, and utopic. Following José Muñoz, "Queerness should and could be about a desire for another way of being in both the world and time, a desire that resists mandates to accept that which is not enough."[4] The youth consistently confronted the limits of others' capacities to engage with their genders and responded by creating spaces (trapdoors) that invited ambiguity. By building and caring for these trapdoors, youth were learning how to be nobodies together. They skirted adult surveillance and judgment by dreaming into reality worlds that did not rely on East City High's gendered metrics and logics. These were queer utopias that signified worlds they desired to inhabit in the future while also making them real in the present through their everyday practices. I am inspired by Eric Stanley's theorizing on ungovernability, offering that it is critical to pay attention to youth's world-making because trans and queer people "teach us not only that we need another world but that it's already here."[5] In this chapter, I explore three sites of world-making that youth chose to share with me: the tech booth, their writing, and the band hall.

The Tech Booth

Trapdoors are liminal spaces that provide escape in part through their embrace of unknowability. They are not tethered to rigid notions of visibility and recognizability. Further, trapdoors are not predictable or inevitable. Their ambiguity connects trapdoors to queer utopia, for they invite the possibility of hope. Yet, crucially, trapdoors are queer utopias that already exist. They are practices of world-making that illustrate how youth can dream different realities into existence and also live differently now because of those dreams. Muñoz proposed that "utopia is a stage, not merely a temporal stage, like a phase, but also a spatial one."[6] I offer that at East City High, one form of utopia was in fact stage adjacent—it was a tech booth.

There were two tech booths at East City High. One was in the theater studio, up a small flight of stairs, and it doubled as Ms. Mack's office. The other was a glass box on a narrow platform in the back of East City High's auditorium. Ms. Mack split the Senior Theater Company's curriculum into two main segments. In the first part of the year, all students worked on a big production that they performed in the auditorium in the first week of March. For the rest of the year, Ms. Mack divided up the class to rehearse and stage three smaller, student-directed plays. They performed these plays in the theater studio in June.

Both booths were literally located on the periphery of either the classroom or the auditorium. They were forgotten spaces, unobserved by adults and ignored by most students. Raeyun and Ostrich, who were the two main crew members, cultivated this lack of attention, keen to have a space away from the notice of others. Instead of neglecting the tech booth as out of the way or unimportant, I am interested in how Raeyun and Ostrich fostered the potential of the tech booth's marginal location to become nobodies together.

The Tech Booth Is Gay

By the end of November, Ms. Mack had instructed the tech crew to relocate to the booth in the auditorium. Raeyun and Ostrich asked me to accompany them. We spent the next few months mostly out of view, up a steep staircase hidden in the back of the large auditorium. During these periods, Raeyun and Ostrich passed the time writing stories, playing video games, and scrolling through memes and Instagram posts, pausing to show me their favorite ones, which typically meant the gayest ones. All the while, we chatted: about the latest school gossip, Ostrich's bee pun account online, their teachers, their families, video games, and a litany of random topics, like ghost stories. Ostrich explained it this way, "Especially in the booth, I feel like one of the perks of being in tech, while you can watch what's going on and that's pretty entertaining, you can also self-absorb yourself into something, and it's super easy to just block out everything else." Being involved in tech was not a path toward being a somebody in theater. Tech kids did not get the accolades or the spotlight on the big night. Tech work is background work. Often, tech kids were meant to be invisible. During performances, they dressed in all black so they could move around unseen during the show. The tech crew was skilled at this work. Throughout the year, Ms. Mack, who referred to tech as "the least creative part of the play," tended to forget that anyone was up in the booth. While Ms. Mack did not care much for tech, Raeyun and Ostrich did. Furthermore, their association with the tech crew brought them together and facilitated their creation of a small trans community of care. Since no one paid attention to the tech booth, our moments there together were often uninterrupted lengths of time when the three of us could just talk and hang out, interacting with queer and trans desire in ways that went beyond what was imaginable the rest of the day.

One month before the first matinee, Raeyun, Ostrich, and I were up in the tech booth with little to do. Ostrich, who was in charge of sound, showed off the Minecraft house he had been building. In Breakfast Club just a few days previous, Ostrich had showed me image after image of Minecraft constructions made to look like penises. Up in the booth, as Ostrich was teaching me how supply and demand worked in the world of Minecraft, I asked how that rule coincided with all the penises. Raeyun burst out laughing and said, "We love this! Nothing is better than talking about dicks!" Over the course of the year, Raeyun and Ostrich had started using the phrase "we love this," referring to the proclivities of all three of us, especially while in the tech booth. When watching YouTube videos, scrolling through memes, and recounting stories from class, Raeyun or Ostrich would respond for all of us with either "we love this" or "we don't love this." For instance, gay content on Instagram, K-pop's soft men, videos of dogs falling asleep: "we love this." Ms. Mack yelling at students for one reason or another, homework in general, staying after school for extra rehearsals: "we don't love this."

While Ostrich played Minecraft, Raeyun worked intermittently on collecting and reformatting images for a multimedia element in the production. Raeyun had to find a photo of a trampoline and upload the image to Ms. Mack's iPad. He devised a plan to make this task more interesting by using editing software to color in a rainbow trim on the trampoline. Ostrich and I thought this was hilarious, and we watched as Raeyun meticulously transformed the previously bland trampoline into a gay one. When Raeyun proudly displayed the finished product, Ostrich spoke for all of us, announcing, "we love this."

Ostrich and Raeyun's use of this phrasing both implied and constructed a shared sensibility. Through these pronouncements, they bolstered their growing friendship and pulled me into community with them. Neither of them was connected to a larger trans community at East City High. On several occasions, Raeyun and Ostrich had lamented the school's lack of a trans community. Raeyun explained, "I think that's, like—because a lot of the trans population at East City—I don't know about a lot—but most of them just want to be, like, normalized and just sort of blend in and just be, like, normal people." Raeyun thought perhaps there were other trans guys at the school, but he did not know of them because they did not present themselves as trans and were perhaps wary of being positioned as anything but normal. Though Raeyun likewise had his own desires to blend in, he also felt strongly about being trans. The tech booth was a rare space where he did not have to resolve the tensions he experienced regarding trans visibility.

As I discussed in chapter 4, Raeyun daily balanced his desires to emulate the K-pop idol aesthetic with his need to be legible as a trans guy. However, in the tech booth, Raeyun disregarded concerns about "proper" masculinity and instead gushed to Ostrich and me about the crop tops, heels, makeup, and glamorous outfits he yearned to wear one day. "The aesthetic for K-pop groups is—sometimes it's like hard stuff, harnesses and sheer clothing, and sometimes it's just flower crowns and really pink clothing. And I'm just like, 'Wow, can I pull it off?'" When discussing fashion goals, Raeyun often imagined an even gayer, more flamboyant future for himself, a time when he could dress how he wanted without recourse. This type of hope for the future is central to utopic imagining. Since Raeyun did not have to worry about proving his gender to us, he had the space to express other desires and enact a variety of trans identities. In the privacy that the booth provided, Raeyun scrolled through photos of his most coveted looks, pointing out details that he wanted to make sure neither Ostrich nor I missed.

In the spring, Raeyun secured tickets to an NCT concert with a friend. The next school day, exhausted but still glowing with excitement, Raeyun earnestly described the show while in the tech booth. For most of that period, the three of us watched a slide show on Raeyun's phone full of photos and videos of extravagant outfits and set pieces. Raeyun could barely speak because he had screamed so loudly at the concert. He kept returning to his surprise and delight at seeing performers with "the same skin tone" as him. Raeyun explained how K-pop idols were often whitewashed, and he had been concerned of that happening at the concert. Sitting in the tech booth, Raeyun shared how it felt, as someone who dreams of being a professional musician, to see parts of his identities reflected on the stage. Raeyun was introverted, and outside the tech booth, he rarely spoke about himself. However, inside the tech booth, Raeyun and Ostrich were building a different world together, one animated by the care they showed each other and their genders. This world welcomed Raeyun's vulnerability.

While moving through most spaces in the school, Raeyun and Ostrich worked hard to be legible as trans guys. During Elizabeth Rahily's study with parents of trans kids, she noted the heightened scrutiny of femme trans boys, indicating the increased pressure on trans youth to perform gender in alignment with conventional expectations.[7] This dynamic was pervasive in Raeyun's and Ostrich's lives. They dropped the "they" pronoun, chose to dress in more recognizably masculine ways, and picked names that aligned with others' gendered expectations. They also navigated adults' transphobia daily, making decisions about whether to correct people when they misgendered and deadnamed them. While they prioritized a particular form of legibility most of the time, Raeyun and Ostrich had a hidden space on the periphery of theater class where they did not have to work as hard. Ostrich and Raeyun could forget about the rest of theater company as well as the myriad negotiations of their daily lives. As Ostrich had remarked, in the tech booth it was easy to block everything else out. They could joke about being super gay without worrying about who overheard and how that person might respond. Importantly, unlike in the rest of Theater Company, we used the right names and pronouns for each other. In the tech booth, Raeyun and Ostrich could take up space, a position that Raeyun mostly associated with whiteness. They had created another world, a place where they could not only count on having their genders and names respected but also celebrate penises and be flamboyant. In the tech booth, Ostrich and Raeyun could relax, and they could dream. It was their trapdoor, an important world on the periphery of theater class that they directed.

The Tech Booth Is for Guys

Raeyun and Ostrich were not the only inhabitants of the tech booth. Spencer, a grade 12 student, was a sporadic visitor. Spencer was a "cool guy," always wearing the latest trends, carrying his skateboard around the halls of East City High, and dating one of the more popular girls in his grade. Unlike many of the students in Senior Theater Company, Spencer consistently remembered Raeyun's and Ostrich's pronouns and names. In fact, he was one of the only students to continue correcting Ms. Mack when she misgendered them. Spencer called them both "bro," a recognition of their masculinity. He was older than Raeyun and Ostrich, and his acknowledgment mattered to them. When Spencer was in the booth, Raeyun and Ostrich laughed at his jokes, listened to his stories, and just generally followed his antics.

Spencer influenced the type and tone of the tech booth conversations, shifting the dynamic away from super gay to more conventionally masculine. Ostrich, Raeyun, and Spencer took turns uploading videos, showing each other their favorite content. Spencer was not as interested in the flamboyantly gay material that Raeyun and Ostrich preferred on non-Spencer days, though he would watch their selections. Spencer liked macho YouTube videos that depicted men attempting feats that a person (or maybe just I) would not believe possible unless they saw it with their own eyes. When no one else was in the auditorium, Spencer would lower the projector screen, hook up his phone to the system, and stream videos on the big screen. If Ms. Mack came to check on the students, Spencer would get busted, and we would go back to just chatting in the booth.

On one such day, Raeyun was in a bad mood because he had PE next period, and they were about to start the dance unit. In this unit, students had to create groups and then make up dances to perform in front of their entire class. Raeyun did not want to dance in a group or present for anyone. Spencer encouraged Raeyun to talk to his PE teacher, saying, "You should be able to dance solo if you want, bro." Raeyun did end up asking Mr. Gonzalez if he could work on his own, though Mr. Gonzalez told him no. It was the only time I witnessed Raeyun ask Mr. Gonzalez for an accommodation of his own accord. Perhaps Raeyun was already intending to pull Mr. Gonzalez aside and advocate for himself. It is also possible that Raeyun was bolstered by Spencer's encouragement. I am not interested in concretizing Raeyun's motivations. Rather, I was compelled by Raeyun's decision to broach his concerns with Spencer about participating in the dance unit as a trans guy. I rarely witnessed Raeyun, a shy kid, discuss aspects of his personal life with anyone but very close friends. Moreover, outside the tech booth, Raeyun and Spencer had limited interaction. The intimacy of this type of conversation and the closeness that it signified was tethered in some way to the tech booth. What about the tech booth made possible their relationship and Raeyun's vulnerability? I suggest that the tech booth's liminality and separateness allowed for the youth to engage with each other differently. They were away from the purview of others and the attendant possibility of observation and judgment. Set off to the side and forgotten about in the tech booth, the students had the opportunity to create a space that allowed them to care about each other as well as their own desires and needs.

* * *

The tech booth was not just one kind of space. It was a hangout, a room to watch videos and scroll through internet content; a place to process life, where students could pause and think through their days; and a super-gay getaway, an escape from the cisheteronormativity that ruled the rest of East City High. In the world that Ostrich and Raeyun built in the tech booth, they could be flamboyantly gay trans men, bros, guys who waxed poetic about penises, and guys who lusted after femme fashion. Since they had created the tech booth as they desired, they were able to exist as they needed and wanted. The tech booth became a space outside the normative, daily structures at East City High. It was a complicated space that contained multitudes and, therefore, allowed them to live in their complexities. The tech booth was a world of opportunity and desire that Raeyun and Ostrich created because they needed a place that did not require stability and simplicity from them.

Writing

In November, Raeyun and I attended a pep rally together. The gymnasium was not big enough for the entire population of East City High to simultaneously attend an event, so teachers signed up their classes to attend either the third-period rally or the fourth-period boys' volleyball playoff game against a rival west-side team. Raeyun had PE third period, and we filed into the event with the rest of his class to find seats in the bleachers. As the other students filled in the stands, teachers stood directing traffic on the sidelines. Meanwhile, two girls with face paint and ribbons in their hair danced around the gymnasium, screaming inspirational chants into microphones. Raeyun put in his headphones, took out his phone, and started working on one of his novels. I nodded at him and motioned toward an empty spot in the back of the gymnasium, and we made an escape.

Raeyun and I leaned against the back wall, a step removed from the bleachers' loud, cramped conditions. We could hear teachers yelling at students to stay seated, but we were just out of view, obscured by the crowd. Raeyun took out his headphones and told me about his latest novel. It was a story about a selectively mute person. When by himself, the protagonist sang all the time, but no one could get to know him because he was too shy to talk to anyone. As Raeyun explained the multiple plot twists in his novel, Mr. Gonzalez walked by and noticed us. "Is everything okay?" Mr. Gonzalez mouthed to me. I gave him a quick signal that we were fine, and Mr. Gonzalez moved on to supervise the rally. Raeyun was allowed to stay standing in the back because he was standing with me.

During the pep rally, Raeyun mostly concentrated on his novel as students competed in musical chairs, a balloon-popping challenge, and an event that consisted of keeping a beach ball in the air. A group of boys dominated musical chairs by shoving all the girls off their chairs after they had already sat down. At the sound of shouting, Raeyun looked up, shook his head, and said, "This is absurdly aggressive." Then he went back to tapping out dialogue and narrative on his phone. Throughout the school day, several participants regularly turned to their phones to write stories and D&D campaigns. In this section, I explore their writing as trapdoors, secret passages they created to imagine other ways of existing when they confronted the limitations of East City High. This "queer feeling of hope in the face of hopeless heteronormative" is a utopic vision that animated their practices of world-making.[8] I am interested in their desire to write and in the way, through writing, youth escaped the gendered constraints of school.

Writing Queerness

After school one day, Scarecrow Jones led me the long way around East City High's fields to eventually end up at a café for an interview. Toward the end of our conversation, we started talking about daydreaming. Scarecrow Jones told me that during class, they daydreamed about the plots of stories. They described the process of writing their latest piece, called *M'dominique*. "It was kind of like one day I was, like, 'Fuck, I'm going to write today. I feel like writing. I don't know what about.' So, just started writing, and I came up with, like, two-thousand-something words in, like, three hours." As Scarecrow Jones spoke, they took out their phone to email me their queer, gender-bendy tale. "And it was, like, this fleshed-out plot, and I was like, 'Fuck yeah. Straight.' The main character is, like—is never given a name. The idea is that, like, they use 'I,' so the idea is, like, it's you, but it's not second person—never given a gender, never given a name." Still telling me about their story, they shared the link and set their phone down on the table. "Their best friend—they've got a best friend—his name is Dominique, and he kind of likely has a boyfriend, so, but, like, that's not—the story's not about that. It's not about *that*. It's about all these other things. But the characters are just characters, and these are just things that people are."

In *M'dominique*, Scarecrow Jones did not contend with ideas of not being "trans enough" or aligning with others' gendered expectations. They intentionally wrote the story without resolving the readers' questions about the protagonist's gender and sexuality. As I discussed in chapter 4, Scarecrow Jones grappled with the ripple effects of their gender unknowability. Similar to the character in their story, Scarecrow Jones's fluid gender affected their understanding of their sexuality. Their writing honored this confusion, challenging the reader to question why we thought we needed these answers. This story and their escape into writing was a trapdoor of their own design. Scarecrow Jones, who was highly selective about disclosing their gender and pronouns, had created another world through writing in which gender was intentionally confusing and beautiful in its illegibility.

Scarecrow Jones often wrote in school when they did not understand what was happening in class. "Like in math class," they explained, "I never understand anything the teacher says anyway, so why would I even go through the pain of trying to decipher it in my head?" Instead, Scarecrow Jones brainstormed ideas for stories. "I have the workbook. She's teaching out of the workbook. Why don't I just read the workbook later?" When not engaged in class, Scarecrow Jones escaped into their own imagination, choosing a different place to exist.

Each of my participants who wrote, wrote on their phones. They always had their phones on them; it was convenient. Whenever they were inspired, they could just pull out their phones and work on a story. Officially, cell phones were not allowed at East City High, though teachers had a fairly casual approach to that policy. Most teachers reminded students to stay off devices and reprimanded them for disobeying during lessons while also permitting unobtrusive usage, like listening to headphones during independent work periods. Only a few teachers ever confiscated phones, and several teachers regularly incorporated them into class by asking students to look up information on their phones during lessons. Youth's phones facilitated their building of fantasy worlds and narrative escapes. Within seconds, youth could easily access a secret passageway out of the classroom and away from East City High by simply slipping a phone out of their pocket and opening a document.

Fantastical Genders in Fantastical Worlds

Raeyun often mediated his behavior in classes in relation to a cohort of white boys in his French Immersion program whom he referred to as the "rowdy boys." Since French Immersion was a small, specialized track, Raeyun mostly had classes with the same students every year. As previously noted, Raeyun understood whiteness as taking up space, and these boys took up significant space in his classes, at times bringing lessons to a halt. Raeyun had developed a coping strategy for enduring their many antics: he wrote. Raeyun found that writing during class helped him stay focused, including allowing him to dodge whatever trouble the rowdy boys stirred up. Raeyun could be ensconced in a story while the rowdy boys threw books across the room, teased the teacher, or muttered slurs at him and his classmates.

Raeyun wrote songs and gaymances, which were mostly fan fiction involving K-pop idols. As you may have already surmised, K-pop was important to Raeyun. "I guess you could say in a sense that K-pop helped me figure out my gender identity. Yeah, it kind of just made me realize how much I wanted to be them in a sense but not really, yeah. It kind of just made me realize how masculine I wanted to be." Beyond wanting to dress like K-pop idols, Raeyun envied the ways the men related to each other. "I think it was, like, for the first little bit, it was their bodies, but then after a while, it started turning into their ability to be with each other, just exist with each other, and exist with themselves." Raeyun laughed, adding, "I mean, that sounds like it made me gay, but, you know, it kind of did in a way. It kind of made me realize that, like, it was, I wanted to be something closer to that." Raeyun coveted the fluid way K-pop men interacted with each other, interactions he read as "super gay." "I felt like they were experiencing something I felt like I was missing out on." Since at the time he did not have any affectionate, intimate relationships with other boys, Raeyun felt like he was missing out on something special.

In Raeyun's fan fiction, he took inspiration from K-pop idols' on-air affection and weaved narrative worlds in which they enacted queer love with an eye toward femme fashion. He explained that "K-pop boys are low-key, like, super gay for each other," so it was easy to "ship" his favorite idols.[9] Through his K-pop fandom, Raeyun explored the expansiveness of masculinity, maleness, and closeness among men of color. By writing into existence the outfits, interactions, and romances of K-pop idols, Raeyun followed a secret passageway into a realm where gender and sexuality operated according to less constraining norms than at East City High. Raeyun created space for himself and his desires, often when in classrooms where he was being denied that space. While sitting in the tech booth, waiting for PE to start, or tuning out the rowdy boys, Raeyun could easily step into that other world just by pulling out his phone.

Barry also drew inspiration from already-existing realities when writing. Barry was a Dungeon Master, and I would often find him sitting in the band hall during his spares writing out campaigns on his phone. As a Dungeon Master, Barry was in charge of creating D&D campaigns, a role he took very seriously. Dungeons & Dragons is a collaborative storytelling system, and building a campaign is akin to building a world. While D&D has been heavily critiqued for the racism and misogyny inherent to the game, it has also been lauded as full of potential and possibility.[10]

Though oppressive hierarchal structures are built into the world, the game ultimately depends on those who are playing it and how they design campaigns and embody their characters. As the creative force behind campaigns, Barry spent hours carefully thinking through all elements of the fantasy realms he crafted. His campaigns were political, fantastical, and super queer. Barry styled them after his favorite musicals and artists, constructing worlds that reflected his values and aspirations.

In the winter, Barry asked if he could teach me how to play. He loaned me his D&D books, helped me create a character, and introduced me to the world. "It's escapist in so many ways," Barry excitedly explained. "Gay everything is super cool in this world. That's just a fact." In the worlds of his design, Barry developed and played characters whose genders and sexualities expanded beyond what felt possible for him in school. Before Barry came out even to himself, he created Merdith. "I was like, 'It feels right for this character to be gay.'" When Barry played D&D, he was able to "go someplace else, often someplace as yet unknown."[11] While playing Merdith, Barry tested out queerness among his friends in an inviting world.

Whenever Barry had a spare moment during the day, he slid his phone out of his pocket to work on a campaign. Once, on a field-trip day for Barry's film class, Barry arranged for us to leave Social Justice 12 early to ensure we were punctual. We arrived at the film classroom before the teacher and sat on the floor in the hall outside the locked door. Barry immediately took out his phone and opened the document to his current campaign. He had recently seen a performance of *Cabaret* at a local college, and he was obsessed with the show. He returned to see the performance four times and then watched the production with Alan Cumming. In class, he would scroll through photos, showing me all his favorites while saying, "Alan Cumming is a fucking bisexual icon." Barry's parents took him the first time he went to see *Cabaret*. Barry, who never discussed his gender or sexuality with his family, asked his mother what she thought about the fluidity in the performance. He told me that his mother shrugged off the question, saying that "she guessed one of the characters was kind of gay." Now Barry was sculpting a D&D campaign modeled after *Cabaret*, making a thievery guild based on the musical's nightclub. In his D&D world, Barry did not have to explain gender, the vast complexities of gender bending, or why being gender nonconforming was not the same as being gay. He could just write queerness into the world, making fluidity possible without having to do the work of making it legible and knowable to people he was worried would not understand. Barry looked to D&D as "a way you can escape from your real world in a lot of different ways." By writing expansive characters and sculpting worlds that operated according to alternative norms, Barry also created other ways of being gendered that were not recognizable in the school. He was creating trapdoors, constructing utopic realms to explore himself and embody other ways of being that did not require coherent explanations.

What Is the Problem with Writing?

Vixen always had two or three writing projects on the go. They were publishing a fan-fiction novel online and writing several other creative pieces: *Light of the Revenant*, *Jack Rabbit*, *The Pirate King*, and *Shine*, to name just a smattering of their titles. "I feel like I was just literally ... born to be a writer," they explained. Vixen was constantly writing. When in school, Vixen was often sitting in the back of a class on their phone, typing away. "I have to be a writer because if I don't get my ideas onto the page, they will just stay in here and drive me nuts," Vixen told me. Sometimes Vixen and I worked on their stories together. We would sit next to each other in class, discussing character arcs and brainstorming possible plot developments. Their characters and story lines became inside jokes for us. We would reference them together like a secret code.

A couple of months into the project, Vixen stopped attending school. While a few of their teachers pulled me aside in the hall to inquire about Vixen's whereabouts, other people seemed entirely unaware. According to policy, Vixen's French teacher explained, "It's a teacher's responsibility to notice if a student is absent for a long period of time, and then they contact the counselor, who may or may not have any idea what is going on. Then they get in touch with the student and come up with a plan." She informed me that Vixen's counselor, Mr. Langlois, had no idea, but "it's hard to notice with students who skip a lot, like Vixen." Vixen was often positioned as "at-risk" and a "problem" at East City High because of their casual approach to school attendance, drug use, class background, family situation, and mental health issues. It was almost two months before teachers fully realized that Vixen had not been in school.

Similar to Vixen's departure, their returns to East City High happened in spurts and according to a logic that, while comprehensible to Vixen, was lost on many of the adults at the school. During the first several weeks when Vixen was trying to restart school, they were constantly colliding with educators' ableist and normative timelines for turning in work and completing high school. Vixen explained how challenging it was to come back to school while dealing with depression and then have to confront others' notions of the "right" way to move through school. "The worst thing about mental illness is that it feels like time stops for you, but it keeps going for everyone else. And then other people just expect you to have caught up and be right where they are once you are 'feeling better.'" Vixen was living according to "crip time," which is "a challenge to normative and normalizing expectations of pace and scheduling. Rather than bend disabled bodies and mind to meet the clock, crip time bends the clock to meet disabled bodies and minds."[12] Alison Kafer entangles queer and crip time, offering that, according to cisheteronormative conventions, queer people are already doing the wrong things at the wrong time. Vixen worked to value their relationship to time as a queer, genderfluid, and neurodivergent person, but they struggled with the persistent discordance between queer, crip time and East City High time. "The hardest part is trying to recover. You can't just be caught up, and the pressure and stress of trying to be recovered is almost worse than feeling your crappiest." Part of Vixen's challenge in returning to East City High was daily experiencing the gaps between what they felt was possible for themself and what everyone else positioned as the immutable standard.

During our conversation about time and recovery, Vixen and I were sitting on the couch in the drama hallway, waiting for a scene to end in Ms. Mack's grade 8 theater class. There was a Senior Theater Company matinee that day that Vixen was required to attend, even though Ms. Mack had already given away their part. However, Vixen also needed to write an in-class essay that they had missed in French class. They wanted support talking to Ms. Mack. Many adults at East City High had opinions about the best way for Vixen to catch up, and they were unwilling to listen to Vixen's ideas on the matter. Now that Vixen was more regularly attending school, they had to contend with a litany of encroaching deadlines and requirements if they wanted to graduate. They had struggled to get themself to school only to face more work on a collapsed time frame. I witnessed them make difficult decisions about which classes to attend, projects to complete, and courses to drop in order to "catch up" and finish high school.

As we sat in the drama hallway, Vixen told me why they would not return to English class until they finished a major, late assignment: "I know the moment I walk in, Ms. Allen will ask for the assignment, and if I don't have it, I will feel embarrassed and like I've disappointed her." The stress of mounting deadlines and projects only continued, and Vixen decided to drop English. "I like English, but I don't like English, but I do like English," Vixen explained. Vixen loved writing, but they disliked their English course and had struggled all year with the constraints, rules, and assignments in the class. Ironically, Vixen would often skip English class to instead work on their own writing or read their favorite books.

Even when Vixen was not going to school, they would regularly hop on a bus, texting me on their way to meet them at a nearby café. We met up multiple times a week and on weekends. While at the café, Vixen would read their writing out loud, and we would workshop ideas for stories. At one point in the winter, Vixen spent weeks reading me the first book in their favorite trilogy. It took place in a fantasy kingdom and revolved around a gay love story. Given their flair for the dramatic and skills as an actor, Vixen reveled in this activity. They affected different voices for the parts and fully embodied the roles. However, Vixen did not just perform this novel; they also analyzed it. They would pause and explain why they thought the author was such a good writer, drawing on analytical tools that they probably learned at school: character development; showing, not telling; and their attention to pay in / pay out. Though Vixen was not attending theater or English class, they chose to meet me at a café just a few blocks from school to act out scenes of star-crossed gay love from a fantasy world and then conduct literary analysis. They were consistently positioned as a bad or struggling student, but Vixen loved learning.

As with other participants, Vixen also wrote on their phone. Since Vixen was already labeled as a problem student, they were more frequently disciplined for this behavior. Their reputation framed their actions. While teachers may have been willing to give other students the benefit of the doubt, people were rarely that generous with Vixen. Ms. Mack confiscated Vixen's phone during class, reprimanding them for their disrespect and lack of commitment to the production. None of the other participants ever had their phones taken away. Teachers also often scolded Vixen for not paying attention, telling them to get off their phone. Vixen was frustrated by this constant chiding. "There's too much of an inherent idea that if I'm on my phone, I'm not listening," they remarked. "But a lot of times, I am. Like, I'm one of those people—I'm better at listening if I'm doing something else." There was little space or understanding for Vixen's neurodivergence, including the stimming practices (or self-stimulating behaviors) that helped them concentrate. Instead, teachers often assumed that they were making trouble or trying to evade work.

Despite how often Vixen got in trouble for being on their phone, they were still very frequently on their phone, writing stories. It is unlikely that teachers knew that Vixen was not just messing around or scrolling aimlessly. Vixen was building fantasy kingdoms, crafting intricate dialogue, and developing complex character arcs. While Vixen may have been physically sitting on the benches in Senior Theater Company, in the back row of Social Justice 12, or in any seat in any class, they were actually someplace else entirely. Vixen was somewhere in the depths of a vast, fantastical world of which even they barely knew the bounds.

Though Vixen was skilled at guarding their vulnerability, making it through an entire school day was often challenging. One morning, about a month into Vixen's latest return to school, they texted me to meet them at our regular café at noon. Their plan for the day was to make it to French class last period. Until then, they asked me to sit with them. Vixen read me the latest installment of one of their novels. After a couple of hours, Vixen checked the time on their phone and slumped back in their chair. I asked if they were heading to French, and they shook their head. "I just don't feel like I can go," they told me. For Vixen, writing was a utopic act of world-making, a trapdoor that gave them hope. It let them escape for a time while trying to make it through a school day. Through writing, Vixen created a place to belong and distance from their teachers' expectations and judgments. While they frequently struggled to find the type of care they needed at East City High, in the worlds they built, Vixen had the space and time to exist that they desired.

The Band Hall

The band hall was a small hallway off the main corridor on the east side of the auditorium. The hallway led to the music room, where the band and choir practiced, as well as a door out to the garden. There was a table and an odd assortment of chairs along one wall. Older students in the music program had their lockers in the band hall. The lockers were painted to look like piano keys. In January, Barry and Ms. Man urged me to ask Ms. Whittaker, their favorite band teacher, if I could use one of the empty lockers. I did, and afterward I wound up spending more and more time in that space before school and in between periods.

Many of the students in the music program had difficult relationships with their new director, Ms. Bartley. They struggled with her conventional, disciplinary approach to teaching band and choir as well as her rigid ideas about gender. There is an assumption that the arts are a safe space for queer and trans people.[13] At East City High, some students joined the music program because of the perception that it was a safe space. As Barry explained, "A lot of gay kids go into music." However, the music program was not an uncomplicated queer haven.

One day, Ms. Man stopped me in the hall to process a transphobic incident from choir. Ms. Bartley had teased a girl for singing the tenor part, saying it would turn her into a guy. Barry later recounted the same story, explaining that part of the issue was Ms. Bartley's insistence on gendering the sections by referring to sopranos/altos as "ladies" and tenors/basses as "guys." Barry relayed the moment from choir: "[Ms. Bartley] was like, 'Oh man, all this time being called a guy, by the end of the year, Taylor's going to be wearing dude's clothes. It's going to be confusing her.'" Ms. Man and Barry were both upset by the event, but neither felt confident in approaching Ms. Bartley. "It's difficult going to Ms. Bartley and talking to her about her shortcomings," Barry explained, "because she's really super defensive about stuff like this." Barry wanted to talk to Ms. Bartley because he was invested in the music program and wanted to protect it. "I care so much about this music program, and I just want it to succeed," he told me. Several students, including Barry and Ms. Man, were concerned that Ms. Bartley's demeanor and style would affect the quality and culture of the program. Beyond the success of the music program, many youths cared specifically about the band hall. In this section, I explore how youth interacted with that space as a form of world-making by attending to the meanings with which they imbued the band hall and the work they put into keeping it safe. I am interested in what queer and trans youth made possible through this utopic act of escape and creation.

Band Hall Is the New GSA

One day in February, Barry and I planned to meet in the band hall at the end of school. Rehearsals for the musical theater club's production of *Into the Woods* had just started, and I was set to accompany Barry to rehearsal. Before making our way up to the third floor, Barry changed into a tight-fitting sweatshirt that he had grabbed out of his locker and arranged it on his body like a crop top. He then catwalked down the hall, swaying his hips and prancing. "Do you like it?" he asked his friends. Folks applauded and cheered him on. Bolstered by their praise, Barry continued sashaying through the band hall as the majority of East City High's student population hustled to exit the school through the main corridor just adjacent to his performance, seemingly unaware of it.

Not all students in the music program hung out in the band hall, and not all students who spent time in the band hall were in the music program. Barry explained, "It's more so that when band is over, some people just stay there because it's where they feel happiest or safest, and some people leave because they have a lot of other places where they feel happy and safe." As Malatino discusses, trans people cultivate arts of living when confronted with cultures that are "depending on where you're at and who you are, either thinly accommodating or devastatingly hostile."[14] At East City High, those youths who did not have other places in the school to go where they felt cared for stayed in the band hall and created their own safety and happiness—their own arts of living. These youths were joined by a group of mostly queer and trans grade 11 and 12 students who were not officially affiliated with the music program. There was a dedicated crew whom I could reliably find in the band hall at some point during the day. Youth were somehow always there—before school, during their spares, at lunch, after school—as if they took turns watching over the space. They were excited for me to hang out there because of our shared interest in gender and sexuality.

While a few youths from the band hall had started out the year participating in the GSA, most of the queer and trans students who gathered in that space did not attend that club. The small number who had initially been members had stopped going and instead ate Friday lunch in the band hall. Why were queer students choosing the band hall over a club that had specifically been created to foster safety and inclusion for them? "This is where all the queer kids hang out," a grade 12 student who was not in band or choir told me at lunch one day while suggesting that I should eat with them. I asked why queer students hung out there, and they responded, "I don't know. I just like it here."

As I briefly discussed in chapter 4, after a beginning-of-the-year rush of interest and curiosity, the GSA at East City High winnowed down to a small handful of members. Those students were predominantly white and a mix of straight, queer, and questioning. The education scholar Cris Mayo offers that GSAs are important, for they are spaces that acknowledge "attachment to one another as related to their desire to go somewhere else and not have to feel like outsiders."[15] Though the students in the GSA articulated a trans-affirming perspective, lunch was short, and trans topics were never their priority. Just a couple of months into the year, almost all the trans and nonbinary students had given up on the GSA. I also stopped attending because Scarecrow Jones, Ostrich, and Ms. Man, the participants who had initially gone to the GSA, had all decided to spend their Friday lunchtime elsewhere. They each explained in their own ways how their experiences were not reflected in the space. However, they indicated that the GSA did not foster a sense of belonging or nurture their desire not to be outsiders while at school. Scholars have found that trans youth who encounter obstacles in accessing safe spaces find and create other places where they are valued and acknowledged.[16] I noticed this dynamic among my participants: Ostrich left the GSA to instead eat with another neurodivergent friend and play video games together, Scarecrow Jones joined a different club, and Ms. Man chose the band hall.

Barry and I discussed the queerness of the band hall versus the GSA multiple times throughout the year. He had a theory. "I think there's less of a precedent [in the band hall] because with, like, the GSA, like, no matter who's running it, by actively deciding to go there, you're really kind of like putting a lot of stuff barefaced," he explained. Participating in the GSA, he said, is "being like, 'This is me deciding to actively be a queer person.' And that's kind of—it can be a scary thing for some people." While students *attended* the GSA, arriving as members or part of the executive to work through items on an agenda once a week, youth just showed up to the band hall and hung out whenever they had time. Though by no means a formal or demanding club, the GSA was a space that specifically revolved around nonnormative gender and sexuality. The youth in the band hall were mostly queer, but queerness was not the focus of that space.

Barry had briefly participated in the GSA in grade 8, but he had a bad experience with another member, whom he referred to as a "gaykeeper."[17] During the year, both Ms. Man and Vixen also described negative interactions with this gaykeeper. Barry told me, "It was just always that mentality of, like, he was the authority on these types of things, ... and, like, you weren't part of the community unless he said so." Since Barry was not confident in his sexuality, he did not believe he had a right to take up space in the GSA, so he left. However, Barry never questioned his right to be in the band hall, both because he was an active participant in the music program and because stated and recognizable queerness was not a prerequisite. If a person wanted to be in the band hall, if they felt comfortable hanging out there, then they were welcome. "With the band hall, it's a space that's very kind of off to the side from the rest of the school, which is really nice, so it's got—it's a bit slower, and if you're already there and you're already the type of person." Barry's comments reflected what I heard from many other students: they felt cared for in the band hall. This care was not incidental. I offer that this care was the result of the work that youth put into making this space a community.

The band hall, like the tech booth, was a liminal space. It was off to the side and unnoticed unless it mattered to you. People could (and often did) walk directly past the band hall without realizing, which facilitated students in cultivating the space as separate and unremarkable. Barry described the band hall as a place that youth arrived at if they needed and desired that type of world. "When there's naturally, not a precedent, but a natural way of queer people flocking towards these types of programs, um, you'll just kind of—there's going to be likeminded people, and then someone's going to walk by, and they'll have the rainbow pin, and you're like, 'Okay, oh, okay.'" Muñoz explains, "Queerness should and could be about a desire for another way of being in both the world and time, a desire that resists mandates to accept that which is not enough."[18] While students saw the GSA as requiring particular forms of gender and sexual identities, they considered the band hall as a more open, fluid space. Furthermore, many youths thought the GSA prioritized certain forms of queer experience over others in their meetings and discussions, a decision that ultimately led to most trans and gender-nonconforming students leaving the group. The GSA's increasingly narrow demographic did not encourage their participation. Queer and trans youth desired another way to exist at East City High, so they built their own utopic escape. In the world of the band hall, they could be queer and trans, but those identities did not have to define them. Likewise, the band hall was not as overwhelmingly white as the GSA. The presence of racialized trans and gender-nonconforming youth in the band hall communicated an inviting atmosphere that the GSA perhaps aspired to but struggled to emulate.

I ultimately came to see the band hall as an integral queer and trans community at the school. While Barry attributed the camaraderie in the band hall to music, the presence of youth from outside the music program complicates this understanding. I suggest that the band hall community did not happen by accident or simply as an offshoot of band and choir. Rather, queer and trans students from all over East City High carefully built the band hall into their own world by consistently choosing to care about it.

Meet Me in the In-Between

Students were often passing time together in the band hall in between more structured moments of their day, like choir rehearsal, sports games, their classes, and other scheduled activities. In many ways, the band hall existed on the periphery and in the in-betweens of the school, both physically and metaphorically, given its location off to the side and how students used it as a space to hang out when there was nowhere else that they *had* to be. I argue that the youth made use of this in-betweenness to disrupt the rules, norms, and filters of their daily lives. They turned the band hall into a secret passageway, just out of the way enough to exist without notice.

One day in the spring, the regular crew debated a rumor that Elsa was going to have a boyfriend in *Frozen 2*. Students were dismayed at this heteronormative development and lambasted the Disney and Hollywood trend of forcing characters into straight relationships and just relationships period. One student asked, "Why can't there be self-love or asexuality or love of your friends and family?" Another agreed, "Why does there always have to be marriage?" The students frequently engaged in these critical conversations, analyzing the cisheteronormative structures they confronted in society and at East City High in particular. They discussed learning about male and female reproductive systems in biology class, lamenting how the teacher explained that they had to learn about boys first because "it's more straightforward." They disagreed that biology was binary and were frustrated by the sexist messaging underlying that presentation.

Another day, Barry and I were walking to film class when we ran into Spencer. He told us that there was a substitute teacher and not to bother attending. Barry swiveled around midstep and led me to the band hall, where we joined the youth who had spares that period. The band had a major field trip planned to Los Angeles in May, and students frequently ended up discussing this trip when together. That day, the youth in the band hall were celebrating their success in overturning a long-standing rule that required gendered uniforms for concerts. As copresidents of the music council, Barry and Taylor had taken on this regulation, which had previously forced girls to wear dresses and boys to wear ties. The students enthusiastically considered possibilities for their LA concert attire. The conversation moved from the uniforms to questions of gender and sexuality more broadly. Youth shared stories about speaking to family members about their sexualities and the harsh discussions they ended up in with more conservative relatives. Matilda, a grade 12 student and former GSA member, described her experience of first coming out as bi and then as a lesbian but feeling uncertain about that label. One student offered, "Sexuality is fluid, and we go through transitions in our thinking about it." The rest of the group pondered these ideas together, agreeing on the importance of having space to change your mind.

The band hall was an example of what Malatino refers to as a "t4t praxis of love." It was "an ideal, a promise, an identifier, a way of flagging an ethic of being. . . . It is about small acts guided by a commitment to trans love, small acts that make life more livable in and through difficult circumstances."[19] The youth worked together to create a space in which trans identity was desirable. They enjoyed being queer and trans and did not understand themselves as vulnerable or at-risk. In the band hall, they fostered this trans desire by expressing care for each other and aiding each other in recognizing the cisheteronormativity in their school and their lives generally. Though youth approached conversations with a critical lens, this dynamic did not mean that they were an overwhelmingly serious group. In response to one youth's story about pushback from their religious grandparents after they came out, a student remarked, "Jesus was a short, brown, polysexual, polyamorous guy." Everyone laughed and then took to their phones, searching out their favorite memes that queered Christianity. The move both supported their band hall community member and confronted normative ideas about queer and trans people that excluded them. However, they did not remain mired in the homophobia and transphobia that they confronted. As they were scrolling on their phones, one young person found a photo of their pride outfit from the previous year and wanted to show it off. Suddenly, I had several phones in my face as youths swiped through rainbow-clad slide shows trying to find the best image of their queerest pride attire to date. The students enacted a t4t praxis of love by engaging with each other and me in a way that highlighted the joy of being queer and trans.

Band Hall Is for Gay Shit

Youth embodied their genders and sexualities differently while in the band hall. They were affectionate with each other, often hugging and cuddling. Barry and a good guy friend greeted each other with kisses on the cheek and would sit with heads in the other's lap. Mark, who looked the part of a gym bro and was captain of the ultimate frisbee team, sang showtunes while in the band hall and made plans for Ms. Man to do his makeup during the trip to LA. Previously, Ms. Man had painted Mark's nails, but when he left the band hall that day and went to the gym, he was called "gay" and teased so badly that he would not let anyone paint them again. With the band trip on the horizon, Mark knew it would be fine to play around a bit more with makeup and nail polish. Barry had also painted his nails for the first time with band kids. "So, I painted my nails and, like, got a lot of compliments. Like, 'Oh, that feels nice.' And it looks really nice, and I just kept doing it." When surrounded by his friends in band, Barry felt supported in transitioning from just thinking about painting his nails to having the confidence to do it. Despite how the youth in the band hall may have otherwise moved through East City High, when they were together in the world they had built, they felt confident in challenging cisheteronormativity and reveling in queerness.

Ms. Man and I had most of our conversations in the band hall. Whenever I arrived in the space, they would sidle up next to me and slide their sketchbook over, introducing their latest work this way: "some gay shit, you know me." They often studied my face as I perused their drawings. Ms. Man enjoyed watching people's reactions to their work. Though Ms. Man was shy and introverted, rarely contributing to group discussions, they loved to share and provoke with their art. In their work, Ms. Man disrupted gendered expectations and confronted societal norms about youth and sexuality. For instance, they made sure that no one gendered the characters in a drawing they proudly displayed of two queer lovers, one grinding their butt against the other. Moreover, Ms. Man often incorporated Vietnamese themes into their comics, pushing back against the whiteness and English dominance of the rest of their day at East City High. Through drawing, Ms. Man not only expressed the queerness and gender nonconformity that they tended to filter out the rest of the day but also created space in contrast to the prevailing whiteness of schooling. They drew comics of queer and trans love stories, sketches of drag queens from *RuPaul's Drag Race*, and tableaus of queer-of-color sex scenes. While I looked through their sketchbook, Ms. Man pointed at their favorite aspects and talked openly about (gender)queerness.

For the entirety of the year, Ms. Man held the project at a distance, insisting that they had nothing valuable to add or say and that I should speak to someone more knowledgeable. Yet, whenever they saw me, they would come over and hand me their sketchbook. When they had their sketchbook out, Ms. Man talked nonstop. One time, as we sat on the floor with our backs against their locker, they told me about a nonbinary substitute teacher from another day and what it was like to hear "they/them" pronouns in the classroom. Another time, I was flipping through stills of their latest comic as they shared how they told their brother about their pronouns and being nonbinary. We were also in the band hall, eating lunch together when they parsed the complexities of approaching a conversation with their mother in Vietnamese about nonbinary gender. Ms. Man felt more comfortable expressing themself and broaching these discussions in the band hall.

Whereas Ms. Man freely circulated their sketchbook to the students in the band hall, they were careful about letting others outside that space see their sexually explicit, gender-bendy artwork. Ms. Man relished the opportunity to share their art in the band hall, where not only was there space for queer, gender-nonconforming art but also the other youths adored Ms. Man's work. Students often asked them to continue comic strips and loudly celebrated their talent and creativity. For Ms. Man, their sketchbook was a conversation starter. Even more, queer art was a way of building community and relating to others. This camaraderie and intimacy were possible because the youth worked together to build a space that welcomed and celebrated these desires.

* * *

The band hall was nestled between the tense dynamics of the music room, a place of potential conflict and discipline, and the public chaos of a main thoroughfare in the school. However, despite its precarious proximity and snug conditions, the world of the band hall was expansive. The band hall was another world, a world created, inhabited, and beloved by a committed group of youth. While in the band hall, youth who did not feel able to oppose the homophobia and transphobia they experienced at East City High processed their thoughts together. They analyzed conversations from classes, peers, and their families and critiqued assignments and films. Several students, like Ms. Man, had left the GSA, a space dominated by white, nontrans youth, and chose to spend their time in the band hall. In this less formal queer community, they supported each other in disrupting oppressive logics that did not serve them.

The youths' critical commitment to disrupting the school's normative structures created space for more capacious relationships to gender. At

East City High, the students navigated others' notions of how to be a boy or a girl, but in the band hall, they helped each other break down this binary logic and explore beyond those boundaries. They had built their own world, an open secret that was both highly visible and somehow invisible to the rest of the school. This trapdoor enabled them to escape the rest of their school lives and exist differently together.

Conclusion

Lacking other communities and places at East City High to explore fluidity, revel in queerness, or try out new ideas and ways of presenting themselves, gender-nonconforming youth built their own worlds out of necessity. Through their world-making, youth found someplace as yet unknown because they needed a place in the school to just exist.[20] Their trapdoors were both physical and fantastical spaces that they could escape into while navigating the cisheteronormativity of East City High. Often these spaces were not noticed by other adults, either because adults were unaware they existed or because youth kept them secret and protected them from interference. Therefore, it is probable that there were many trapdoors that youth were creating to upend and disrupt the conditions that structured the school. Furthermore, these spaces were not discrete—they overlapped in productive ways. Often youth worked on their writing while in the band hall or the tech booth. The entryways they had created for themselves at the school fostered their imaginative outlets and made possible further fantastical exploration.

Trapdoors are created in spaces and institutions that extend opportunities for trans youth only so long as youth are willing to adhere to normative expectations for gender legibility.[21] While East City High articulated a progressive stance toward diversity and inclusion, this welcoming framework relied on youth being legible as gender nonconforming within established parameters of visibility and knowability. However, in their acts of world-making, youth eluded recognition and eschewed normative ideas for what it means and looks like to be trans and gender nonconforming. They refused and resisted the logics undergirding East City High's approach to diversity and inclusion by constructing trapdoors that did not adhere to cisheteronormative expectations. In these spaces, they existed in expansive relationships to their genders. Even for the youth who worked hard to become recognizable as trans, it was integral for them to cultivate worlds that did not demand the labor of legibility. The worlds they built were important spaces of refuge and pauses in their day when they did not have to work as hard to survive schooling or contort themselves to align with others' understandings of trans identity.

Unlike moving through the rest of the school, the worlds that youth built were complicated spaces that did not require them to remain stable, certain, and knowable. Beyond using the correct names and pronouns, gender-nonconforming youth invited expansive ways of relating to gender and sexuality. Through their acts of world-making, youth were learning how to care for themselves, their genders, and each other within an institution that struggled to care for them in all their complexities. Rather than perform the labor necessary to qualify for protection through accommodations, youth's world-building was a praxis of care that honored their desires. They were learning how to be nobodies together, creating communities outside adult surveillance as well as others' gendered expectations and standards. Unlike the other forms of labor I have discussed, youth's work in this chapter centered their desires to explore, embody, and live in their genders without having to reckon with adults' perceptions of them or what was typically required to survive and navigate the cisheteronormative structures of East City High. World-making practices among youth are integral to consider because they are both utopic and happening now, illustrating that a different world is possible in schools because it already exists.

Conclusion

From Risk to Desire

In May, on the fiftieth anniversary of the decriminalization of homosexual sex in Canada, Mr. Hill began a unit on queer and trans issues in Social Justice 12. This unit held particular importance for him. At the start of the year, Mr. Hill had come out as gay to the students in this course. He explained that when he was assigned to teach a class on social justice, he realized that he could no longer keep his sexuality hidden at school. During one of the last lessons in this unit, Mr. Hill announced that he wanted to talk about "transgender and gender identity issues." After a month of focusing on questions about the origins of sexuality (nature or nurture?), reading articles covering statistics on the queer community and rates of homophobia, and discussing pride politics, it was finally time to consider gender. Mr. Hill opened with a question for the class: "How do you know someone's gender?" Immediately, Barry responded, "You ask them!" Mr. Hill laughed and rephrased his question. He had wanted to explain the differences between "sex" and "gender." Mr. Hill described gender as the expression of sex. "It's masculine and feminine; it's how we perform in society," he told the class. Next, he had students define the terms "cisgender" and "transgender" before moving on to a group activity. Standing in front of the whiteboard, Mr. Hill uncapped a marker and asked, "What issues do people who are not cis face? There are a lot," he said, "so start listing!"

My intention is not to criticize Mr. Hill's lesson. Rather, I highlight this moment to emphasize how pervasive risk discourses were in relation to trans identity at East City High. Even in a social justice class, students learned about trans topics through the lens of hardship and struggle. Though Mr. Hill cared about queer and trans students, his support was informed by this understanding. During the activity, the students shouted out problems: lack of basic respect, constant suspicion, people policing boundaries of trans identity, harassment, higher rates of suicide, lack of medical attention, denied employment, denied opportunities, violence, and accessing bathrooms. They were adept at identifying the challenges involved in being trans in North American society.

As a progressive Canadian school that prioritized a multicultural approach to diversity and inclusion, East City High was committed to accepting trans students. As I have discussed, adults at the school largely tackled this work through accommodation practices. Though well-intentioned, accommodation approaches are reactionary strategies that offer support primarily for recognizable trans youth on an individual basis. These practices rely on the notion that trans is a visible, knowable gender identity as well as an identity that requires added protection in schools. In short, in this context, being trans means that a person will encounter problems, but accepting adults can support students in overcoming them. Accommodation approaches assert that when adults notice that a student is trans, their task is to work with that individual student to help them fit in by providing tailored concessions. Underlying this framework is the notion that there is something risky about being trans in school and that, therefore, adults need to be able to identify who is trans in order to then keep them safe from harm. At East City High, this approach was guided by a district-wide trans-inclusive policy and the good intentions of teachers, administrators, and staff. Recognizable trans youth were accepted in part because of the multicultural ideals that directed adults' attitudes and interactions with students who were positioned as "different." After all, in the words of Ms. O'Connor, "East City High is really good about that stuff."

Since I left East City High in early summer 2019, the political context regarding trans-inclusion in schools has shifted. Though accommodations approaches remain the dominant framework in the Lower Mainland of British Columbia, across North America, we are likewise witnessing mounting backlash against any mention of gender and sexuality in schools. At a recent school board trustee campaign event in a northern district of British Columbia, one candidate articulated her impetus for running: pushing back against queer- and trans-inclusive curricular programming and antiracist policies in schools. "Children don't see differences," the candidate announced, "and pointing them out just focuses attention on that."[1] This district was one of eight across the province where a conservative parents'-rights group backed a slate of school board candidates. In some districts, these conversations revolved around book banning; in others, the focus was on attempts to restrict the curriculum in schools. Often, the condemnation of queer and trans issues in schools is happening alongside the denouncing of antiracist teaching and learning.

These attacks have catapulted trans youth into mainstream discourse. Currently, conversations about queer and trans youth are prevalent across the news, media, and legislation. Notions of risk are rampant throughout the attempts to restrict youth's lives and access to information and care as well as people's various endeavors to advocate on behalf of young people. Legislators, parents, and activists on all sides of the issues position children and youth as vulnerable and in need of protection. Reactionary and conservative adults position youth as at-risk from learning about "controversial" topics like gender, sexuality, and race in schools, while more progressive advocates warn of the possibilities of harm in censoring this knowledge and banning access to health care.

In this conclusion, I revisit central themes of the book to underline the limitations of understanding gender nonconformity through the lens of risk. I consider how the rising backlash against antioppressive curricula and support in schools draws on the language of concern, deploying fears over children and youth's safety as justification for violent and restrictive policies and pedagogy. These moves point to the weaknesses of accommodation approaches, which have focused on making schools safe for individual students instead of reworking harmful, foundational schooling structures. Rather than position trans youth as especially vulnerable, I advocate for cultivating a pedagogy of desire—for creating schools that desire youth to be and grow up trans. The worlds that the youth in this study were building in the tech booth, through their writing, and in the band hall were animated and fostered by this desire. I close by turning to the youths' ideas for transforming schools.

The Meaning of Safety

In September 2022, the Virginia Department of Education reversed its previous policy for transgender students in schools, which had been adopted just a year earlier. According to the latest proposal, students will now be required to provide legal documentation for pronoun changes and must use the bathroom and locker room that matches the gender marker on their birth certificate.[2] This situation is dire for many reasons and creates an impossible dilemma for gender-nonconforming and nonbinary youth who have no possibility of acquiring legal proof of their genders or accessing facilities that "match." The earlier law, developed by the former governor, had instructed the Department of Education to abide by the "Model Policies," a set of guidelines meant to assist schools in accommodating trans students. A key tenet of the "Model Policies" was to maintain "a safe and supportive learning environment free from discrimination and harassment for all students."[3] However, after the most recent election in Virginia, the newly elected Republican governor drew on that same sentence in the "Model Policies" to justify the removal of protections for trans youth. Both governors named the vulnerability of youth as well as adults' responsibilities in protecting them while they are in school, yet the resulting policies were dramatically different.

From the rejection of textbooks that discuss race in Florida to the criminalization of gender-affirming care in Texas and Alabama to the school board elections in British Columbia, the language of concern is pervasive in the proliferation of antitrans fearmongering and legislation as well as pushback on antiracist curricula. The language of concern obscures the systemic cisheteronormativity, transphobia, and racism informing people's actions, justifying their behavior as motivated instead by worry and the presumed good intentions of adults to keep a young person safe. As lawmakers and politicians ramp up their fight against teaching and learning about gender, sexuality, and race in schools, it is evident that the rhetoric of "protecting" youth is inextricable from upholding dominant societal structures, such as whiteness and cisheteronormativity. More specifically, the language of concern undergirds adults' anxieties over the implications of teaching students accurate history for the stated reason of fear of making youth feel bad or guilty. It is likewise present in the discussions compelling legislative attacks against trans youth, for gender nonconformity is positioned as a social contagion—a risky ideology that youth will fall victim to if exposed. Through adults' anxieties, they indicate who they perceive young people to be and desire them to grow up into: white, cisgender, heterosexual, and otherwise normatively aligned. At East City High, adults' investment in a "feel good" approach to diversity and inclusion precluded the blatant racism and transphobia fueling these curricular and legislative bans. Educators were encouraged to accept "difference" rather than legislate against it. However, returning to Sunera Thobani's theorizing on Canadian politics, the multicultural recognition of otherness upholds hegemonic expectations for students, reproducing a population in need of protection and a dominant, white population positioned as tolerant because of its good intentions to be accepting of difference.[4]

Across these interrelated legislative moves, we can hear echoes of Scarecrow Jones's rejection of the language of concern and their disdain at the adultist and ableist paternalism of teachers who undermined their capacity to know and articulate their own gender. They explained how adults at the school would not directly indicate their discomfort with gender nonconformity, "but they'll be like, 'Hmm, what does that mean for you? What, how do you know? Are you sure? But you're a child.'" Scarecrow Jones was frustrated with the way adults devalued their own knowledge of their gender under the guise of keeping them safe. In both the language of the recent legislation and the pushback against it, young people are positioned as in need of protection—from the state, "woke" ideology, high rates of suicidality, and their own machinations. Trans youth are framed as vulnerable and at-risk, in need of saving by adults. This perspective makes impossible the idea that anyone could desire gender nonconformity for a young person.

At East City High, I observed adults reference this vulnerability as a reason to be cautious in supporting a young person's desire to transition or as justification for their fear-based response to finding out that a student was trans. They used the language of concern to temper their own transphobia, excusing their lack of desire for a young person to be trans with their knowledge that being trans was attendant with added obstacles and harm. Though inspired by different reasons than conservative politicians and parents'-rights groups, educators' inability to desire gender nonconformity among their students shares important underpinnings with the uproar over trans identity as a social contagion. Both the conservative "social contagion" perspective and the educators' protective stance includes the presumption of a normative, "correct" way for a young person to grow into adulthood. Likewise, there is the notion that gender nonconformity is risky and that, if one cares for a young person, one will not wish such a challenging life for them.

At East City High, educators absolved themselves of the possibility of transphobic harm by framing their interactions with youth as a result of worry. They indicated that they were acting with youth's best interests at heart, out of genuine concern for their well-being. Madame Blanchet drew on this framework during our conversation following the opinion piece on "transgender bathrooms" in Raeyun's class. She expressed concern for Raeyun's safety while also permitting transphobic arguments about bathrooms and sexual predation. This situation underscored how safety, like diversity, is an empty container; it can be deployed and weaponized for drastically different intentions.[5] When we rely on the "good" intentions of adults to keep youth safe, we likewise submit to the mercy of shifting notions of safety. As political contexts fluctuate, as in Virginia, so do the meanings of vulnerability and safety. One year, a Department of Education may determine that youth are vulnerable because they encounter transphobic bullying, while the following year, youth may be positioned as vulnerable because educators teach openly about gender, race, and sexuality.

Beyond the volatility of elected officials, the emptiness of safety as a framework highlights the limitations of accommodation approaches as well as strategies to support youth that emerge from adult concern. "Nice" educators, like Madame Blanchet or Ostrich's counselor, Ms. O'Connor, wanted to protect youth whom they perceived as at-risk; yet their efforts emphasized the dominant assumption that being trans and gender nonconforming made youth vulnerable. It was impossible for adults to desire youth to be or grow up trans because that was akin to wishing them a lifetime of struggle and hardship. Instead of cultivating schools with a desire for gender nonconformity, educators worked to accept youth whom they recognized as trans. Moreover, the pervasive belief that gender nonconformity was a risk factor in a young person's life compelled adults to particular forms of action. They worked to provide concessions and protect youth from what were presumed to be potential dangers. Locating safety for trans youth in schools as a response to their vulnerability both tethered youth to risk and demanded that they become recognizably trans to qualify for protection. I explored the weaknesses in these approaches in chapter 2, and I underline them in closing to argue instead for cultivating school environments that desire gender nonconformity.

The Limits of Visibility

At East City High, safety was defined as protecting trans youth from discrimination and helping them "fit in" while at school. These goals relied on two intertwined ideas that circulated at East City High. The first was the belief that schools were fundamentally safe places. The conceit was that, from time to time, there may be a student who encountered obstacles at school. However, since most teachers and staff understood the school to generally operate in the best interests of youth, they likewise believed that they could work with that anomalous young person to mediate their inclusion and, thus, success. This negotiation depended on the second idea: that educators could tell who was trans. The pervasive assumption was that gender nonconformity was visible and recognizable as a legible identity. Adults believed that they knew who was trans and, therefore, would be able to protect trans students who needed their support. This perspective directed adults' interactions with youth and offers of assistance. For instance, Mr. Gonzalez found workarounds for Raeyun in PE; however, that class maintained its foundation in biologically essentialist ideas about gender and ability. While Raeyun was able to discern a path through the gendered travails of his PE lessons, his labor and Mr. Gonzalez's accommodation efforts did not alter the structural violence of PE. The understanding was that PE was generally a safe space for students. It is likely that Mr. Gonzalez will utilize similar strategies when he encounters another trans student whom he *recognizes* as trans. Yet, this experience did not transform his approach to the curriculum or his ideas about the relationship between gender, ability, health, and fitness. Trans-inclusive strategies that focus on accommodating individual students leave intact the oppressive organizational mechanisms of schools and schooling.

Over the year, I witnessed nice adults at East City High express care and concern for the trans youth whom they knew existed. Mr. Hill was caring for Vixen when he told them how to change their name, and Mr. Gonzalez responded from a place of concern when he pulled Raeyun aside and let him make important decisions regarding his assessment. However, I was never in a class in which an adult created space for the possibility of gender nonconformity without being asked to by a young person or in response to the presence of a *known* trans youth. In fact, during Mr. Hill's unit on gender in Social Justice 12, he was flummoxed by a conversation on this topic that emerged during a class discussion. Students shared their belief that it was not always possible to tell who is trans and that support in the school should not rely on visibility. In response, Mr. Hill asked, "How do you support people if you can't refer to them directly because you can't tell?" For Mr. Hill, it was integral to know who was trans because, as a teacher with the good intentions to keep youth safe, he needed to know whom to protect. Barry explained that it was not necessary to know, saying, "We need to teach people to not see the world in such a limited way."

Teachers, counselors, and administrators shared the predominant belief that the structures of binary gender only affected *visibly* trans and gender-nonconforming youth. Though grounded in cisheteronormativity, the idea of visibility has expansive reach. Teachers, counselors, and administrators relied on their assumptions and expectations about what gender nonconformity "looks" like to guide their interactions with students. Since notions of visibility often correspond to a "white middle-class epistemological bias that does not necessarily resonate for queer subjects marked by racial difference," who has access to visibility is already constrained.[6] As I have explored throughout this book, in North America, norms of whiteness, settler colonialism, and ability are inextricable from ideas about what it means and looks like to be gender nonconforming. The reliance on visibility only further reifies normative constructions of gender legibility, or what Barry would call the bureaucracy of gender. All youth who did not perform their genders according to these ideas were not recognized or acknowledged.

Moreover, the privileging of visibility promoted the perspective that cisheteronormativity was only a problem for trans and gender-nonconforming youth. If there were no youth in a class who were visibly trans and gender nonconforming, the assumption was that gendered language, activities, and expectations were not an issue. However, cisheteronormativity, and the power structures that inform it, remains a violent, organizing principle of schools. All students are subjected to and policed by these expectations, for no one can fit into these ideals perfectly all the time. Dismantling the cisheteronormativity of schooling would expand possibilities for all youth, not just those whom teachers could point to as not belonging.

In chapter 2, I examined how accommodation approaches emerged from the understanding both that schools are generally safe places for youth and that specific youth need assistance to "fit in." Rather than addressing structural injustices endemic to schooling, accommodation practices focus on individual students experiencing hardship. They offer solutions aimed at including these students back into the everyday operations of the school with the least amount of possible disruption. Since accommodation approaches are reactionary, arising in response to the needs of individual students, they often place the onus on those students to make themselves visible or otherwise knowable as requiring concessions or qualifying for assistance. These approaches are ill equipped to enact systemic changes within the school. Their reliance on visibility as a metric for support and overly individualistic focus hinders their impact, and therefore, accommodation practices often enable schools to persist as inequitable, exclusionary institutions.

Accommodation strategies are likewise limited because they continue to view trans and gender-nonconforming youth as vulnerable and at-risk in schools. Instead of reckoning with the many ways schools have been created to deny their existence, accommodation approaches position trans youth as in need of protection and always already vulnerable. As Travers notes, "often the best outcome one can hope for, it seems, is that individual trans kids will be accommodated."[7] Until we can envision nonnormative lives and futures for youth, the goal of keeping students safe in schools will always have the potential to be undermined by adults' inability to imagine a world in which existing as trans is possible, beautiful, and desirable.

The Hard Work of Desire

At East City High, trans and gender-nonconforming youth were at times accommodated, at times unnoticed, at times erased, and at times met with violence. Thinking alongside Malatino, trans life becomes possible in this type of culture through care work. "This work—like all care work—is about fostering survival; it is maintenance work that must be done so that trans folks can get about the work of living."[8] I have focused this book on youth labor because, throughout the year, I witnessed youth perform significant labor to go about the work of living at East

City High. The labor they performed addressed myriad elements of their experiences of being gender nonconforming at school. Their labor was about easing their interactions with teachers and peers by discerning when to correct people who misgendered and deadnamed them, deciding which aspects of their gender to share and in which spaces, learning how to trust their own knowledge of their genders, and building places of refuge that did not require narrow forms of gender legibility from them. Undergirding all these aspects was care—their care for themselves, their genders, and the trans communities they were attempting to create in the school. In the absence of the care that the youth needed and desired from adults, they navigated how to foster this ethic and support for themselves. It is critical to take this labor seriously. Though frequently unnoticed, trans youth are already creating other, queerer worlds in which to live.

During my year at East City High, I frequently wound up in conversations with young people who were exasperated by adults not taking them and their labor seriously. The dynamic of undervaluing, disrespecting, and not caring about youth's experiences had far-reaching effects at the school. It was present when adults discounted the work of student activists, like Tamar and Eliza, as well as when educators were wary to trust youth who requested name and pronoun changes. Likewise, it circulated when Ms. Mack nonchalantly informed youth that she would misgender them. She laughed off this comment, believing it was not transphobic. The idea that youth are incapable of articulating their own genders and lives is connected to the dominant frameworks used to distinguish between youth and adults. In North America, youth are positioned as inchoate versions of their future selves who rely on adult protection to safely move through the phases of development toward normative adulthood. These developmental events are mired in ableist and capitalist concepts of success (independent living, home ownership, acquiring a profession) as well as white, colonial, and cisheteronormative partnership models of family (heteromonogamous marriage, kids).[9] This framework is propelled by the paternalistic belief that adults know better than youth. In Elizabeth Rahily's research with parents, she noted that even among families that ultimately supported their trans children, there was a belief that no young person would want to be trans. Rahily observed how parents drew on medicalized and ableist language as they articulated their assumptions about the "right" way to grow up and their sense that gender nonconformity signaled that something had gone awry.[10] As I have discussed throughout this book, desiring youth to grow up trans, disabled, or in any way outside of normative paradigms is framed as perverse because these desires would represent a failure of youth to safely traverse their development and become "successful" adults.

On the basis of these models for growing up, we cast youth as less able than adults to understand themselves and make decisions about their own lives and, therefore, as less human. According to this perspective, since youth are not yet fully formed, their growth must be protected so they may develop into adults free from risk and harm.[11] This understanding of youth intersects with and is informed by racist, ableist, and colonial histories that have assigned marginalized communities to the status of children and as wards of the state.[12] If living outside or in rejection of white, settler colonial, ableist frameworks is tethered to risk, then what is the meaning of protection? As I examined in the first section of this conclusion with a brief look at recent curricular and legislative bans across North America, positioning someone (including communities and nations) as in need of protection can also be a strategy to deny their personhood and humanity. For instance, it can be used as justification for enacting restrictive and violent policy and legislation, such as the removal of textbooks that teach about Black history or banning the mention of queer sexualities in schools. I observed this protectionist dynamic at East City High when Ms. O'Connor listened sympathetically to Ostrich's request for a name and pronoun change but, behind his back, delayed following through. She interacted with Ostrich as a vulnerable young person, in part because he was neurodivergent. She believed that Ostrich was less able to handle the challenges of high school than other youth were and that being trans would be an added vulnerability in his life. Therefore, she saw it as her duty as a nice educator to protect him from these harms.

Since youth were infrequently taken seriously by adults at East City High, they worked to listen to themselves and each other. In this book, I have centered youth labor as an act of noticing and care for the ways that they worked to navigate the school, the curriculum, and their relationships with adults and peers and, critically, to build worlds in which their genders, lives, and bodies were not discounted. I documented three forms of youth labor. The first was the labor to understand and forgive adults' transphobia, which often involved reframing violence against them as misunderstandings or acts of care. The second was the labor of filtering their gender expressions and making decisions about what parts of their genders to share depending on their awareness of East City High's cisheteronormativity. Beyond those two, complicated practices, I discussed how gender-nonconforming youth actively intervened at East City High. This final form was the labor they performed to desire their transness and queerness by creating their own worlds within the school that invited the fluidity and ambiguity that was otherwise denied them. Despite the pervasive pressures to be and become legible as trans according to recognizable parameters (to be trans somebodies), gender-nonconforming youth at East City High developed their own relationships to safety, legibility, and gender nonconformity over the year. Through their labor, I witnessed their desire for complex trans identities that were not possible elsewhere in the school. Inspired by their care and their labor, I consider what it might mean for educators to desire youth to be trans.

A Pedagogy of Desire

Throughout this book, I have called on educators to cultivate a desire for gender nonconformity, but what would it mean for educators to enact this desire in schools? To consider this question, I return to Eve Tuck's call for an end to damage-centered research.[13] While Tuck was writing specifically about colonial research imposed on and extracted from Indigenous communities and nations, she offers important provocations for the implications of continuously theorizing communities as composed of victims who are at-risk. I think alongside her letter to ponder the necessity of an epistemological and cultural shift in the way we understand gender-nonconforming and trans identities, especially in schools.

In Tuck's piece, she acknowledges that there was previously a need for recording hardship and damage.[14] Like Tuck, I am presently able to engage in research that rejects risk discourses because other scholars have done the important work of documenting harm and struggle in my communities. However, it is now critical to invest in additional ways of thinking about our lives. Trans people are always more than our pain, our suffering, and our hardship. We need language, activism, and pedagogy that reflect our complexities and our joy. Tuck offers that "desire-based research frameworks are concerned with understanding complexity, contradiction, and the self-determination of lived lives."[15] These frameworks do not deny the real violence inflicted on and experienced by our communities. Trans youth experience intense violence, and this violence is mounting. Crucially, desire-based research situates violence within its systemic roots. For trans youth, the violence they experience is not inherent to being gender nonconforming. Rather, trans youth are made vulnerable to structural violence by a society that has deemed them undesirable and less human, monstrous. Recently, trans journalists and supporters published an open letter criticizing the *New York Times* for its coverage of trans issues.[16] The authors of this letter noted that the newspaper has been contributing to violence against trans people by participating in rhetoric (specifically focused on trans youth) that questions our right to exist. If media coverage and legislative bans are attacking trans people's existence, then I offer that to move forward, we need to desire trans existence. In schools, endeavoring to protect youth will always be a game of catch-up if we do not shift our approach to actively wanting trans people to be present and thriving.

Desire already permeates schools. As I have discussed in this conclusion, conventional notions of childhood and youth are framed by normative desires for young people to grow up according to a prescribed trajectory informed by white, colonial, ableist, and cisheteronormative metrics of adulthood and success. If educators are committed to creating schools that welcome queer and trans lives, we need to radically rework our understanding of how to grow up in part by confronting and disrupting the idea that being trans means risk. Inviting queerness and gender nonconformity into schools requires expanding our ideas about who young people are and can be, a reimagining that is only possible when we cease to subscribe to limited notions of "successful" development and adulthood. This is an epistemological shift: we need to come into the belief that being and growing up to be trans *is* a desirable way to exist.

Enacting a pedagogy of desire is importantly distinct from accepting trans youth only after we recognize their presence. Acceptance is a reactionary position that responds to crises rather than a necessary rewriting of society's ideas of gender nonconformity, a move that might make youth's constant protection unnecessary. A pedagogy of desire is an active stance that communicates: we want trans youth to exist. Rather than tolerating, accepting, or even celebrating trans young people when they announce themselves in schools, this shift entails making it clear that being and growing up trans is wanted, desired, and joyful. This means making it clear that trans youth are vital members of our schools and society, even if we cannot tell that they are present. Think about the care that youth in the band hall expressed for each other and their gender nonconformity: they intentionally built that world to have a refuge where they could exist together as a community outside and in rejection of the oppressive norms of East City High. Students flocked to that space and worked to protect it because they knew they were wanted and cared for while there. Furthermore, they understood that their presence in that space did not rely on performing any specific type of gender or sexual identity.

Engendering this change in schools requires a radical transformation of mind-set, and I am under no illusion that this process will be easy or quick. However, as we work to reshape our cultural conceptions of gender, there are likewise material, concrete moves to pursue. In the next section, I share youth's ideas for how to transform schools. Here I offer that desiring youth to be trans necessitates first untethering gender nonconformity from risk. This reframing needs to happen in the way we think about gender and to take place across all levels of schooling, from the policies we create to the ways we teach and talk about trans topics. In the past decade, there has been a push to "include" trans issues in the curriculum, a move encapsulated through programs like SOGI 123. However, following my examination of accommodation approaches, inclusion is not sufficient. If adults still believe gender nonconformity to be mired in risk, then they will convey this precarity when they incorporate trans topics. For instance, when educators teach about trans lives by centering pain and struggle, such as during Mr. Hill's Social Justice 12 lesson, they are concurrently communicating that being trans *is* pain and struggle. Students were quick to identify issues faced by trans people in part because this is the information most readily available to them. How would they relate to gender nonconformity in their own lives if they were as able to list out trans joy? Critically, it is not just content but also adults' tone and word choice that depicts trans people as vulnerable. Educators' discomfort with trans lives and, at times, reluctance to discuss them indicate to youth that there is something "wrong" with being trans. An adult endeavoring to protect a trans student does not disrupt this sense of "wrongness." Rather, that approach underlines it. Ostrich ultimately agreed that it was paramount to approach aspects of social and medical transition with caution and wariness because he had learned that, especially for youth, these were potentially dangerous, irreparable decisions. Therefore, he balanced his yearning for a binder, for instance, against the information he was receiving from his counselor and his father that he might be harmed in the process.

The reworking of ideas about gender nonconformity must go beyond the classroom. Schools need to stop framing trans youth as problems that need solutions through their responses to youth coming out and their requests for support, the language in policy, and the campaigns they undertake to implement diversity and inclusion. For decades, schools have predominantly told a singular story about gender nonconformity—one encased in risk. If we want to care for trans youth, we need to tell a new story. I believe that part of that rewriting involves removing gender as a category of distinction in schools.

At the end of the year, I was standing with Raeyun in the hallway as he searched for the date of his literacy exam. There was a long list of names posted outside the main office. Students were identified by their name, their student number, and their gender. Why was it necessary to state students' genders when informing them of the date of their literacy exam? The gendered operation of schools and schooling is so ingrained at this point that to many people, it seems mundane and even invisible. Students are separated by gender in PE class and evaluated based on gendered standards, teachers refer to students as "boys and girls," attendance lists identify students by their genders, graduation photos have different outfits for boys and girls, bathrooms and locker rooms are split by gender, students audition for gendered parts in theater, and despite best intentions, educators often hold different expectations for students' behavior and success on the basis of their gender. Schools are so infused with gender that there is a sense that it is impossible they could function any other way. To tell a new story about gender, schooling needs to move past both essentialist thinking and the practice of relying on gender as a key method of identifying and knowing students. It is time to stop believing that a young person's gender provides necessary data on their interests, their sexuality, their ability, and other critical elements of their life.

In the workshops on gender and sexuality that I have led with PE teachers, they ask, "How else can we organize a PE class fairly and safely if not by separating students by gender?" At first, it seems unbelievable that there could be another approach. The idea has been instilled over decades that PE classes function best when gendered. Yet, I ask them to consider what work they understand gender to be doing in these spaces. Together, we wonder how PE could be structured instead by students' levels of experience, interest, and goals. If we unpack the false assumption that boys are both more interested in and skilled at certain physical feats, we can move toward creating PE spaces that invite varying modes of participation and encourage multiple levels of engagement (and even fun!). Students can self-select based on the activity into tracks based on interest, skill, and competition level. This pedagogical move is supported by recent research in physical and health education as one of several ways to move beyond gendered classrooms.[17]

Dean Spade argues, "Trans people are told by the law, state agencies, private discriminators, and our families that we are impossible people who cannot exist, cannot be seen, cannot be classified, and cannot fit anywhere." However, he continues, "Inside this impossibility . . . lies our specific political potential."[18] Not only are trans people possible, but in confronting the myriad refusals of our existence, we have the capacity to imagine "someplace yet unknown."[19] It may seem impossible to organize schools without relying on gender as a mechanism in the process. However, the six youths I moved alongside for the year built entire worlds to honor the possibilities of their trans lives. In their trapdoors, they eschewed the ideas that restricted and constrained their movements and enactments of gender nonconformity the rest of the time at East City High. Importantly, they not only dreamed of trapdoors and queer utopias but also actively created other spaces to exist. Following Muñoz, these worlds invited the possibility of hope, and transforming schools demands these radical practices of hope.[20] Educators need to join trans youth in this world-building by recognizing the potential and feasibility of this project.

In calling on schools to remove gender as a category of distinction, I am not advocating for abolishing gender altogether. The youth in this study cared about their genders. However, they also cared about fluidity and ambiguity. They cared about being able to trust their own processes and ideas about gender nonconformity. They daily made space for expansive relationships to trans identity, working both to understand and to resist the normative expectations for trans legibility that dominated. Inspired by the desires that propelled their labor, I want to push the field of education to let go of the idea that we need to know youth's genders in order to care for and teach them. What do teachers, counselors, and administrators believe they know when they think they know a young person's gender? Why is this information pertinent to educating a young person or keeping them safe while in school? If we can cease to enforce gendered expectations and ideas in schools, we can foster the space for *all* youth to create their own relationships with their genders. By abolishing gender as a category of distinction among students, we can upend the outsized role that gender plays in school. That is the work needed to create schools that function more like the worlds that gender-nonconforming youth desire.

Listening to Youth

"We're smarter than they think we are," said Vixen as they vented about how underappreciated and devalued youth and their ideas were at East City High. We had been talking about the recent unit on LGBTQ issues in Social Justice 12. Vixen was a vocal critic in the class. They were frustrated at the level of the content, and they frequently interjected to share their ideas and knowledge. "I feel like they implemented it, like, 'Oh yeah, this is what you can talk about,' . . . assuming that we were all a little dumber than we actually are. But what they didn't realize is that we're well past that." Vixen had initially looked to Social Justice 12 as a course that would welcome them in their complexity as well as challenge them in their thinking. However, even in a space that centered conversations on gender and sexuality, youth felt thwarted by adults' underestimation of them. In this book, I have centered listening to youth and taking them seriously. Throughout the year, they shared with me their views on how to change schools, and as this book draws to a close, I present these ideas.

We Need a Cultural Shift

In the third week of June, I was waiting in the front hall for Scarecrow Jones at the end of the day. They emerged into the hallway still in their PE clothes: a black T-shirt and black sweatshirt shorts with a black hoodie tied around their waist. I gave them a surreptitious nod, and they pointed toward the west doors. We joined up as we exited the fluorescent lighting of the school into a bright, summery afternoon to walk to a nearby café. As we sat across from each other with a table full of snacks, Scarecrow Jones laid out their dreams for re-creating East City High. For starters, Scarecrow Jones had a simple demand: "Educate the staff." Throughout the year that we spent together, Scarecrow Jones consistently underlined how teachers' lack of awareness and knowledge about queer and trans students and issues had vast implications for the youth at East City High. "It's not just the education for the students," they explained. "It's how the students are treated in everyday life."

Often, when the youth and I ended up talking about the presence (or not) of queer and trans topics at East City High, they expressed their manifold frustrations with their teachers' inexperience and discomfort. They wanted more from the adults in their lives and felt let down by how little was offered. Students desired direct and transparent conversations on gender and sexuality. Moreover, they shared how their teachers' uneasiness and hesitancy to speak openly about queerness and transness perpetuated East City High's cisheteronormative culture. They were clear that teachers' lack of education was a multifaceted issue. Many adults at East City High did not know enough about gender and sexuality to teach students, while some had inaccurate information that caused harm. Furthermore, this dynamic contributed to the culture of cisheteronormativity and transphobia that youth confronted daily. Adults' ignorance and discomfort made it difficult for students to learn about being queer and trans, let alone trust their teachers with the complexities of their genders. As I have explored, this context demanded multiple forms of labor from the youth, and they were exhausted at having to work so hard.

To transform schools, youth wanted to start by training teachers so they knew enough about gender and sexuality to incorporate this knowledge into the curriculum without it feeling awkward at best and harmful at worst. Early in the year, Raeyun told me that for a while, he had not thought he was trans because of a workshop in grade 4 in which the teacher defined transgender as a person who wanted to "change their genitals." That was not how Raeyun felt about his body, so he figured he must not be trans. It was not until Raeyun met a trans girl in Theater Company in grade 8 that he learned how trans can be more expansive than what his teacher presented. Raeyun frequently returned to this story, using it as an example of why it mattered not just that you learned about trans topics in school but *how* you learned about them. He felt sad for his younger self and wanted teachers to have access to better information.

Students were adamant that educating teachers was never going to be sufficient to generate cultural shifts. Scarecrow Jones explained, "You can't learn about [queer and trans people] if it's from some counselor talking out their ass through some paper they received two days ago. That's not going to work." The collusion of queer and trans erasure, inaccurate information, and obvious teacher discomfort all contributed to the cisheteronormative culture that permeated East City High. The youth wanted to learn at a school that uplifted the idea that their lives and genders were possible and desirable. They viewed educating teachers about their humanity as a pivotal, though rudimentary, step in that process. "The way that schools deal with this kind of thing as a whole is not great," Scarecrow Jones remarked. They wanted teachers to go through trainings; however, they couched their idea within an extensive critique of that approach. Mainly, they knew that just telling teachers not to be homophobic and transphobic would never create the necessary cultural shifts. "It's like they kind of read a book about it once, and then they're like, 'We're the expert,' and they put up a bunch of signs and told the teachers, 'Don't say the f-slur.' Like, I feel like that's all that's been done," Scarecrow Jones explained as they described their observations of antihomophobia and antitransphobia work at East City High. "Nothing is really changing. And it doesn't matter how much is changing within your administration or within the minds of the staff, they're not changing their behavior." While they felt that it was crucial for teachers and staff to learn the correct language and information to incorporate queer and trans topics in their classrooms, they were likewise not convinced that just learning this information would translate into a less cisheteronormative context at school. "That's what we see and hear and feel, their behavior. And if that doesn't change, it doesn't matter how good-hearted they are. It's still—they're just—nothing's changing."

Until work was focused on transforming the culture of East City High, trans youth would continue to confront the transphobia of "nice" adults who did not understand them and, often, positioned them as at-risk. As I have explored, this context demanded significant labor from the youth. Over the year, I witnessed youth pull teachers aside to correct them on their names and pronouns, ask for workarounds in classes when it felt impossible to participate, raise their hands and interject so that queer and trans lives were mentioned during lessons, and teach each other about gender and sexuality when they were not learning about it from anyone else. Youth took on the responsibility of teaching their teachers about trans issues because they needed the adults in their lives to have this information. However, that labor was not only draining but also uncomfortable. Raeyun expressed frustration with how hard he had to work to educate teachers about his transness at East City High. "I really wish that my teachers would come to me asking the questions 'cause it was really awkward for me as someone who wasn't really close to any of their teachers to go up to them and be like, 'Oh yeah, I'm actually trans.'" Instead of asking for space in class, Raeyun wanted teachers to proactively create it.

Raeyun spoke openly about how difficult it was to defy the cisheteronormative assumption in classes. "I feel like it was really awkward, and I got really scared a lot of the time," Raeyun told me. "It would have been very useful for the teachers to come up and ask, 'Hey, what are your pronouns?' and just be more hands-on . . . 'cause when I had to do it all by myself, it was very daunting." Raeyun was intimidated at the prospect of approaching his teachers and asking for accommodations. He did not want to make himself visible as trans. Though Raeyun regularly performed this labor at East City High, he found it scary and uncomfortable. Raeyun wanted teachers to anticipate the possibility of his existence.

Though Raeyun suggested that teachers approach gender-nonconforming and trans students, this idea relies on mechanisms of visibility that he regularly confronted and challenged during the year. As Scarecrow Jones argued, just providing teachers with tools and strategies was never going to be enough to transform schools. Teachers could use the "correct" language and incorporate trans topics into their lessons, but, Scarecrow Jones contended, if adults still believed that gender nonconformity was cause for concern, then they would also communicate those harmful ideas. Regardless of how many "safe space" stickers teachers plastered on their doors or trainings they attended, nothing would change in schools until there was a cultural shift toward desiring gender nonconformity.

We Need More Queer and Trans Adults

All year, Barry shared with me a plethora of ideas for how to fix the education system. He even wanted to be a teacher so he could chip away at the problem himself. "I think a radical shift in people's opinions would be nice," Barry told me. "I'm not expecting it, but it would be real cool." Barry had big ideas for overhauling schools, but he also cared about East City High specifically and spent time pondering what could change to make life better and more possible there. "I don't know. It's like—it's—more conversations like the ones that we've been able to have here would be nice, 'cause people just feeling the ability to talk about these things, maybe not with anybody but with somebody." Our conversations mattered to Barry in part because we cultivated a space that desired a capacious gender nonconformity. Barry wanted people in school to care that queer and trans people existed and, crucially, to want them to exist. He viewed our time together as integral since he did not have to work to believe that his gender nonconformity was valid. Though Barry articulated a hope that our dynamic could translate into schools, he also doubted it would. However, along with other youth in the study, Barry believed that having more queer and trans adults around might be a start in the right direction. This seemingly simple desire was shared by most of the youth in the study. When I asked the youth what they wanted to change in schools, they often began by listing several practical solutions, like switching the language in dance classes from "boys and girls" to "leads and follows" and having access to a gender-neutral bathroom. They frequently moved beyond these concrete examples to highlight the need for queer and trans adults who could assist them in creating supportive spaces in the school.

East City High had a large staff, yet there were only a couple of out queer adults in the school. Most of the youth in the study had never had an openly queer teacher and, prior to my arrival at the school, had little to no relationship with queer or trans adults at all. For many, there was a sense that life might be easier at school if there were more queer and trans adults. Though this suggestion appears mired in a visibility logic that promotes the idea that the mere presence of queer and trans people works to dismantle cisheteronormativity, the youth presented it in more complex terms. Vixen explained how their experiences in school were different because of their queerness and genderfluidity. Unlike adults at the school who tethered this difference to risk and harm, Vixen understood it as just different. They were not interested in assimilating to East City High's dominant cisheteronormative culture, and Vixen wanted relationships with adults who were knowledgeable about (gender)queerness and would value their nonconformity. Since queer and trans youth navigated distinct challenges in school, Vixen argued that they should have their own resources, supports, and staff capable of catering to the uniqueness of their life. Vixen described one possible scenario: "A good idea might be to have a health counselor and then also an LGBTQ health counselor, you know? Because then they can really help LGTBQ students with their specific problems that have to do with them being LGBTQ." Like other youth in the study, Vixen did not trust that cis and straight adults would be able to provide the same level of care to queer and trans students. This hesitancy to regard nonqueer and nontrans adults as potential mentors in school underscores how unsupported and uncared for they generally felt.

As I have explored throughout this book, youth worked hard to intervene at East City High by imagining into existence other, queerer worlds. At times, these were fantastical and imaginary worlds, like Barry's D&D campaigns, Raeyun's K-pop fan fiction, and Vixen's and Scarecrow Jones's fictional narratives. Other times, these were physical trapdoors, places like the band hall or the tech booth where youth could live outside and in rejection of the normative gendered expectations that otherwise shaped their days. They developed these spaces because they needed and desired escapes from the overwhelming cisheteronormativity that prevailed at East City High. However, creating and maintaining these worlds required substantial labor from the youth. Many of the young people expressed desire for support from adults in these efforts. They did not just want more trapdoors; they wanted school-facilitated spaces where they could feel acknowledged, understood, and cared for by queer and trans adults. They wanted places at East City High where they could live in defiance of cisheteronormativity without having to work so hard.

Gender Is Complicated!

One afternoon toward the end of the school year, Ostrich and I sat together drinking bubble tea. We were talking about what could change at East City High to make life better for him. Ostrich stuck to the basics. He told me that he just wanted teachers to know that "gender is not fully binary. It's not just male and female." Though Ostrich's statement was succinct, this idea was anything but simple for him. All year, Ostrich navigated complex questions of legitimacy, working hard to be respected as a trans guy. He dropped "they/them" pronouns, chose a name that would help his teachers stop misgendering him, and tempered his queer desires and flamboyance to assist in being perceived as a guy. Ostrich's comment bolstering the importance and validity of nonbinary genders speaks to the tensions he experienced around gender ambiguity and legibility. How would Ostrich's relationship to his gender be different if he did not have to work so hard to prove its validity within a binary framework? What if adults like Ms. O'Connor just listened to him when he said he was trans instead of believing that his transness meant that he was extra "vulnerable"?

Throughout our year together, I observed youth express not just frustration with the labor required of them to exist as gender nonconforming but also surprise and confusion. Why was it so difficult for adults to understand that gender was not fully binary? Why would adults not just listen to youth when youth told them that gender was more complicated? Vixen was a consistent proponent for gender that was confusing. They were not interested in other people's ideas about gender nonconformity or people's ideas about much else. "I don't think you always need to be able to tell [someone's gender]," Vixen explained. "And then sometimes if you don't know, why does it matter? Why is it any of your business? I don't think it really needs to be broadcast to every stranger. I don't think it matters." Vixen found little space for this type of fluid relationship to gender while at East City High. They worked hard to intervene and create that space, but it was often more challenging for Vixen to perform this labor than for other youth since they were positioned as a "problem" student. They regularly spoke of how no one listened to or believed them. This dynamic extended to their movements through the school as a nonbinary, neurodivergent person. They were consistently misgendered and tasked with fitting into neurotypical expectations, even when they explicitly asked for support and understanding.

Youth regularly lamented the invisibility and seeming impossibility of nonbinary genders at East City High. They described the school as a place where it felt increasingly possible to be gay or lesbian but where it remained challenging to live any form of ambiguity. The youth wanted space for nonconformity and to feel like it was possible to exist without set ideas and expectations for being trans, nonbinary, and genderfluid. They wanted adults to catch up to their understandings of gender and to trust them when they articulated their lives, bodies, and experiences. Though youth described being gender nonconforming and nonbinary at East City High as challenging, they also moved through the school in ways that upended and resisted pervasive norms of visibility and legibility. Scarecrow Jones, Ms. Man, Barry, Vixen, Ostrich, and Raeyun all lived complicated relationships with their genders. Beyond just existing, they intervened and disrupted the cisheteronormativity of East City High by building other worlds that defied the limited gendered logics that otherwise dominated. Through their queer, utopic acts of worldmaking, youth were creating the spaces they needed and desired. We need to take their labor seriously and pay attention to how gendernonconforming youth are already transforming schools.

ACKNOWLEDGMENTS

I have been (and still am) taught, inspired, and encouraged by numerous educators in a variety of forms. I am grateful to the friends, colleagues, teachers, instructors, professors, and mentors who take the time to nurture my curiosity and share their passion for learning. This book is a testament to all of you.

To my editor, Ilene Kalish, thank you for believing in this project from the start. You pushed me in critical ways that grew this book into what it is, and you were always patient and encouraging. And of course, thank you to Travers for connecting me with Ilene. You are a rare find in academia: a great softball player, friend, and colleague.

I am grateful for the hard work and encouragement of my dissertation committee: Drs. Lisa Loutzenheiser, Sarah Hunt, and LeAnne Petherick. Thank you for your years of labor, advice, and support. Your questions, knowledge, and care challenged me and my research in invaluable ways. I was also immensely fortunate to receive support throughout my graduate studies. The Vanier Canada Graduate Scholarship through the Social Sciences and Humanities Research Council made it possible for me to spend an entire year at East City High with the youth. Its funding also paid for all the snacks we ate during our hangouts, so thank you very much!

Many people have read and discussed this work with me over the years. A thank you seems insufficient for how deeply I appreciate your time and your ideas, but here it is anyway! Thank you to every friend and colleague who engaged with this book in its various iterations. A very special thank you to the friends who read, revised, and bolstered me throughout this project: Rachel Brydolf-Horowitz, Hélène Frohard-Dourlent, and Sam Stiegler. As well, Naomi Ostwald Kawamura and Margaret O'Sullivan, our writing group was instrumental in keeping me on track at key moments early on in this project. We will always be the Real Committee.

Thank you to my queer and trans family, near and far. Finishing a book takes a community, and I am honored that you are mine. Thank you especially to Danica for being a partner, friend, and all-around joy, and Fievel, my cat, who lovingly watched me write basically every part of this book.

This book would not have been possible without all the people at East City High who made space for me, both formally and informally. Thank you to the administrators, teachers, and staff who welcomed me into the school and into their classrooms. Thank you to the many students who hung out with me in classrooms, hallways, and all over the school. It would have been a much lonelier year without your great company.

To all the trans and nonbinary people, especially youth, just living and exuding trans joy, thank you. We build queerer worlds together.

And finally, to Barry, Ostrich, Ms. Man, Raeyun, Scarecrow Jones, and Vixen, thank you for inviting me into your lives and into your worlds. I am grateful for the year we spent together and the times we have shared since. This book is because of you—your labor, your care, your brilliance, and your fierceness.

APPENDIX

What Grade Are You In?

Toward the end of the year, I was sitting in the back of Social Justice 12 in my usual seat next to Vixen while the class worked on its final projects. I had been attending this class since September and had grown close with several students. In chapter 2, I discussed how earlier in the year I had supported Tamar and Eliza, who were students in Social Justice 12, in an attempt at advocating for a multistall, gender-neutral bathroom. Now they had turned this campaign into their final class project. While students were quietly working, Tamar walked over to inquire if Vixen would write a personal statement in support of the bathroom. Vixen enthusiastically agreed. Then Tamar turned to me and hesitantly said, "I feel like you're an adult . . . ?" Vixen and I both laughed, and I asked Tamar if that was a question or a statement. Tamar explained, "I just think of you as a student, but I guess you're not, and probably it's better for these statements to come from students." All three of us laughed for a moment, and I told Tamar that I thought she was right. However, Tamar already knew that I was not a student. She had previously asked for advice on applying to universities and expressed a desire to be a student in my class one day. I do not think she suddenly forgot. Rather, her question speaks to the blurriness surrounding my presence at East City High.

When Tamar walked away, Vixen and I chatted about adults' confusion surrounding me in the school, specifically whether I counted as an adult. In classic Vixen fashion, they shrugged, rolled their eyes, and declared, "I mean, according to whose definition?" There is an assumption within ethnographic studies that all researchers are recognized and treated as adults. However, being recognized as an adult, and thus a full person, relies on being legible within society.[1] While there is a growing understanding that gender is not binary, currently there is still little sense of nonbinary adulthood.[2] Given the lack of understanding about nonbinary genders generally and, specifically, the dearth of models of nonbinary adulthood, being legible as a nonbinary adult is complicated. In this appendix, I consider the assumption that all researchers are understood as adults through the concept of nonadulthood, which I developed to examine how I navigated ethical accountability and data generation as a nonbinary researcher at East City High.

THEORIZING ADULTHOOD

The presumption that all researchers are read and recognized as adults has framed methodological inquiries into researcher-participant relationships and ethnographic fieldwork. In this section, I consider adulthood as a socially constructed category that is the result not simply of growing older but of growing up in adherence with agreed-on parameters. I use the term "nonadult" to signal those people against whom understandings of normative adulthood are shored up and reinforced. Nonadults, though perhaps grown in age and self-identifying as adults, are not consistently recognized as adults by others in society. The pervasiveness of conventional expectations surrounding adulthood and its invisibility as a default category for researchers are revealed through contrast to those of us who move through the world (and our research sites) as nonadults.

The social construction of adulthood is already part of youth research, for a salient aspect of scholarship discusses how notions of youth cohere around their contrast to adulthood.[3] Scholars examine how adulthood is a stage of life that people reach not just by growing older but by growing up in a specific direction, marked by passage through recognizable checkpoints along a socioculturally prescribed trajectory.[4] Becoming an adult hinges on the perceived success of a person within established white, settler, cisheteronormative, ableist, and capitalist structures: leaving home, living independently, gaining financial security, getting monogamously married, and having children.[5] Similar to the work of gender, people cannot simply claim adulthood for themselves; rather, others must also recognize them as having achieved adulthood. Adherence to cisheteronormative gendered standards and expectations is an integral facet of this process of recognition.

There is power in determining who "counts" as an adult, for "adulthood is a metaphor for membership in society through the attainment of full personhood."[6] Importantly, acknowledgment of someone as an adult is not a static, immutable determination. Who is labeled an adult, and when such persons acquire this label, is also a question of power. For instance, while white, affluent, and otherwise normatively positioned children have the privilege of being afforded the assumption of innocent childhood when interacting with the state, racialized, Indigenous, and gender-nonconforming children often have adulthood imposed on them.[7] They are forced into adulthood in order to serve harsher prison sentences and to bear the responsibility for their actions. As such, their adulthood is not the recognition of full personhood; rather, it is a mechanism by which to deny them this personhood.

Adulthood, if understood as a normative category that differentially bestows legibility and as a social construct conditioned by hegemonic structures that are not neutral, is ultimately about power, not age. "Normative adulthood is produced and reified through contrast between adults and others not seen to be adult, including children, adults with disabilities, gender diverse adults, women who are voluntarily childless, and, increasingly, young adults, with a focus on the notion of a prolonged 'emerging adulthood.'"[8] I use the concept of nonadulthood to reveal the construction of adulthood as a power-wielding category and to highlight adulthood's unremarked-on exclusivity in ethnography.

BECOMING A NONADULT

Though I had some inclination of the way I might be understood at East City High on the basis of several years of experience as a youth worker who was infrequently read as an adult, I could not have anticipated the extent to which my nonadult status would shape my relationships with the participants and other students as well as inform the role I developed in the school over the course of the study. However, it became evident early on that my challenge during fieldwork was not going to revolve around downplaying my adulthood in order to build rapport with youth, as is often discussed in ethnographic scholarship, but rather in navigating the ethical quandaries and complexities involved in being a nonadult researcher in a high school.[9] As I observed and reflected on the ways that students were positioning me and how I moved through the school, I realized that being a nonadult was a critical element of the study. I was present in the school to generate research with youth whom

I intended to advocate for and support during as well as after the study. Given my background in youth work, I understood our relationships to be meaningful and positive for my participants. Though mentorship and research are not often combined, I believe that ethical accountability required acknowledging the importance of reimagining a researcher-participant relationship, especially when I was the only nonbinary (non)adult that my participants knew.

I followed youth's lead in cultivating this blend of mentorship and research. For instance, Raeyun and I went on what he referred to as "trans field trips." Raeyun wanted to look at packers and binders. He was nervous to order these products online and have them delivered to his house, where his parents might intercept the package. There was a store in our neighborhood that sold them, but Raeyun had not previously known about it. We walked there together after school one day. On our way, Raeyun told me, "It would be so great if there was a trans club, because the GSA is not that kind of space." He explained that with a trans club, both youth who were out and those who were not would be able to get together and "go take care of trans necessities." He described getting haircuts together, shopping for binders, and braving the awful experience of buying clothes.

In the store, Raeyun tried on binders, but they were all too expensive. As we were leaving, the owner told us that the store was going to announce a sale: 20 percent off everything in the store. Raeyun's face lit up, and he asked if we could come back. We made a plan to return the next week after school. As I walked him to the bus, he told me, "You're the only trans adult that I know." He asked if we could be our own trans club. Raeyun and I bonded over shared understandings of andromasculine gender nonconformity, like the first time you appreciate the greater pocket depths in men's jeans. "I feel like no cis guys would get that moment," Raeyun said. "If they listen to me, they would just be like, 'They're just pockets.'" Our trans club ranged from silly conversations about pockets to more meaningful acts of collectivity. I brought him pronoun pins for his backpack, and we talked about trans issues on the sidelines of PE, in the back row of his planning class, and up in the tech booth. In November, Raeyun and I observed Trans Day of Remembrance (TDOR) together, which was not recognized by East City High. He had never heard of it before. "It's so cool this day exists," he told me.

We sent each other TDOR posts back and forth on Instagram throughout the day.

I was aware that students' security around me as well as their informal ways of relating to and incorporating me into their contexts in the classroom aided me in generating interesting data. I heard and witnessed more because I did not stand out as an adult in a youth space. Boundary work was therefore a constant, complicated task with the students. Students confided in me about their lives and welcomed me into conversations about teachers and other students with whom they had issues. Though at times these discussions revolved around fairly benign themes, several students disclosed serious matters. I was cognizant that my nonadult status invited this trust and confidence. I followed up with students, privately, after disclosures to make sure they were safe and to ascertain if further steps needed to be taken regarding reporting. By checking in with students in this manner, I distinguished myself from their peers and became an adult. I noticed this shift once when, during a hangout with Vixen, their current safety became a question. Though we had been working together for months and Vixen understood that I was a researcher and an adult, they were surprised and disappointed that I would react as such. Almost as a rule, Vixen did not tell adults what was happening in their life. At that moment, I betrayed them by becoming an adult in their eyes and caring whether they lived or died. Vixen did not speak to me for days. During our bout of silence, I wondered if Vixen would leave the study. I was concerned not just about their withdrawal but about the destruction of a relationship we had been building for months. I had reacted in accordance with my ethical responsibility toward them, but Vixen, like many of my participants, did not predominantly interact with me as an adult with those responsibilities. Despite my repeated discussions with students about my role in the school, they positioned me in the ways that made the most sense to them.

AGE, GENDER, AND WHITENESS

It is impossible to untether how I was consistently positioned as a student from the ways I was misgendered. Was I policed for using the women's staff bathroom because of perceptions that I was a student or beliefs that I was inappropriately gendered for that space? How would I ever know? Nearly every day, a teacher shifted their demeanor toward me partway through our interaction because they had mistaken me for a student. Teachers regularly passed by me, overlooked me, or just did not meet my eye in the hallway because they did not recognize me as an adult. The difference in the way teachers greeted and engaged with me when they believed me to be a student versus when they realized I was an adult researcher was stark and a disconcerting illustration of how adults position youth in schools. Since adults' inability to perceive me as an adult was entangled in my gender nonconformity, these shifts in behavior and attitude were also a challenging dynamic that I negotiated daily in order to navigate an age-striated research site that did not have space for a person who looks like me. Frequently, adults' positioning of me as a student was intertwined with their perception of me as a teenage boy, an unstable impression that provoked in them the desire to figure out the "truth" of my gender. When I explained myself as a doctoral student and an adult, they interpreted these responses as information about my gender in addition to age. Their confusion about my age was not removed from their discomfort regarding the ambiguity of my gender, and many believed that if they could determine one for certain, they would "solve" the other.

As a white settler scholar in Canada, I am afforded countless privileges, among them moving through society with relative safety and increased ease and opportunity. At the same time, as a nonbinary person, I am regularly policed regarding my status as an adult. My whiteness frequently serves as protection in these regulatory moments. My multiple privileges also served as a form of protection from the intertwined policing of my gender and age in the school. In general, I was not viewed as a threat, in large part due to my whiteness. When found to be in the "wrong" space, like a staff bathroom, my whiteness protected me from punishment. I was (often) afforded the benefit of the doubt and the opportunity to explain myself. As mentioned, many times, people's confusion around my gender resulted in people positioning me as a teenage boy. My whiteness allowed me to blend in while among youth. I became just another "young" person passing time in the hallways, in the back of a classroom, in the cafeteria, and on the school grounds. Teachers, counselors, and administrators infrequently noticed me during the year because as a white, nonbinary person, I could easily disappear into a crowd of students.

People perceived me as a person who had yet to grow up, which is a more palatable version of a nonadult, in contrast to when, informed by ableist, racist, and colonial logics, nonadulthood is imposed on people in order to deny them personhood. Interpretations of me as a teenager were always tenuous, for though a person may have viewed me as a young man in one context, this understanding of me was unstable and tended to collapse over the course of our interaction. However, when people realized their mistake, and I explained my role as a researcher in the school, no one questioned whether I was telling the truth. Frequently adults found their mistakes funny because, once they thought they *knew* who I was, they no longer felt as uncomfortable about me. Instead, they perceived me as someone who did not understand how to be an adult. My whiteness shielded me from their fear.

Adults were not the only ones who experienced this confusion surrounding my gender and age. At the start of the study, I introduced myself as a graduate student and explained my project every time I entered a new class. There were many students who heard my spiel multiple times. However, even after months of these introductions, I could be midconversation with a student who would pause and ask, "Wait, what grade are you in?" or a student who understood that I was not in high school but was certain that I could not be more than twenty years old, even though I was in my midthirties. Once while Barry and I were walking down the hall after math class, he joked with me about how people did not think of me as an adult. Adulthood was on Barry's mind at that moment since it was the week before his eighteenth birthday. He mused about the ways people interacted with me, noting that I had a slight mustache and some chin hair, which he assumed would help people perceive me as older. Then he added, teasing, "Nothing says adult like faint facial hair." Barry's understanding of me as a person who was not read as an adult by others was intertwined with his perception of my gender nonconformity. However, ideas about who grows facial hair are not just gendered but racialized, and the tethering of facial hair to masculinity is a specifically racialized construction.

THE ETHICS OF NONADULTHOOD

Research ethics are not just about preventing harm. Rather, ethics necessarily includes acknowledging our accountability to the participants in our studies as well as others who may be affected by our presence. The youth I worked with may have connected to me as a nonadult, but I did have access to resources and power that they did not. Their trust in me was important, and it was my ethical responsibility to follow through for them. For this reason, I said yes to students who asked for support over the course of the year, whether it was supporting Eliza and Tamar in fighting for a gender-neutral multistall bathroom at the school or shopping for binders with Raeyun. Similarly, two weeks before the end of school, I accompanied Vixen to the vice principal's office to assist in a difficult conversation. In order to graduate, all grade 12 students had to complete a litany of forms and response questions. This packet was due months previously, but Vixen sporadically attended school and had not yet turned it in. Vixen was frequently labeled "at-risk" in the school, in part due to their many absences. I knew many sides of Vixen, far beyond the similar tropes that get repeated about queer and trans youth in trouble. I knew that they really wanted to graduate and, likewise, that they were nervous about handing in the packet this late on their own, so we went together. Our earlier standoff and period of silence may have contributed to Vixen asking me for help. Though Vixen's understanding of me as a nonadult bolstered our relationship and invited a unique type of closeness, they also came to realize that my adulthood might be useful to them. Sitting next to Vixen in the administrator's office, I was certainly not a peer high school student. At the same time, Vixen had a relationship with a youth worker at the school, and they did not ask this adult person for support. My liminality may have made Vixen feel more comfortable and able to reach out in these situations. Being a nonadult certainly facilitated students' minimization of our age differences, but it also let students call on my adulthood when they needed an advocate or trans mentor. Part of my work and responsibility as a nonadult researcher was to understand the ways participants were positioning me, to acknowledge the uniqueness of being a nonadult researcher, and then to respond and be accountable to the importance of that role in the school and in their lives.

NOTES

INTRODUCTION

1. All the participants chose their own pseudonyms. Some chose just one name, while others selected first and last names. I created the pseudonyms for the adults and other students who appear in this text. Additionally, many participants used more than one pronoun, and their pronouns changed over the study. At the end of fieldwork, I asked all the participants which pronouns to use when writing about them.
2. NCT is a popular K-pop band first introduced in 2016.
3. Beauchamp, *Going Stealth*.
4. "Deadnamed" is a term that describes when someone refers to a trans person by their birth name. It is meant to convey the violence of this naming. While not all trans people relate to the term "deadname" or feel as if it accurately describes their relationship with names, several students felt strongly about burying their previous identities. For a discussion that complicates this terminology, please see Putzi, "COVID-19 and Archival Research."
5. Glenn, "Creating a Caring Society"; Malatino, *Trans Care*.
6. Muñoz, *Cruising Utopia*; Tourmaline, Stanley, and Burton, *Trap Door*.
7. Martino, Kassen, and Omercajic, "Supporting Transgender Students in Schools."
8. Martino, "Supporting Transgender Students"; Travers, *Trans Generation*.
9. Martino, "Supporting Transgender Students"; Martino, Omercajic, and Kassen, "We Have No 'Visibly' Trans Students"; Travers, *Trans Generation*.
10. Goble, "[City redacted for anonymity] School Closures."
11. Ahmed, *On Being Included*.
12. Ahmed, 69.
13. Statistics Canada, "Census Profile."
14. BC Ministry of Education, "Teacher Statistics."
15. Huynh, and Woo, "Asian Fail."
16. This vice principal later transferred.
17. Martino, Kassen, and Omercajic, "Supporting Transgender Students in Schools."
18. Airton, "Leave 'Those Kids' Alone"; Greteman, *Sexualities and Genders in Education*; Hackford-Peer, "In the Name of Safety."
19. Halberstam, *Trans**; Rasmussen, *Becoming Subjects*.
20. Fetner et al., "Safe Spaces"; Greytak, Kosciw, and Diaz, "Harsh Realities"; Meyer and Sansfacon, *Supporting Transgender and Gender Creative Youth*; Payne and

Smith, "LGBTQ Kids, School Safety, and Missing the Big Picture"; Taylor and Peter, *Every Class in Every School*; Veale et al., *Being Safe, Being Me*.
21 Thorpe and Greteman, "Intimately Bound to Numbers," 75.
22 Gilbert, *Sexuality in School*; Mayo, *Disputing the Subject of Sex*; Talburt, "Constructions of LGBT Youth."
23 Brockenbrough, "Queer of Color Agency in Educational Contexts."
24 Martino, Omercajic, and Kassen, "We Have No 'Visibly' Trans Students."
25 Talburt, "Constructions of LGBT Youth," 117.
26 Greteman, *Sexualities and Genders in Education*; Mayo, "Pushing the Limits of Liberalism."
27 Gill-Peterson, *Histories of the Transgender Child*; Kafer, *Feminist, Queer, Crip*; Sedgwick, "How to Bring Your Kids Up Gay."
28 Stryker, *Transgender History*, 6.
29 Stryker, 6.
30 Bettie, *Women without Class*; Brockenbrough, "Queer of Color Agency in Educational Contexts"; Pascoe, *Dude, You're a Fag*; Ray, "School as a Hostile Institution."
31 Bettie, *Women without Class*; Ray, *Making of a Teenage Service Class*; Robinson, *Coming Out to the Streets*.
32 Tuck, "Suspending Damage."
33 Greteman, *Sexualities and Gender in Education*; Tuck, "Suspending Damage."
34 Dyer, "Queer Futurity and Childhood Innocence"; Gilbert, *Sexuality in School*; Greteman, *Sexualities and Gender in Education*; Mayo, "Disruptions of Desire."
35 Tuck, "Suspending Damage," 409.
36 Tuck, 417.
37 hooks, *Ain't I a Woman*; Crenshaw, "Demarginalizing the Intersection of Race and Sex"; Glenn, "From Servitude to Service Work"; Parreñas, *Servants of Globalization*.
38 Mies, *Patriarchy and Accumulation*; Federici, *Wages against Housework*; Glenn, "From Servitude to Service Work"; Pratt, *Working Feminism*.
39 Boris and Parreñas, *Intimate Labors*; Folbre, "Measuring Care"; Green and Lawson, "Recentring Care"; McDowell, "Work, Workfare, Work/Life Balance."
40 Folbre and Nelson, "For Love or Money—or Both?"
41 Cox, "Gendered Spaces of Commoditised Care"; Glenn, "Creating a Caring Society."
42 Glenn, "Creating a Caring Society," 84.
43 Glenn, 86.
44 Malatino, *Trans Care*, 7.
45 Malatino, 3.
46 Malatino; Meadow, *Trans Kids*; Rasmussen, "Beyond Gender Identity?"; Travers, *Trans Generation*.
47 Meadow, *Trans Kids*, 45.
48 Malatino, *Trans Care*; Robinson, *Coming Out to the Streets*.
49 Malatino, *Trans Care*.

50 Tourmaline, Stanley, and Burton, introduction to *Trap Door*, xxiii.
51 Aizura, "Unrecognizable"; Beauchamp, *Going Stealth*; Tourmaline, Stanley, and Burton, *Trap Door*.
52 Beauchamp, *Going Stealth*.
53 Aizura, "Unrecognizable," 609.
54 Tourmaline, Stanley, and Burton, introduction to *Trap Door*, xxiii.
55 Bettie, *Women without Class*; Brockenbrough and Boatwright, "In the MAC."; Pascoe, *Dude, You're a Fag*; Ray, *Making of a Teenage Service Class*; Robinson, *Coming Out to the Streets*; Thorne, *Gender Play*: Travers, *Trans Generation*.
56 Serano, "Detransition, Desistance, and Disinformation"; Stryker, *Transgender History*.
57 Sutherland, "Trans Enough."
58 Bradford and Johnson, "Transnormativity," 2.
59 Bradford and Johnson.
60 Butler, *Gender Trouble*.
61 Aizura, "Unrecognizable"; Butler, *Gender Trouble*; Gill-Peterson, *Histories of the Transgender Child*; Stanley, *Atmospheres of Violence*; Stryker, *Transgender History*.
62 Butler, *Gender Trouble*, 22–23.
63 Butler, 22.
64 L. Simpson, *As We Have Always Done*, 52.
65 De Leeuw, "If Anything Is to Be Done"; Dean, *Remembering Vancouver's Disappeared Women*; Haig-Brown, *Resistance and Renewal*; Hunt, "Relationality of Justice"; Million, *Therapeutic Nations*; Patzer, "Residential School Harm"; A. Simpson, "Whither Settler Colonialism?"; L. Simpson, *As We Have Always Done*.
66 De Leeuw, "If Anything Is to Be Done"; Haig-Brown, *Resistance and Renewal*; Marker, "Indigenous Resistance."
67 De Leeuw, "If Anything Is to Be Done."
68 Gill-Peterson, *Histories of the Transgender Child*.
69 Lesko, *Act Your Age!*
70 Beauchamp, *Going Stealth*; Kafer, *Feminist, Queer, Crip*; McRuer, *Crip Theory*.
71 McRuer, *Crip Theory*.
72 Awkward-Rich, "She of the Pants and No Voice"; Bychowski et al., "Trans*historicities."
73 Schalk, *Black Disability Politics*, 11.
74 De Leeuw, "If Anything Is to Be Done"; Lesko, *Act Your Age!*; Spade, *Normal Life*; Sykes, *Queer Bodies*.
75 Baynton, "Slaves, Immigrants, and Suffragists"; Thobani, *Exalted Subjects*.
76 Rahily, *Trans-Affirmative Parenting*; Travers, *Trans Generation*.
77 Bettie, *Women without Class*; Pascoe, *Dude, You're a Fag*; Ray, *Making of a Teenage Service Class*; Thorne, *Gender Play*.
78 Blackburn, "Disrupting the (Hetero)Normative"; Brockenbrough and Boatwright, "In the MAC"; Cruz, "LGBTQ Street Youth Talk Back"; Stiegler, "On Doing Go-Along Interviews."

79 Shelton, "Queer Ethnography."
80 Gill-Peterson, *Histories of the Transgender Child*, 207.
81 Gill-Peterson; Prosser, *Second Skins*; Travers, *Trans Generation*.
82 Gill-Peterson, *Histories of the Transgender Child*; Prosser, *Second Skins*; Rasmussen, Rofes, and Talburt, *Youth and Sexualities*; Talburt, "Constructions of LGBT Youth"; Travers, *Trans Generation*.
83 Wilchins, *Read My Lips*.
84 Childers, "Promiscuous Analysis"; Jackson and Mazzei, *Thinking with Theory*; MacLure, "Wonder of Data"; Ringrose and Renold, "Normative Cruelties."
85 Jackson, "Posthumanist Data Analysis of Mangling Practices," 742.
86 Tuck and Yang, "Unbecoming Claims."
87 Gieseking, "Where We Go from Here," 722.
88 Ahmed, *On Being Included*.
89 Thobani, *Exalted Subjects*.
90 Ahmed, *On Being Included*; Castagno, *Educated in Whiteness*; Lewis and Diamond, *Despite the Best Intentions*.
91 Cover, "Conditions of Living"; Fetner et al., "Safe Spaces"; Greytak, Kosciw, and Diaz, "Harsh Realities"; Taylor and Peter, *Every Class in Every School*.
92 Thobani, *Exalted Subjects*, 160.
93 Tourmaline, Stanley, and Burton, *Trap Door*.

CHAPTER 1. EAST CITY HIGH'S DIVERSITY CULTURE

1 Ahmed, *On Being Included*, 69.
2 Ahmed, 69.
3 Castagno, *Educated in Whiteness*.
4 Huynh and Woo, "Asian Fail."
5 Social Justice 12 is an elective course unique to British Columbia that was created as the result of a court case filed in 1997. Peter and Murray Corren, local gay educator-activists, brought the case to the British Columbia Human Rights Tribunal, arguing that the Ministry of Education discriminated against lesbian, gay, bisexual, and queer people in the school curriculum. Before the tribunal heard the case, the Ministry of Education decided to settle. The resolution is known as the "Settlement Agreement," and it lays out changes to curriculum policy, including the development of Social Justice 12.
6 Joshee and Winton, "Past Crossings," 22.
7 Joshee and Winton, 17.
8 Joshee and Winton, 18.
9 Thobani, *Exalted Subjects*, 148.
10 Thobani, 160.
11 Castagno, *Educated in Whiteness*; Lewis and Diamond, *Despite the Best Intentions*.
12 Castagno, *Educated in Whiteness*; Kumashiro, *Troubling Intersections*; Lewis and Diamond, *Despite the Best Intentions*; McCready, "Some Challenges."
13 Frohard-Dourlent, "I Don't Care What's under Your Clothes," 68.

14 Huynh and Woo, "Asian Fail"; Thobani, *Exalted Subjects*.
15 Ahmed, *On Being Included*, 71.
16 Ahmed; Ward, *Respectably Queer*.
17 Ahmed, *On Being Included*, 57.
18 Given the ongoing violent history of colonially imposed language and naming, I did not create pseudonyms for the Indigenous teachers and staff. They chose their own.
19 Patzer, "Residential School Harm."
20 Million, *Therapeutic Nations*; Patzer, "Residential School Harm."
21 Lewis and Diamond, *Despite the Best Intentions*, 58.
22 Patzer, "Residential School Harm," 166.
23 Ahmed, *On Being Included*, 69.
24 Meyer, *Gender, Bullying, and Harassment*, 11.
25 Ahmed, *On Being Included*, 69.
26 Ahmed, 80.
27 Castagno, *Educated in Whiteness*.
28 Daigle, "Spectacle of Reconciliation."
29 Daigle, 711.
30 Beauchamp, *Going Stealth*; Kafer, *Feminist, Queer, Crip*.
31 Beauchamp, *Going Stealth*; Kafer, *Feminist, Queer, Crip*.
32 Beauchamp, *Going Stealth*.
33 Beauchamp, 85.
34 In Canada, people use both "bathroom" and "washroom" to refer to these spaces.
35 Ahmed, *On Being Included*; Ball, Maguire, and Braun, *How Schools Do Policy*.
36 Ahmed, *On Being Included*.

CHAPTER 2. ACCOMMODATING TRANS YOUTH

1 Emens, "Accommodation," 19.
2 Spade, *Normal Life*, 208.
3 Martino, Kassen, and Omercajic, "Supporting Transgender Students in Schools"; Meyer and Keenan, "Can Policies Help Schools Affirm Gender Diversity?"; Travers, *Trans Generation*.
4 Airton, "Leave 'Those Kids' Alone"; Greteman, *Sexualities and Genders in Education*; Loutzenheiser, "Can We Learn Queerly?"
5 Tourmaline, Stanley, and Burton, introduction to *Trap Door*, xxiii.
6 Kafer, *Feminist, Queer, Crip*; McRuer, *Crip Theory*.
7 Martino, "Supporting Transgender Students," 5.
8 Herriot, Burns, and Yeung, "Contested Spaces."
9 Herriot, Burns, and Yeung.
10 Martino, Kassen, and Omercajic, "Supporting Transgender Students in Schools," 755.
11 Travers, *Trans Generation*, 76.
12 Travers, 76.

13 Loutzenheiser, "Who Are You Calling a Problem?"
14 Ahmed, *On Being Included*, 6.
15 Ahmed, 6; Ball, Maguire, and Braun, *How Schools Do Policy*.
16 Hamraie, "Beyond Accommodation"; Ray, "School as a Hostile Institution"; Shalaby, *Troublemakers*; Sykes, *Queer Bodies*.
17 Frohard-Dourlent, "I Don't Care What's under Your Clothes."
18 Bettie, *Women without Class*; Castagno, *Educated in Whiteness*; Kehily, *Sexuality, Gender and Schooling*; Kumashiro, *Troubling Intersections of Race and Sexuality*; Lewis and Diamond, *Despite the Best Intentions*; Marker, "Indigenous Resistance and Racist Schooling"; McCready, "Some Challenges Facing Queer Youth Programs"; Pascoe, *Dude, You're a Fag*; Ray, "School as a Hostile Institution."
19 Sutherland, "Trans Enough."
20 Travers, *Trans Generation*, 56.
21 Meyer and Keenan, "Can Policies Help Schools Affirm Gender Diversity?," 744.
22 For examples and discussion of the positive effects of these policies, see Herriot, Burns, and Yeung, "Contested Spaces"; Holmes and Cahill, "School Experiences of Gay, Lesbian, Bisexual and Transgender Youth"; Ingrey, "Limitations and Possibilities for Teaching Transgender Issues."
23 ARC Foundation, "SOGI 123: Teaching Resources."
24 Ahmed, *Queer Phenomenology*; Castagno, *Educated in Whiteness*.
25 Martino, Omercajic, and Kassen, "We Have No 'Visibly' Trans Students."
26 Sykes, *Queer Bodies*; Travers, *Trans Generation*.
27 Hokowhitu, "If You Are Not Healthy, Then What Are You?"; Norman, Hart, and Petherick, "Indigenous Gender Reformations"; Sykes, *Queer Bodies*.
28 Norman, Hart, and Petherick, "Indigenous Gender Reformations"; Petherick, "Race and Culture."
29 Baynton, "Slaves, Immigrants, and Suffragists."
30 Travers, *Trans Generation*.
31 Sykes, *Queer Bodies*.
32 Hamraie, "Beyond Accommodation"; Jung, "Textual Mainstreaming."
33 Martino, Kassen, and Omercajic, "Supporting Transgender Students in Schools," 761.
34 Kafer, *Feminist, Queer, Crip*, 43.
35 Sykes, *Queer Bodies*.
36 Martino, Kassen, and Omercajic, "Supporting Transgender Students in Schools"; Meyer and Keenan, "Can Policies Help Schools Affirm Gender Diversity?"
37 Martino, Kassen, and Omercajic, "Supporting Transgender Students in Schools," 753.

CHAPTER 3. THE LABOR OF UNDERSTANDING AND FORGIVENESS

1 Thobani, *Exalted Subjects*.
2 Meadow, *Trans Kids*.
3 Malatino, *Trans Care*, 5.

4   Frohard-Dourlent, "I Don't Care What's under Your Clothes."
5   Travers, *Trans Generation*, 54.
6   Ahmed, *On Being Included*; Ball, Maguire, and Braun, *How Schools Do Policy*.
7   Berlant, "Subject of True Feeling."
8   Castagno, *Educated in Whiteness*; Youdell, *Impossible Bodies, Impossible Selves*.
9   Loutzenheiser and Moore, "Safe Schools, Sexualities, and Critical Education," 154.
10 Greteman, *Sexualities and Genders in Education*; Loutzenheiser, "Who Are You Calling a Problem?"; MacIntosh, "Does Anyone Have a Band-Aid?"; Quinan, "Safe Space."
11 Fields et al., "Beyond Bullying"; Greteman, *Sexualities and Genders in Education*.
12 Castagno, *Educated in Whiteness*; Frohard-Dourlent, "I Don't Care What's under Your Clothes"; Travers, *Trans Generation*.
13 Castagno, *Educated in Whiteness*, 10.
14 Adair, "Bathrooms and Beyond"; Beauchamp, *Going Stealth*; Frohard-Dourlent, "I Don't Care What's under Your Clothes"; Kafer, *Feminist, Queer, Crip*; Travers, *Trans Generation*.
15 Carter, "Nothing Better or Worse"; Pascoe, *Dude, You're a Fag*; Rosenfeld Halverson, "InsideOut"; Verner Chappell, Ketchum, and Richardson, "High School Curriculum."
16 Malatino, *Trans Care*, 2, 3.
17 Wentling, "Trans* Disruptions," 469.
18 Gill-Peterson, *Histories of the Transgender Child*; Stockton, *Queer Child*.
19 Ahmed, *On Being Included*; Castagno, *Educated in Whiteness*; Ward, *Respectably Queer*.

CHAPTER 4. THE LABOR OF GENDER LEGIBILITY

1   Mayo, *Gay-Straight Alliances*.
2   Ahmed, *On Being Included*, 42.
3   Beauchamp, *Going Stealth*; Jung, "Textual Mainstreaming"; Kafer, *Feminist, Queer, Crip*; Million, *Therapeutic Nations*; Morgensen, "Settler Homonationalism"; Simpson, *As We Have Always Done*; Slater, Agustsdottir, and Haraldsdottir, "Becoming Intelligible Women"; Spade, *Normal Life*.
4   Stryker and Currah, introduction to "Postposttranssexual."
5   Beauchamp, *Going Stealth*.
6   Aizura, "Unrecognizable."
7   Catalano, "Trans Enough?," 419.
8   Malatino, *Trans Care*, 38.
9   Butler, *Gender Trouble*, 22.
10 Rahily, *Trans-Affirmative Parenting*.
11 Malatino, "Pedagogies of Becoming."
12 Meyer and Sansfacon, *Supporting Transgender and Gender Creative Youth*; Pyne, "Gender Independent Kids"; Travers, *Trans Generation*.

13 The Medical Services Plan (MSP) is the provincial health-care program that all residents in British Columbia are required to enroll in and that is free for citizens and permanent residents.
14 Travers, *Trans Generation*.
15 Rahily, *Trans-Affirmative Parenting*.
16 Oh and Oh, "Unmasking Queerness," 9.
17 Huynh and Woo, "Asian Fail."
18 Temple Newhook et al., "Critical Commentary on Follow-Up Studies."
19 Malatino, *Trans Care*, 39.

CHAPTER 5. THE LABOR OF WORLD-MAKING

1 Smudging is a practice used by some Indigenous nations. It involves burning sacred herbs or medicines.
2 Tourmaline, Stanley, and Burton, introduction to *Trap Door*, xxiii.
3 Tourmaline, Stanley, and Burton, xxiii.
4 Muñoz, *Cruising Utopia*, 96.
5 Stanley, *Atmospheres of Violence*, 113.
6 Muñoz, *Cruising Utopia*, 99.
7 Rahily, *Trans-Affirmative Parenting*.
8 Muñoz, *Cruising Utopia*, 28.
9 "Shipping" refers to a common practice in fan fiction in which the author envisions a relationship between two characters or people who are not romantically connected in the original work or are not dating in real life.
10 Garcia, "Privilege, Power, and Dungeons & Dragons."
11 Tourmaline, Stanley, and Burton, introduction to *Trap Door*, xxiii.
12 Kafer, *Feminist, Queer, Crip*, 27.
13 Bartolome and Stanford, "Can't I Sing with the Girls?"; Carter, "Nothing Better or Worse"; Pascoe, *Dude, You're a Fag*; Payne, "Heterosexism, Perfection, and Popularity."
14 Malatino, *Trans Care*, 5.
15 Mayo, *Gay-Straight Alliances*, 7.
16 Brockenbrough and Boatwright, "In the MAC."
17 A "gaykeeper," as explained by Barry, is a gatekeeper specifically within the queer community.
18 Muñoz, *Cruising Utopia*, 96.
19 Malatino, *Trans Care*, 44.
20 Tourmaline, Stanley, and Burton, introduction to *Trap Door*, xxiii.
21 Tourmaline, Stanley, and Burton, xxiii.

CONCLUSION

1 Petersen, "Prince George School Trustee Candidates."
2 Sasani, "Virginia Reverses School Protections."
3 Sasani.
4 Thobani, *Exalted Subjects*.

5 Ahmed, *On Being Included*.
6 Brockenbrough, "Queer of Color Agency in Educational Contexts," 36.
7 Travers, *Trans Generation*, 74.
8 Malatino, *Trans Care*, 41.
9 Halberstam, *Queer Art of Failure*; O'Dell, Brownlow, and Bertilsdotter Rosqvist, "Different Adulthoods"; Riggs and Bartholomaeus, "It's Just What You Do"; Slater, Agustsdottir, and Haraldsdottir, "Becoming Intelligible Women."
10 Rahily, *Trans-Affirmative Parenting*.
11 Gilbert, *Sexuality in School*; Stockton, *Queer Child*; Travers, *Trans Generation*.
12 Castañeda, *Figurations*; de Leeuw, "If Anything Is to Be Done."
13 Tuck, "Suspending Damage."
14 Tuck, 415.
15 Tuck, 416.
16 *New York Times* contributors, letter to Philip B. Corbett.
17 PHE Canada, *Spirit Report*.
18 Spade, *Normal Life*, 41.
19 Tourmaline, Stanley, and Burton, introduction to *Trap Door*, xxiii.
20 Muñoz, *Cruising Utopia*.

APPENDIX

An early version of this appendix was previously published as L. Slovin. "What Grade are You In? On Being a Non-Binary Researcher." *Curriculum Inquiry* 50, no.3 (2020), 225–41.
1 Spade, *Normal Life*; Stryker, *Transgender History*.
2 Airton, "De/Politicization of Pronouns."
3 Gilbert, *Sexuality in School*; Lesko, *Act Your Age!*; Stockton, *Queer Child*.
4 Blatterer, "Contemporary Adulthood"; Halberstam, *In a Queer Time and Place*; Slater, Agustsdottir, and Haraldsdottir, "Becoming Intelligible Women"; Stockton, *Queer Child*.
5 Blatterer, "Contemporary Adulthood"; Halberstam, *In a Queer Time and Place*; Riggs and Bartholomaeus, "It's Just What You Do"; Silva, "Constructing Adulthood"; Slater, Agustsdottir, and Haraldsdottir, "Becoming Intelligible Women."
6 Blatterer, "Contemporary Adulthood," 780.
7 Meiners, "Trouble with the Child."
8 O'Dell, Brownlow, and Bertilsdotter Rosqvist, "Different Adulthoods," 350.
9 Pascoe, *Dude, You're a Fag*.

BIBLIOGRAPHY

Adair, Cassius. "Bathrooms and Beyond: Expanding a Pedagogy of Access in Trans/Disability Studies." *Transgender Studies Quarterly* 2, no. 3 (2015): 464–68.

Ahmed, Sara. *On Being Included: Racism and Diversity in Institutional Life*. Durham, NC: Duke University Press, 2012.

———. *Queer Phenomenology: Orientations, Objects, Others*. Durham, NC: Duke University Press, 2006.

Airton, Lee. "The De/Politicization of Pronouns: Implications of the No Big Deal Campaign for Gender-Expansive Educational Policy and Practice." *Gender and Education* 30, no. 5 (2018): 790–810.

———. "Leave 'Those Kids' Alone: On the Conflation of School Homophobia and Suffering Queers." *Curriculum Inquiry* 43, no. 5 (2013): 532–62.

Aizura, Aren. "Unrecognizable: On Trans Recognition in 2017." *South Atlantic Quarterly* 116, no. 3 (2017): 606–11.

ARC Foundation. "SOGI 3: Teaching Resources." 2019. https://bc.sogieducation.org.

Awkward-Rich, Cameron. "'She of the Pants and No Voice': Jack Bee Garland's Disability Drag." *Transgender Studies Quarterly* 7, no. 1 (2020): 20–36.

Ball, Stephen J., Meg Maguire, and Annette Braun. *How Schools Do Policy: Policy Enactments in Secondary Schools*. London: Routledge, 2012.

Bartolome, Sarah J., and Melanie E. Stanford. "'Can't I Sing with the Girls?': A Transgender Music Educator's Journey." In *Marginalized Voices in Music Education*, edited by Brent C. Talbot, 114–36. New York: Routledge, 2018.

Baynton, Douglas. "Slaves, Immigrants, and Suffragists: The Uses of Disability in Citizenship Debates." *PMLA* 120, no. 2 (2005): 562–67.

BC Ministry of Education. "Teacher Statistics—2013/2014—Province—Public Schools." 2014.

Beauchamp, Toby. *Going Stealth: Transgender Politics and U.S. Surveillance Practices*. Durham, NC: Duke University Press, 2018.

Berlant, Lauren. "The Subject of True Feeling: Pain, Privacy, and Politics." In *Cultural Pluralism, Identity Politics, and the Law*, edited by Austin Sarat and Thomas R. Kearns, 49–84. Ann Arbor: University of Michigan Press, 2001.

Bettie, Julie. *Women without Class: Girls, Race, and Identity*. Oakland: University of California Press, 2014.

Blackburn, Molly V. "Disrupting the (Hetero)Normative: Exploring Literacy Performances and Identity Work with Queer Youth." *Journal of Adolescent & Adult Literacy* 46, no. 4 (2002): 312–24.

Blatterer, Harry. "Contemporary Adulthood: Reconceptualizing an Uncontested Category." *Current Sociology* 55, no. 6 (2007): 771-92.

Boris, Eileen, and Rhacel Salazar Parreñas. *Intimate Labors: Cultures, Technologies, and the Politics of Care*. Stanford, CA: Stanford University Press, 2010.

Bradford, Nova J., and Austin H. Johnson. "Transnormativity." In *The Sage Encyclopedia of Trans Studies*, edited by Abbie E. Goldberg and Genny Beemyn, vol. 2, 869-71. Thousand Oaks, CA: Sage, 2021.

Brockenbrough, Ed. "Queer of Color Agency in Educational Contexts: Analytic Frameworks from a Queer of Color Critique." *Educational Studies* 51, no. 1 (2015): 28-44.

Brockenbrough, Ed, and Tomás Boatwright. "In the MAC: Creating Safe Spaces for Transgender Youth of Colour." In *Cultural Transformations: Youth and Pedagogies of Possibility*, edited by Korina Mineth Jocson, 165-82. Cambridge, MA: Harvard University Press, 2013.

Butler, Judith. *Bodies That Matter: On the Discursive Limits of "Sex."* New York: Routledge, 1993.

———. *Gender Trouble: Feminism and the Subversion of Identity*. New York: Routledge, 1990.

Bychowski, M. W., Howard Chiang, Jack Halberstam, Jacob Lau, Kathleen P. Long, Marcia Ochoa, C. Riley Snorton, Leah DeVun, and Zeb Tortorici. "Trans*historicities: A Roundtable Discussion." *TSQ: Transgender Studies Quarterly* 5, no. 4 (2018): 658-85.

Carter, Bruce Allen. "'Nothing Better or Worse than Being Black, Gay, and in the Band': A Qualitative Examination of Gay Undergraduate Participating in Historically Black College or University Marching Bands." *Journal of Research in Music Education* 61, no. 1 (2013): 26-43.

Castagno, Angelina E. *Educated in Whiteness: Good Intentions and Diversity in Schools*. Minneapolis: University of Minnesota Press, 2014.

Castañeda, Claudia. *Figurations: Child, Bodies, Worlds*. Durham, NC: Duke University Press, 2002.

Catalano, D. Chase J. "'Trans Enough?': The Pressures Trans Men Negotiate in Higher Education." *TSQ: Transgender Studies Quarterly* 2, no. 3 (2015): 411-30.

Childers, Sara M. "Promiscuous Analysis in Qualitative Research." *Qualitative Inquiry* 20, no. 6 (2014): 819-26.

Cover, Rob. "Conditions of Living: Queer Youth Suicide, Homonormative Tolerance, and Relative Misery." *Journal of LGBT Youth* 10, no. 4 (2013): 328-50.

Cox, Rosie. "Gendered Spaces of Commoditised Care." *Social & Cultural Geography* 14, no. 5 (2013): 491-99.

Crenshaw, Kimberlé. "Demarginalizing the Intersections of Race and Sex: A Black Feminist Critique of Antidiscrimination Doctrine, Feminist Theory and Antiracist Politics." *University of Chicago Legal Forum* 1, no. 8 (1989).

Cruz, Cindy. "LGBTQ Street Youth Talk Back: A Meditation on Resistance and Witnessing." *International Journal of Qualitative Studies in Education* 24, no. 5 (2011): 547-58.

Daigle, Michelle. "The Spectacle of Reconciliation: On (the) Unsettling Responsibilities of Indigenous Peoples in the Academy." *EPD: Society and Space* 37, no. 4 (2019): 703–21.

Dean, Amber Richelle. *Remembering Vancouver's Disappeared Women: Settler Colonialism and the Difficulty of Inheritance.* Toronto: Toronto University Press, 2015.

de Leeuw, Sarah. "'If Anything Is to Be Done with the Indian, We Must Catch Him Very Young': Colonial Constructions of Aboriginal Children and the Geographies of Indian Residential Schooling in British Columbia, Canada." *Children's Geographies* 7, no. 2 (2009): 123–40.

Dyer, Hannah. "Queer Futurity and Childhood Innocence: Beyond the Injury of Development." *Global Studies of Childhood* 7, no. 3 (2017): 290–302.

Emens, Elizabeth F. "Accommodation." In *Keywords for Disability Studies*, edited by Rachel Adams, Benjamin Reiss, and David Serlin, 18–21. New York: New York University Press, 2015.

Federici, Silvia. *Wages against Housework.* Bristol, UK: Power of Women Collective and Falling Wall Press, 1974.

Fetner, Tina, Athena Elafros, Sandra Bortolin, and Coralee Drechsler. "Safe Spaces: Gay-Straight Alliances in High Schools." *Canadian Sociological Association* 49, no. 2 (2012): 188–207.

Fields, Jessica, Laura Mamo, Jen Gilbert, and Nancy Lesko. "Beyond Bullying." *Contexts* 13, no. 4 (2014): 80–83.

Folbre, Nancy. "Measuring Care: Gender, Empowerment, and the Care Economy." *Journal of Human Development* 7, no. 2 (2006): 183–99.

Folbre, Nancy, and Julie A. Nelson. "For Love or Money—or Both?" *Journal of Economic Perspectives* 14, no. 4 (2000): 123–40.

Frohard-Dourlent, Hélène. "'I Don't Care What's under Your Clothes': The Discursive Positioning of Educators Working with Trans and Gender-Nonconforming Students." *Sex Education: Sexuality, Society and Learning* 16, no. 1 (2016): 63–76.

Garcia, Antero. "Privilege, Power, and Dungeons & Dragons: How Systems Shape Racial and Gender Identities in Tabletop Role-Playing Games." *Mind, Culture, and Activity* 24, no. 3 (2017): 232–46.

Gieseking, Jack. "Where We Go from Here: The Mental Sketch Mapping Method and Its Analytic Components." *Qualitative Inquiry* 19, no. 9 (2013): 712–24.

Gilbert, Jen. *Sexuality in School: The Limits of Education.* Minneapolis: University of Minnesota Press, 2014.

Gill-Peterson, Jules. *Histories of the Transgender Child.* Minneapolis: University of Minnesota Press, 2018.

Glenn, Evelyn N. "Creating a Caring Society." *Contemporary Sociology* 29, no. 1 (2000): 84–94.

———. "From Servitude to Service Work: Historical Continuities in the Racial Division of Paid Reproductive Labor." *Signs* 18, no. 1 (1992): 1–43.

Goble, Deborah. "[City redacted for anonymity] School Closures: Preliminary List Released." *CBC*, June 20, 2016.

Green, Maia, and Victoria Lawson. "Recentring Care: Interrogating the Commodification of Care." *Social & Cultural Geography* 12, no. 6 (2011): 639–54.
Greteman, Adam J. *Sexualities and Genders in Education: Towards Queer Thriving.* Queer Studies and Education. Cham, Switzerland: Palgrave Macmillan, 2018.
Greytak, Emily A., Joseph G. Kosciw, and Elizabeth M. Diaz. "Harsh Realities: The Experiences of Transgender Youth in Our Nation's Schools." Gay, Lesbian and Straight Education Network (GLSEN), 2009.
Hackford-Peer, Kim. "In the Name of Safety: Discursive Positionings of Queer Youth." *Studies in Philosophy and Education* 29 (2010): 541–56.
Haig-Brown, Celia. *Resistance and Renewal: Surviving the Indian Residential School.* Vancouver: Arsenal Pulp, 1988.
Halberstam, Jack. *In a Queer Time and Place: Transgender Bodies, Subcultural Lives.* New York: New York University Press, 2005.
———. *The Queer Art of Failure.* Durham, NC: Duke University Press, 2011.
———. *Trans*: A Quick and Quirky Account of Gender Variability.* Oakland: University of California Press, 2018.
Hamraie, Aimi. "Beyond Accommodation: Disability, Feminist Philosophy, and the Design of Everyday Academic Life." *PhiloSOPHIA* 6, no. 2 (2016): 259–71.
Herriot, Lindsay, David P. Burns, and Betty Yeung. "Contested Spaces: Trans-Inclusive School Policies and Parental Sovereignty in Canada." *Gender and Education* 30, no. 6 (2018): 695–714.
Hokowhitu, Brendan. "If You Are Not Healthy, Then What Are You? Healthism, Colonial Disease and Body Logic." In *Health Education: Critical Perspectives*, edited by Katie Fitzpatrick and Richard Tinning, 31–47. New York: Routledge, 2014.
Holmes, Sarah E., and Sean Cahill. "School Experiences of Gay, Lesbian, Bisexual and Transgender Youth." *Journal of Gay & Lesbian Issues in Education* 1, no. 3 (2004): 53–66.
hooks, bell. *Ain't I a Woman: Black Women and Feminism.* Boston: South End, 2014.
Hunt, Sarah. "The Relationality of Justice: Rethinking Legal Pluralism and Everyday Decolonization." University of Toronto, April 19, 2016.
Huynh, Kenneth and Benjamin Woo. "'Asian Fail': Chinese Canadian Men Talk about Race, Masculinity, and the Nerd Stereotype." *Social Identities* 20, nos. 4–5 (2014): 363–378.
Ingrey, Jennifer C. "The Limitations and Possibilities for Teaching Transgender Issues in Education to Preservice Teachers." In *Supporting Transgender and Gender Creative Youth: Schools, Families, and Communities in Action*, edited by Elizabeth J. Meyer and Annie Pullen Sansfacon, 97–110. New York: Peter Lang, 2014.
Jackson, Alecia Y. "Posthumanist Data Analysis of Mangling Practices." *International Journal of Qualitative Studies in Education* 26, no. 6 (2013): 741–48.
Jackson, Alecia Y., and Lisa A. Mazzei. *Thinking with Theory in Qualitative Research: Viewing Data across Multiple Perspectives.* New York: Routledge, 2012.
Joshee, Reva, and Susan Winton. "Past Crossings: US Influences on the Development of Canadian Multicultural Education Policy." In *Multicultural Education Policies in*

Canada and the United States, edited by Reva Joshee and Lauri Johnson, 17–27. Vancouver, BC: UBC Press, 2007.

Jung, Julie. "Textual Mainstreaming and Rhetorics of Accommodation." *Rhetoric Review* 26, no. 2 (2007): 160–78.

Kafer, Alison. *Feminist, Queer, Crip*. Bloomington: Indiana University Press, 2013.

Kehily, Mary Jane. *Sexuality, Gender and Schooling: Shifting Agendas in Social Learning*. London: Routledge, 2002.

Kumashiro, Kevin K., ed. *Troubling Intersections of Race and Sexuality: Queer Students of Color and Anti-Oppressive Education*. Lanham, MD: Rowman and Littlefield, 2001.

Lesko, Nancy. *Act Your Age! A Cultural Construction of Adolescence*. New York: Routledge, 2012.

Lewis, Amanda E., and John B. Diamond. *Despite the Best Intentions: How Racial Inequality Thrives in Good Schools*. New York: Oxford University Press, 2015.

Loutzenheiser, Lisa. "Can We Learn Queerly? Normativity and Social Justice Pedagogies." In *Social Justice Pedagogy across the Curriculum*, edited by Thandeka K. Chapman and Nikola Hobbel, 121–44. New York: Routledge, 2010.

———. "'Who Are You Calling a Problem?': Addressing Transphobia and Homophobia through School Policy." *Critical Studies in Education* 56, no. 1 (2015): 99–115.

Loutzenheiser, Lisa, and Shannon D. M. Moore. "Safe Schools, Sexualities, and Critical Education." In *The Routledge International Handbook of Critical Education*, edited by Michael W. Apple, Wayne Au, and Luis Armando Gandin, 150–62. New York: Routledge, 2009.

MacIntosh, Lori B. "Does Anyone Have a Band-Aid? Anti-Homophobia Discourses and Pedagogical Impossibilities." *Educational Studies* 41, no. 1 (2007): 33–43.

MacLure, Maggie. "The Wonder of Data." *Cultural Studies, Critical Methodologies* 13, no. 4 (2013): 228–232.

Malatino, Hil. "Pedagogies of Becoming: Trans Inclusivity and the Crafting of Being." *Transgender Studies Quarterly* 2, no. 3 (2015): 395–410.

———. *Trans Care*. Minneapolis: University of Minnesota Press, 2020.

Marker, Michael. "Indigenous Resistance and Racist Schooling on the Borders of Empires: Coast Salish Cultural Survival." *Paedagogica Historica* 45, no. 6 (2009): 757–72.

Martino, Wayne. "Supporting Transgender Students and Gender-Expansive Education in Schools: Investigating Policy, Pedagogy, and Curricular Implications." *Teachers College Record* 124, no. 8 (2022): 3–16.

Martino, Wayne, Jenny Kassen, and Kenan Omercajic. "Supporting Transgender Students in Schools: Beyond an Individualistic Approach to Trans Inclusion in the Education System." *Educational Review* 74, no. 4 (2020): 753–772.

Martino, Wayne, Kenan Omercajic, and Jenny Kassen. "'We Have No 'Visibly' Trans Students in Our School': Educators' Perspectives on Transgender-Affirmative Policies in Schools." *Teachers College Record* 124, no. 8 (2022): 66–97.

Mayo, Cris. *Disputing the Subject of Sex: Sexuality and Public School Controversies*. Lanham, MD: Rowman and Littlefield, 2004.

———. "Disruptions of Desire: From Androgynes to Genderqueer." In *Philosophy of Education 2007*, edited by Barbara S. Stengel, 49–58. Urbana, IL: Philosophy of Education Society, 2007.

———. *Gay-Straight Alliances and Associations among Youth in Schools*. Queer Studies and Education. New York: Palgrave Macmillan, 2017.

———. "Pushing the Limits of Liberalism: Queerness, Children, and the Future." *Educational Theory* 56, no. 4 (2006): 469–87.

McCready, Lance Trevor. "Some Challenges Facing Queer Youth Programs in Urban High Schools: Racial Segregation and de-Normalizing Whiteness." *Journal of Gay & Lesbian Issues in Education* 1, no. 3 (2004): 37–51.

McDowell, Linda. "Work, Workfare, Work/Life Balance and an Ethic of Care." *Progress in Human Geography* 28, no. 2 (2004): 145–63.

McRuer, Robert. *Crip Theory: Cultural Signs of Queerness and Disability*. New York: New York University Press, 2006.

Meadow, Tey. *Trans Kids: Being Gendered in the Twenty-First Century*. Oakland: University of California Press, 2018.

Meiners, Erica R. "Trouble with the Child in the Carceral State." *Social Justice* 41, no. 3 (2015): 120–44.

Meyer, Elizabeth J. *Gender, Bullying, and Harassment: Strategies to End Sexism and Homophobia in Schools*. New York: Teachers College Press, 2009.

Meyer, Elizabeth J., and Harper Benjamin Keenan. "Can Policies Help Schools Affirm Gender Diversity? A Policy Archaeology of Transgender-Inclusive Policies in California Schools." *Gender and Education* 30, no. 6 (2018): 736–53.

Meyer, Elizabeth J., and Annie Pullen Sansfacon, eds. *Supporting Transgender and Gender Creative Youth: Schools, Families, and Communities in Action*. New York: Peter Lang, 2014.

Mies, Maria. *Patriarchy and Accumulation on a World Scale: Women in the International Division of Labour*. London: Third World Books, 1986.

Million, Dian. *Therapeutic Nations: Healing in an Age of Indigenous Human Rights*. Tucson: University of Arizona Press, 2013.

Morgensen, Scott Lauria. "Settler Homonationalism: Theorizing Settler Colonialism within Queer Modernities." *GLQ: A Journal of Lesbian and Gay Studies* 16, nos. 1–2 (2010): 105–31.

Muñoz, José E. *Cruising Utopia: The Then and There of Queer Futurity*. New York: New York University Press, 2009.

New York Times contributors. Letter to Philip B. Corbett, associate managing editor for standards at the *New York Times*, February 15, 2023. https://nytletter.com.

Norman, Moss E., Michael Hart, and LeAnne Petherick. "Indigenous Gender Reformations: Physical Culture, Settler Colonialism and the Politics of Containment." *Sociology of Sport Journal* 36, no. 2 (2019): 113–23.

O'Dell, Lindsay, Charlotte Brownlow, and Hanna Bertilsdotter Rosqvist. "Different Adulthoods: Normative Development and Transgressive Trajectories." *Feminism & Psychology* 28, no. 3 (2018): 349–54.

Oh, Chuyun, and David C. Oh. "Unmasking Queerness: Blurring and Solidifying Queer Lines through K-Pop Cross-Dressing." *Journal of Popular Culture* 50, no. 1 (2017): 9–29.

Parreñas, Rhacel Salazar. *Servants of Globalization: Woman, Migration and Domestic Work*. Stanford, CA: Stanford University Press, 2001.

Pascoe, C. J. *Dude, You're a Fag: Masculinity and Sexuality in High School*. Oakland: University of California Press, 2007.

Patzer, Jeremy. "Residential School Harm and Colonial Dispossession: What's the Connection?" In *Colonial Genocide in Indigenous North America*, edited by Andrew Woolford, Jeff Benvenuto, and Alexander Laban Hinton, 166–86. Durham, NC: Duke University Press, 2014.

Payne, Elizabeth C. "Heterosexism, Perfection, and Popularity: Young Lesbians' Experiences of the High School Social Scene." *Educational Studies* 41, no. 1 (2007): 60–79.

Payne, Elizabeth C., and Melissa Smith. "LGBTQ Kids, School Safety, and Missing the Big Picture: How the Dominant Bullying Discourse Prevents School Professionals from Thinking about Systemic Marginalization or . . . Why We Need to Rethink LGBTQ Bullying." *QED: A Journal in GLBTQ Worldmaking* 0, no. 1 (2013): 1–36.

Petersen, Hanna. "Prince George School Trustee Candidates Tackle Tough Issues in Forum." *Prince George Citizen*, September 29, 2022.

Petherick, LeAnne. "Race and Culture in the Secondary School Health and Physical Education Curriculum in Ontario, Canada: A Critical Reading." *Health Education* 118, no. 2 (2018): 144–58.

PHE Canada. *Spirit Report*. 2022.

Pratt, Geraldine. *Working Feminism*. Philadelphia: Temple University Press, 2004.

Prosser, Jay. *Second Skins: The Body Narratives of Transsexuality*. Gender and Culture Series. New York: Columbia University Press, 1998.

Putzi, Jennifer. "COVID-19 and Archival Research: An Introduction." *Legacy: A Journal of American Women Writers*, February 16, 2022. https://legacywomenwriters.org/conversations/.

Pyne, Jake. "Gender Independent Kids: A Paradigm Shift in Approaches to Gender Non-Conforming Children." *Canadian Journal of Human Sexuality* 23, no. 1 (2014): 1–8.

Quinan, Christine. "Safe Space." In *Critical Concepts in Queer Studies and Education: An International Guide for the Twenty-First Century*, edited by Nelson M. Rodriguez, Wayne J. Martino, Jennifer C. Ingrey, and Edward Brockenbrough, 361–68. Queer Studies and Education. New York: Palgrave Macmillan, 2016.

Rahily, Elizabeth. *Trans-Affirmative Parenting: Raising Kids across the Gender Spectrum*. New York: New York University Press, 2020.

Rasmussen, Mary Lou. *Becoming Subjects: Sexualities and Secondary Schooling*. New York: Taylor and Francis, 2006.

———. "Beyond Gender Identity?" *Gender and Education* 21, no. 4 (2009): 431–47.

Rasmussen, Mary Lou, Eric Rofes, and Susan Talburt, eds. *Youth and Sexualities: Pleasure, Subversion, and Insubordination In and Out of Schools*. New York: Palgrave Macmillan, 2004.

Ray, Ranita. *Making of a Teenage Service Class: Poverty and Mobility in an American City*. Oakland: University of California Press, 2018.

———. "School as a Hostile Institution: How Black and Immigrant Girls of Color Experience the Classroom." *Gender & Society* 36, no. 1 (2022): 88–111.

Riggs, Damien W., and Clare Bartholomaeus. "'It's Just What You Do': Australian Middle-Class Heterosexual Couples Negotiating Compulsory Parenthood." *Feminism & Psychology* 28, no. 3 (2018): 373–89.

Ringrose, Jessica, and EJ Renold. "Normative Cruelties and Gender Deviants: The Performative Effects of Bully Discourses for Girls and Boys in School." *British Educational Research Journal* 36, no. 4 (2010): 573–96.

Robinson, Brandon Andrew. *Coming Out to the Streets: LGBTQ Youth Experiencing Homelessness*. Oakland: University of California Press, 2020.

Rosenfeld Halverson, Erica. "InsideOut: Facilitating Gay Youth Identity Development through a Performance-Based Youth Organization." *Identity* 5, no. 1 (2005): 67–90.

Sasani, Ava. "Virginia Reverses School Protections for Transgender Students." *New York Times*, September 18, 2022.

Schalk, Samantha D. *Black Disability Politics*. Durham, NC: Duke University Press, 2022.

Sedgwick, Eve Kosofsky. "How to Bring Your Kids Up Gay." *Social Text* 9, no. 4 (1991): 18–27.

Serano, Julia. "Detransition, Desistance, and Disinformation: A Guide for Understanding Transgender Children Debates." *Medium*, August 2, 2016.

Shalaby, Carla. *Troublemakers: Lessons in Freedom from Young Children in School*. New York: New Press, 2017.

Shelton, Stephanie A. "Queer Ethnography." In *Encyclopedia of Queer Studies in Education*, edited by Kamden K. Strunk and Stephanie A. Shelton, 513–17. Boston: Brill, 2022.

Silva, Jennifer M. "Constructing Adulthood in an Age of Uncertainty." *American Sociological Review* 77, no. 4 (2012): 505–22.

Simpson, Audra. "Whither Settler Colonialism?" *Settler Colonial Studies* 6, no. 4 (2016): 438–45.

Simpson, Leanne Betasamosake. *As We Have Always Done: Indigenous Freedom through Radical Resistance*. Minneapolis: University of Minnesota Press, 2017.

Slater, Jen, Embla Agustsdottir, and Freyja Haraldsdottir. "Becoming Intelligible Women: Gender, Disability and Resistance at the Border Zone of Youth." *Feminism & Psychology* 28, no. 3 (2018): 409–26.

Spade, Dean. *Normal Life: Administrative Violence, Critical Trans Politics, and the Limits of Law*. Boston: South End, 2011.

Stanley, Eric A. *Atmospheres of Violence: Structuring Antagonism and the Trans/Queer Ungovernable*. Durham, NC: Duke University Press, 2021.

Statistics Canada. "Census Profile." 2021.

Stiegler, Sam. "On Doing Go-Along Interviews: Toward Sensuous Analyses of Everyday Experiences." *Qualitative Inquiry* 27, nos. 3–4 (2021): 364–73.

Stockton, Kathryn Bond. *The Queer Child, or Growing Sideways in the Twentieth Century*. Durham, NC: Duke University Press, 2009.

Stryker, Susan. *Transgender History*. Berkeley, CA: Seal, 2008.

Stryker, Susan, and Paisley Currah. Introduction to "Postposttranssexual: Key Concepts for a Twenty-First Century Transgender Studies." Special issue, *Transgender Studies Quarterly* 1, nos. 1–2 (2014): 1–18.

Sutherland, David Kyle. "'Trans Enough': Examining the Boundaries of Transgender-Identity Membership." *Social Problems* 70, no. 1 (2021): 71–86.

Sykes, Heather. *Queer Bodies: Sexualities, Gender, and Fatness in Physical Education*. New York: Peter Lang, 2011.

Talburt, Susan. "Constructions of LGBT Youth: Opening up Subject Positions." *Theory Into Practice* 43, no. 2 (2004): 116–21.

Taylor, Catherine, and Tracey Peter. *Every Class in Every School: Final Report on the First National Climate Survey on Homophobia, Biphobia, and Transphobia in Canadian Schools*. Toronto: Egale Canada Human Rights Trust, 2011.

Temple Newhook, Julia, Jake Pyne, Kelley Winters, Stephen Feder, Cindy Holmes, Jemma Tosh, Mari-Lynne Sinnott, Ally Jamieson, and Ally Pickett. "A Critical Commentary on Follow-Up Studies and 'Desistance' Theories about Transgender and Gender-Nonconforming Children." *International Journal of Transgenderism* 19, no. 2 (2018): 212–24.

Thobani, Sunera. *Exalted Subjects: Studies in the Making of Race and Nation in Canada*. Toronto: University of Toronto Press, 2007.

Thorne, Barrie. *Gender Play: Girls and Boys in School*. New Brunswick, NJ: Rutgers University Press, 1993.

Thorpe, Justin N., and Adam J. Greteman. "Intimately Bound to Numbers: On the Rhetorics of GLBTQ School Climate Research." *QED: A Journal in GLBTQ Worldmaking* 2, no. 1 (2015): 73–99.

Tourmaline [published under the name Reina Gossett], Eric A. Stanley, and Johanna Burton. Introduction to *Trap Door: Trans Cultural Production and the Politics of Visibility*, xv–xxvi, Critical Anthologies in Art and Culture. Cambridge, MA: MIT Press, 2017.

———, eds. *Trap Door: Trans Cultural Production and the Politics of Visibility*. Critical Anthologies in Art and Culture. Cambridge, MA: MIT Press, 2017.

Travers. *The Trans Generation: How Trans Kids (and Their Parents) Are Creating a Gender Revolution*. Regina: University of Regina Press, 2018.

Tuck, Eve. "Suspending Damage: A Letter to Communities." *Harvard Educational Review* 79, no. 3 (2009): 409–27.

Tuck, Eve, and K. Wayne Yang. "Unbecoming Claims: Pedagogies of Refusal in Qualitative Research." *Qualitative Inquiry* 20, no. 6 (2014): 811–18.

Veale, Jaimie, Elizabeth M. Saewyc, Hélène Frohard-Dourlent, Sarah Dobson, and Beth Clark. *Being Safe, Being Me: Results of the Canadian Trans Youth Health Survey*. Vancouver: SARAVYC, 2015.

Verner Chappell, Sharon, Karyl E. Ketchum, and Lisa Richardson. "High School Curriculum." In *Gender Diversity and LGBTQ Inclusion in K–12 Schools: A Guide to Supporting Students, Changing Lives*, by Sharon Verner Chappell, Karyl E. Ketchum, and Lisa Richardson, 192–211. New York: Routledge, 2018.

Ward, Jane. *Respectably Queer: Diversity Culture in LGBT Activist Organizations*. Nashville: Vanderbilt University Press, 2008.

Wentling, Tre. "Trans* Disruptions: Pedagogical Practices and Pronoun Recognition." *TSQ: Transgender Studies Quarterly* 2, no. 3 (2015): 469–76.

Wilchins, Riki Anne. *Read My Lips: Sexual Subversion and the End of Gender*. Ithaca, NY: Firebrand Books, 1997.

Youdell, Deborah. *Impossible Bodies, Impossible Selves: Exclusions and Students Subjectivities*. Dordrecht: Springer, 2006.

INDEX

ability. *See* disability
ableism, 5, 7, 20–21, 23, 40, 69, 74, 76–78, 88–89, 91–92, 116–17, 152, 171, 176–77, 179, 194–95
acceptance, 9–10, 35–36, 38, 42, 52, 85–86, 107–9, 135–36, 179–80
access, accessibility, 3–4, 57–58, 64–65, 68–69, 98–99, 119–20; to health care, 169; to rights, 8. *See also* accommodations
accommodations, 3–4, 9–11, 13, 23, 64–65, 68–72, 74–75, 77–82, 85–86, 90, 108–9, 144–45, 168–70, 172–73, 175, 180–81; self-identification and, 67. *See also under* trans and gender-nonconforming youth
activism, 59, 62, 176–79
adults, adulthood: concern, 3–5, 39–40, 61–62, 65–66, 72, 74–75, 82, 85–90, 97–98, 108–9, 168, 170–75; legibility of, 24–25, 193–95; nonadulthood, 24–25, 193–200; nonbinary, 24–25, 27, 193–99, 138–39; normativity and, 10–12, 17–18, 20–21, 66, 107–8, 136, 175–81, 184, 186–87; queer and trans, 187–89; in research, 193–97, 199–200; as socially constructed, 194–95; surveillance, 140, 164–65. *See also* childhood; youth
adultism, 91–92, 171
Ahmed, Sara, 7, 35–36, 42, 50, 53, 111–12
Aizura, Aren, 17, 113
allyship, 45–46, 48–49, 56–57, 60–62, 96–97, 110

ambiguity, 4–5, 18–20, 22, 70, 116, 120–21, 129–31, 135–36, 138–40, 177–78, 183, 189–90, 197–98. *See also* trans and gender-nonconforming youth
antisemitism, 55–56
anxiety, 9, 75–76, 94, 112–14, 124–25, 131–36, 170–71
art, 16–17, 26–27, 84, 93–94, 100, 132–33, 149–50, 162–63; of living, 156–57
assemblies, 36–37, 42–52, 62
assimilation, 21

bathrooms, 42–43, 54–61, 64, 68–69, 94–95, 98–99, 167–70, 172, 181–82, 187, 193, 197–200. *See also* locker rooms
Beauchamp, Toby, 2, 57
beauty, 1, 22; of being trans, 5, 121–24, 129, 135–36, 147, 175
belonging, 57, 64–65, 67, 69, 81–82, 154–55, 157, 174
Bettie, Julie, 113
bias, 7–8, 174
binders, 119, 180–81, 196–97
Black History Month, 37–39, 52, 62
body, 2, 15–16, 22–23; accessibility and, 64–65, 75; disciplinary regulation of, 111–12; diversity and, 62–63; marginalization and, 42; normativity and, 9, 28–29, 64–65, 77–79, 89, 98; policing, 23; trans, 111–12, 119–20; "wrong body" narrative, 118–19. *See also* disability
Boushie, Colten, 48–49
Bradford, Nova, 18–19

British Columbia, 5, 7–8, 40, 96, 168–71; Indigenous peoples, 5, 55; Medical Services Plan (MSP), 119–20, 208n13; Ministry of Education, 72, 204n5; "Settlement Agreement," 37, 204n5; SOGI (sexual orientation and gender identity) 123 initiative, 71–75, 180–81. *See also* Canada
bullying, 50–52, 65–66, 92–93, 96, 128, 172
bureaucracy, 111–13, 116–17, 132, 135
Burton, Johanna, 16, 65–66, 135, 138
Butler, Judith, 20–21, 116–17

Cabaret (musical), 150–51
Canada: Citizenship Act, 37–38; Indian Residential Schools Settlement Agreement, 43–44; multiculturalism and, 37–44, 46–47, 61–62, 170–71; Truth and Reconciliation Commission, 43–44. *See also* British Columbia
capitalism, 69, 76, 176–77, 194–95
care, care work, 2–4, 10, 13–18, 86–87, 89–90, 103–4, 107–9, 114, 119, 121–26, 134–36, 139, 175–78; communities of, 11–12, 14–15, 97–98, 103, 125–26, 140–45, 158–59, 161–63, 165, 175–76. *See also* health, health care; labor
cartography, 30–31
Castagno, Angelina, 35–36, 97
category, categorization, 4–5, 10, 29–30, 111–12, 135, 181, 183, 194–95
cell phones, 1, 41, 83–84, 93–94, 127, 145–51, 153–54, 161
childhood: Indigenous, 21, 76, 177; normativity and, 10–11, 107–8, 169, 176–77, 179; as plastic, 21; racialized, 21, 177; trans, 10–11, 28, 107–8, 117, 176–77, 194–95. *See also* adults, adulthood; youth
cisheteronormativity, 4–5, 7, 9, 18, 20–21, 23, 40, 52, 65–69, 73–74, 76–82, 85, 88, 91, 93, 96–97, 107–8, 125–26, 129–31, 135–36, 145, 152, 160–62, 164–65, 170–71, 174, 176–79, 184–90, 194–95

citizenship, 23, 37–38, 57, 77
civil rights movement, 38–39
class, classism, 7, 76–77, 118–19; education and, 6–7; gender and, 18; visibility and, 174
clothing. *See* fashion
coding, 29–30
collectivity, 196–97
colonialism, settler, 18, 20–23, 40, 43–46, 48–49, 52, 55, 62, 76–78, 86–87, 111–12, 116–17, 138, 174, 176–77, 179, 194–95, 198, 205n18
community, 11–12, 14–15, 27, 97–98, 103, 125–26, 140–45, 156–59, 161–63, 165, 176–76. *See also under* care, care work
concern, 3–5, 9, 65–66, 82, 86–90, 95, 170–74, 186–87. *See also* niceness; risk
contagion, 170–71
critical disability studies, 20–21, 23, 66
critical geography, 30
Cumming, Alan, 150–51

data: analyzing, 29–30; as fluid and changing, 29–30
deadnaming, 109, 143, 175–76, 201n4
depression, 9–10, 65–66, 152
desire: as fraught, 4–5; inclusion and, 66, 74–75; labor of, 11–12; 17–18; pedagogy of, 169, 179–81; for recognition, 2; in research, 11–12; for transness and gender nonconformity, 10–11, 28–29, 66, 74–75, 82, 85–86, 89, 107–8, 116–17, 135–36, 140–42, 144–45, 157–59, 161, 165, 169, 171–72, 175–80, 186–89. *See also under* trans and gender-nonconforming youth
Desmond, Viola, 38–39
disability, 10–11, 18, 23, 66, 75–77, 79–80, 82, 88, 98, 111–12, 114, 116–17, 135; accommodations and, 64–65, 68–69; adulthood and, 194–95; chronic illness, 22; citizenship and, 57; compulsory able-bodiedness, 23; crip time,

152–53; in education, 69; gender nonconformity and, 18, 20–21, 23, 116–17, 173; race and, 23; settler colonialism and, 23; visibility and, 174

discipline, disciplinarity, 10–11, 21, 40, 44, 76, 111–12, 155, 163

diversity and inclusion, 3–10, 16–17, 35–37, 42, 52, 58–63, 65–75, 78, 80–82, 85–86, 96–97, 107–8, 138, 164–65, 168–73, 180–81; accommodations and, 64–65; cultural enrichment model of, 35–36, 43–44, 46–49, 61; desire and, 66; "feel good" approach to, 7–8, 36–37, 41–42, 47–48, 50, 52–53, 55, 59–63, 66, 85–86, 107–8; fun, 35–36; nationalism and, 36–44, 46–47, 61–62; safety and, 96–97; training and labor of, 74

drugs and alcohol use, 9–10, 151–52. See also substance abuse

Dungeons & Dragons (D&D), 1–2, 149–51. See also world-making

dysphoria, 79–80, 118–19

East City High, 1–13; All Nations room, 42–43, 137–38; anti-Black racism at, 53–57, 59–61; band hall, 155–64; Breakfast Club, 25–26, 83–84; demographics, 6–8; French Immersion program, 6–7, 35, 41, 148; Gender and Sexuality Alliance (GSA), 35, 110, 157–59, 163; gender-neutral bathrooms, 54–55, 57–61; Indigenous Awareness Week, 42–49, 52; physical education, 64, 75–80; Pink Shirt Day, 50–52; "Policy on Sexual Orientation and Gender Identity," 67–74, 111–12; progressive image of, 6–8, 40–41, 61–63, 108, 168, 173; tech booth, 139–45, 164; Theater Company, 7–8, 100–103, 139–45, 152–53; violence at, 35–36

education: ableism in, 69, 152–53; as age-striated space, 26; backlash to queer and trans-inclusive curricular programming, 168–71; cisheteronormativity and, 3–4, 9–12, 52, 65–69, 73, 79–82, 85, 88, 91, 93, 96–97, 108, 164–65, 174, 185–90; desire and, 11–12, 179–81; disciplinary processes, 44; discomfort and, 47; diversity and inclusion in, 35–36, 38–42, 53–54, 61–62, 67, 72–74; funding and resources, 6–7, 74, 98–99; gender and, 1–4, 9–12, 16–17, 73–74, 181–83; good intentions and, 39–40, 44, 46–47, 55–57, 61–63, 66, 72, 82, 85–89, 96–97, 102–3, 107–8, 172–74; marginalization and, 67–68; normativity in, 152–53, 163–64; queer and trans adults in, 12, 187–89; race and, 47, 52–54, 61–62, 69; safe spaces and, 173, 175; settler colonialism and, 21, 43–46, 48–49, 52, 55, 62, 69, 86–87; systemic oppression in, 50–52, 60–63; transphobia and, 3–4, 9–12, 85–87, 89–91, 94–98, 102–3, 108; violence and, 10, 108. See also East City High; pedagogy

education studies, 8, 96, 108–9

embodiment. See body; disability

enactment, 2, 15–16, 22

equality. See diversity and inclusion

escape, 2–3, 17, 137–39, 145–48, 150–51, 154–56, 159, 163–64, 188–89. See also trapdoors; utopia

essentialism, 29–30, 78, 118

ethnography, 1–2; desire and, 28–29; as movement, 27–28; queer, 27–29; school-based, 11, 27

exclusion, 8, 23, 42, 66–68, 70–71, 77–78, 161, 175

family, 14–15, 176–77

fan fiction, 1, 148–49, 151, 208n9. See also writing

fashion, 1, 22, 68–69, 112, 122–23, 127–29, 142, 145, 149, 160–61, 196. *See also* makeup; nail art, nail polish
fatness, fatphobia, 4–5, 10–11, 20–21, 42–43, 77, 79–80, 89, 118–19
feminism, 13–15
femme, femininity, 1, 21, 103–4, 123–24, 127–29, 135, 143, 145, 149. *See also* gender; masculinity
fitness, 76–78, 80, 173. *See also* physical education
flamboyance, 33–34, 122–24, 128–29, 135, 142–45, 189
fluidity, 27–30, 70, 105, 109, 114, 124, 129–31, 135, 147–51, 158–59. *See also* ambiguity; genderfluid
food insecurity, 6–7, 46–47
Frohard-Dourlent, Hélène, 40
future, futurity, 10–12, 18, 28, 79, 93–94, 117, 139, 142, 175–77. *See also* desire; hope; utopia

gender: adulthood and, 194–95, 197–99; ambiguity and, 4–5, 19–20, 29, 183, 189–90; biology of, 117–22, 160; body and, 22, 77–78, 98; bureaucracy of, 111–13, 116–17, 132, 135; as capacious and fluid, 2–3, 5, 11–12, 18, 27–29, 129–34, 163–65; citizenship and, 57; class and, 18; disability and, 18, 20–21, 23, 75, 173; fitness and, 77–78; gender binary, 10, 15–16, 20, 67, 103–4, 113–14, 189; identity and, 15–16, 119–21; in education, 1–4, 9–12, 16–17, 73–74, 181–83; knowledge and, 115–17, 171, 175–76; labor and, 13–17, 124–25; legibility and, 4–5, 8, 10–11, 15–18, 20–22, 70, 82, 106–7, 150–51, 164–65, 174–76, 189–90; misgendering, 2, 15–17, 22, 102–8, 115, 135–36, 143–44, 175–77, 189–90, 197–98; normativity and, 17–19, 98, 111–12; performing, 19–20, 113; policing, 19–20, 111–12, 119, 124, 127–28, 132–33, 197–98; race and, 18, 20–22, 127–28, 199; settler colonialism and, 20–22; sexuality and, 18–20, 147–51; social recognition and, 15–16, 114, 135–36, 150–51, 194–95; transgressing, 4–5, 132–34; X marker, 8; youth and, 18, 28–29. *See also* femme, femininity; genderfluid; masculinity; nonbinary; trans and gender-nonconforming youth
gender and sexuality studies, 18–19
gender-neutral bathrooms, 53–61, 98–99
genderfluid, 2, 27, 71, 105–7, 119–22, 127, 131–32, 147, 152, 187–88, 190. *See also* nonbinary; trans and gender-nonconforming youth
Gill-Peterson, Jules, 28
Glenn, Evelyn Nakano, 13–15
good intentions, 40, 44, 55, 61, 66, 72, 82, 85–89, 97–98, 102–3, 107–8, 168, 170–74. *See also* niceness; *under* education
Greteman, Adam, 9–10

harm, 4–5, 7–8, 10–11, 32–34, 39–40, 43–44, 57, 60, 63–65, 67–70, 82, 85–86, 89, 91, 96–97, 99, 102–3, 106–8, 119, 168–69, 171–72, 177–81, 184–87. *See also* risk; violence
health, health care, 23, 76–77, 80, 173, 208n13; access to, 169; gender-affirming, 8, 18–19, 118–20. *See also* care, care work
homelessness, 8
homophobia, 5–6, 10, 19–20, 40–41, 50–52, 55–56, 91, 132, 161, 163, 185–86
hope, 45, 113–14, 116, 139–40, 142, 154–55, 182. *See also* desire; future, futurity; utopia
hormone replacement therapy (HRT), 119–20. *See also* health, health care
humanity, 8, 10–11, 20, 131–32, 135–36, 177–79, 185–86

identity: ambiguity of, 4–5; gender and, 15–16, 119–21; risk and, 9–10; as stable, concrete, and knowable, 69–70, 89, 100–101, 115–16, 119–22, 129–34, 168; tensions and dynamics of, 2, 133–34; visibility and, 67
Idle No More, 48–49
immigration, 13–14, 23, 38, 76
inclusion, inclusivity. *See* diversity and inclusion
Indian Act, 21
Indigenous people, Indigeneity, 5–6, 21, 42–43, 137, 205n18; adulthood and, 194–95; erasure of, 21, 40; in education, 42–46, 48–49, 55, 62, 76; overcoding of, 29–30; resistance, 48–49; vulnerability and, 86–87. *See also* colonialism, settler
Indigenous studies, 20–21
individualism, 3–4, 65, 67–70, 78–82, 168, 175
inequality. *See* diversity and inclusion
intersectionality, 19, 23
intervention, 2–3, 5, 11, 13, 30–31, 46–49, 51–52, 67, 87, 98, 119–20, 125–26, 138, 177–78, 189–90

Johnson, Austin, 18–19

K-pop, 1–3, 120–21, 127–29, 142–43, 148–49, 201n2
Kafer, Alison, 79, 152
Kassen, Jenny, 67–68, 78, 80–81
knowledge, knowability, 119–21, 164–65, 171, 175–76; data and, 29–30; knowable populations, 10, 17; of self, 115–17, 121–22, 130–31; resisting, 4–5; unknowability, 138–40

labor: care and, 13–15, 17–18, 86, 90, 103–4, 107–9, 114, 121–26, 134–36, 139, 175–78; of cultivating desire, 11–12; daily acts of, 2–3, 5, 8, 112, 121–22, 124–26, 130–31, 135; of filtering gender expressions, 177–78; gender and, 2–3, 5, 8, 13–17, 30–31, 36–37; going unnoticed, 2–4; as intervention, 5; of making oneself legible, 112–17, 122–25, 127–29, 134–36; racialization of, 13–15; of social recognition, 16–18; of survival, 129; of understanding and forgiveness, 17, 177–78; (un)waged, 13–14; valuing, 175–78, 190; visibility and, 13–14; of world-making, 17–18, 30–31, 138–39, 163–65, 177–80, 182, 188–89; youth, 58, 62–63, 86, 90–91, 97–99, 103–9, 175–78, 184, 186, 188–90. *See also* care, care work
land acknowledgments, 5–6, 49–50, 55, 61, 86–87
land dispossession, 55
legibility, 4–5, 8, 10, 13, 15–18, 20–25, 29–31, 70, 79–80, 82, 86–87, 106–7, 112–16, 118–25, 127–31, 134–35, 138–39, 142–43, 150–51, 164–65, 173–78, 183, 189–90, 193–95. *See also under* adults, adulthood; gender; labor; trans and gender-nonconforming youth
Lewis, Amanda, 44
liminality, 139, 144–45, 158–59, 163–64, 200
locker rooms, 32, 64–65, 68–70, 77, 79, 169–70. *See also* bathrooms

makeup, 1, 122–24, 127–28, 132–33, 142, 161–62. *See also* fashion; nail art, nail polish
Malatino, Hil, 14–16, 90, 103, 114, 118, 124–25, 135–36, 156–57, 161, 175–75
mapping, mental, 30–31. *See also* cartography
marginalization, 7–8, 13–14, 29–30, 42, 46–47, 66–68, 86, 119–20, 177
Martino, Wayne, 67–68, 78, 80–81
masculinity, 1, 18–22, 76–80, 100, 103–4, 114, 118–19, 127–28, 132, 142–44, 148–49, 196–97, 199. *See also* femme, femininity; gender

Mayo, Cris, 157
McRuer, Robert, 23
Meadow, Tey, 15–16
medicalization, 18–19, 23, 89, 111–12, 117, 119–20, 176–77. *See also* transitioning
membership, 69–70
mental illness, 152. *See also* depression
Meyer, Elizabeth, 50–51
microaggressions, 86
militarism, 76–78. *See also* physical education
model-minority myth, 7–8
monster, monstrousness, 10–12, 17, 135–36, 178–79
movement, 20–21, 24–25, 27–30, 68–71, 76–77, 86, 138–39, 182–83, 189–90
multiculturalism, 36–44, 46–47, 61–62, 85–87, 168, 170–71. *See also* diversity and inclusion
Muñoz, José, 18, 139, 158–59, 182
Musqueam (xʷməθkʷəy̓əm) Nation, 5

nail art, nail polish, 25–26, 122–23, 132–33, 161–62. *See also* fashion; makeup
nationalism, 76–78; diversity and, 36–44, 46–47, 61–62. *See also* multiculturalism
NCT (K-pop group), 1, 127, 142–43, 201n2. *See also* K-pop
neoliberalism, 96
neurodivergence, 4–5, 20–21, 88, 118–19, 152–54, 177, 189–90
niceness, 35–38, 40–41, 43–44, 46–47, 61–63, 66, 85–90, 97, 99, 102–3, 107–8, 172–74, 177, 186. *See also* good intentions
nobodiness, 17–18, 116–17, 125–26, 129, 139–40, 165. *See also* trapdoors
nonbinary, 2, 5–7, 9, 22, 24–25, 27, 33–34, 69–70, 75–76, 112–13, 116–22, 125–26, 129–31, 138–39, 162–63, 189–90, 193–94. *See also* genderfluid; trans and gender-nonconforming youth
normativity, 6, 9–11, 14–15, 17–20, 23, 27–28, 64–65, 77–79, 89, 98, 107–8, 111–12, 114, 118–19, 131–32, 135, 142–43, 145, 152, 163–65
Nuxalk Nation, 48–49

Omercajic, Kenan, 67–68, 78, 80–81
Onondaga Nation, 48–49
oppression: in education, 35–36, 40–42, 61–62; structures of, 5, 7–8, 18, 50–52, 56–57, 60–63, 108

pansexuality, 2, 5–6, 92–93, 130–31
parents, 35, 67–68, 71–72, 117–21, 143, 150–51, 168–69, 176–77; parent advisory councils, 6–7; parental rights, 67, 168–69, 171
Parks, Rosa, 38–39, 46–47
Pascoe, C. J., 19–20, 127–28, 132
paternalism, 91–92, 176–77
pathologization, 86–87, 111–12
pedagogy, 47; of desire, 34, 74–75, 116, 169, 178–83. *See also* education
pep rallies, 145–46
performativity, 19–20, 62, 113
physical education (PE), 3–4, 76–80, 144–45, 173, 182. *See also* fitness
plasticity, 21
policing, 2, 19–20, 111–12, 119, 124, 127–28, 132–33, 197–98; of bodies, 23, 42; of Indigeneity, 21; of marginalized communities, 42; violence of, 37
policy, 2–3, 9–10, 37–38, 58–60, 67–74, 80–82, 96, 116, 168–70, 180–81; awareness of, 71–74
poverty, 6–7
power, 17; adulthood and, 195, 199–200; disciplinary, 111–12; imbalances of, 50–52; structures of, 107–8
Prince, 46–47
prison system, 8
privilege, 6–8, 66, 76–77, 96–98, 102, 119–20, 198–99
productivity, 76–77

progress, progressivism, 5–6, 8, 10–11, 35–36, 40–41
pronouns, 3–4, 12–13, 18, 65–66, 68–69, 93, 102–8, 110–11, 122–23, 125–26, 135, 143–44, 162–63, 169–70, 201n1

qualitative research, 29–30
queer and trans studies, 8, 11, 14–16, 20–21, 96
queer, queerness, 1–2, 9–10, 13, 19–21; desire for, 3–4, 11–12, 18, 36–37, 116, 135–36, 158–59, 162–63, 165, 187–89; disability and, 152–53; in education, 72–74, 91–93, 96, 107–8, 116, 135–36; as methodology, 27–29; risk and, 9–12, 34, 65–66, 96; safety and, 96; teachers, 12; visibility, 5–6; world-making and, 18, 113–14, 138–40, 146, 149–51, 155–56, 158–59, 165, 175–76, 182, 188–89. *See also* trans and gender-nonconforming youth

race: adulthood and, 194–95, 198–99; backlash to antiracist teaching and learning, 168–71; body and, 98; citizenship and, 57; disability and, 23; in education, 39–40, 69; gender and, 1, 10, 18, 20–22, 116–17, 127–28, 199; immigration and, 38; labor and, 13–15; masculinity and, 127–28; multiculturalism and, 38; niceness and, 35–36, 39–40; settler colonialism and, 21–22, 44–46; sexuality and, 10; taking up space, 98, 143, 148; transness and, 4–5, 8, 10, 18–19, 60, 82, 118–20, 158–59; visibility and, 174; whiteness, 18–21, 35–36, 38–40, 44–46, 53–54, 56–57, 60, 66, 69, 76–77, 98, 111–12, 114, 116–20, 135, 138–39, 143, 148, 162, 170–71, 176–77, 179, 194–95, 198–99. *See also* white supremacy
racism, 5–7, 20–21, 39–41, 46–47, 52, 61–62, 74, 98, 116–17, 170–71, 177; anti-Asian, 7–8; anti-Black, 35–40, 47, 53–57, 59–61, 69, 76–77, 137; anti-Indigenous, 40, 43–44, 47, 55, 61; disciplining and, 44; in education, 47, 52–54, 60–61; among teachers, 40–41, 53–57, 59–62

Rahily, Elizabeth, 117, 119–21, 143, 176–77
rape culture, 37
recognition, social, 15–19, 22, 66, 114, 135–36, 150–51, 194–95
reconciliation, 43–44, 46, 55, 86–87
refusal, 16–17, 28–31, 38–39, 79–80, 92–93, 103, 135–36, 138–39, 164–65. *See also* resistance; transgression; world-making
reification, 11, 20–21, 43–44, 52, 62–63, 66, 138, 174, 195
reproduction, social, 2–5, 10, 13–14, 20, 35–36, 38, 43–44, 52, 55, 64–65, 67–68, 77–78, 82, 98, 170–71
researcher, 9; adulthood and, 193–200; legibility of, 23–25; relationship with participants, 25–27, 30–31
residential schools, 21, 48–49, 76
resistance, 2–5, 16–17, 27–30, 48–49, 62, 117–18, 125–26, 138–39, 158–59, 164–65, 183, 190. *See also* refusal; transgression; world-making
rhetoric, 51–52
rights, 8, 107–8, 113, 133–34, 158, 178–79; to gender-neutral bathrooms, 58–59, 68–69, 97–99; parental, 67, 168–69, 171
risk, 3–5, 8–12, 23, 28–30, 65–66, 74–75, 82, 85–91, 96–97, 99, 107–8, 151–52, 167–72, 175, 177–81. *See also under* trans and gender-nonconforming youth

safety, 8, 10–11, 57–58, 70, 90, 99, 169–73; fairness and, 75; privilege and, 46; as qualified, 85–86, 89; safe spaces, 9, 45–48, 91–98, 108–9, 155–59, 175
Schalk, Sami, 23

school leaving, 9–10
science, 117–22, 160
Sedgwick, Eve Kosofsky, 10–11
sex, sexuality: adulthood and, 194–95; body and, 98; citizenship and, 57; in education, 73–74; as expansive, 165; gender and, 18–20, 130–31, 147–51; policing, 19–20; race and, 127–28, 162–63; romance and, 11. *See also* gender; queer, queerness; trans and gender-nonconforming youth
sexual assault, 35–36
Simpson, Leanne Betasamosake, 21
SOGI (sexual orientation and gender identity) 123 initiative, 71–75, 180–81
somebodiness, 17–18, 113, 116–17, 125–26, 140–41, 177–78. *See also* nobodiness
Spade, Dean, 64–65, 182
sports, 8, 69–70, 76–77, 118, 159–60. *See also* fitness; physical education (PE)
Squamish (Skwxwú7mesh-ulh Temíxw) Nation, 5
Standing Rock, 48–49
Stanley, Eric, 16, 65–66, 135, 138–39
statistics, 9–10, 167
stereotypes, 7–8, 102
sterilization, 23
stimming (self-stimulating behaviors), 153–54
Stryker, Susan, 10–11
substance abuse, 65–66. *See also* drugs and alcohol use
suicidality, 9–10, 65–66, 167–68, 171
surveillance, 2, 5, 17–18, 127–28, 138–39, 144–45, 165
survival, 2–3, 11–15, 17, 86, 103, 109, 129, 164–65, 175–76

Talburt, Susan, 10
teachers: educating on gender and sexuality, 184–87; good intentions, 39–40, 44, 56–57, 61–62, 66, 69, 72, 82, 85–86, 88–89, 96–97, 102–3, 108–9, 172–74; queer and trans, 187–89; racism and, 40–41, 53–57, 59–62
Teachers College Record, 67
theater, 1, 5–8, 100–103, 139–45, 152–53. *See under* East City High
Thobani, Sunera, 38–40, 42, 46, 170–71
Thorpe, Justin, 9–10
tolerance, 52, 86–87, 170–71. *See also* diversity and inclusion; multiculturalism
Tourmaline, 16, 65–66, 135, 138
trans and gender-nonconforming youth, 1–5, 8–11, 15–16, 18–20, 22, 69, 73–74; access to gender-affirming care, 18–19; accommodations and, 64–65, 68–72, 74–75, 77–78, 80–82, 85–86, 90, 108–9, 168–70, 172–75, 180–81; adulthood and, 193–99; ambiguity and, 4–5, 22, 27–28, 116, 129–36, 165, 187, 183–85, 189–90; attacks on, 168–71; biological explanations for, 117–22; body and, 89, 111–12, 118–20; care and, 14–15, 103, 161, 165, 175–76; class and, 118–19; community and, 142–43, 157, 161, 163; desire and, 10–12, 28–29, 66, 74–75, 82, 85–86, 89, 107–8, 116–17, 135–36, 140–42, 144–45, 157, 161, 165, 169, 171–72, 175–80, 186–89; disability and, 23, 82, 116–19, 135, 174; discursive positioning of, 28–29; expectations for, 22; fatness and, 4–5, 22; homelessness and, 8; identity and, 2–4, 115–16, 119–21; inclusion and, 3–5, 8–10, 36–37, 58–59, 65, 67–75, 78, 80–82, 85–86, 168–69, 173, 180–81; labor of, 2–3, 5, 8, 36–37, 62–63, 86, 108–9, 112–14, 116–17, 121–25, 127–29, 135–36, 175–78, 189–90; legibility of, 2, 4–5, 15–17, 22, 29–31, 79–80, 82, 86–87, 113–14, 116–25, 127–31, 134–36, 138–39, 142–43, 147, 164–65, 173–78, 183, 189–90; medical-

izing, 117, 119–20; monstrousness and, 10–12, 17, 20, 135–36, 178–79; narrow understanding of, 2–5, 10, 16–21, 67–70, 80–82, 91–92, 106–7, 111–22, 129–30, 135–36; not "trans enough," 2, 111–22, 129–36; overcoding of, 29–30; neurodivergence and, 4–5; normativity and, 18–19, 114, 118–19, 131–32, 135, 142–43, 164–65; pathologizing, 86–87; in prison system, 8; privileging of stability and coherence, 111–13, 117–19; race and, 4–5, 8, 22, 60, 82, 116–20, 135, 158–59, 174; risk and, 3–5, 8–12, 23, 28–30, 36–37, 65–66, 68–69, 74–75, 82, 85–91, 96–97, 107–8, 167–72, 175, 178–81; safety and, 9, 85–86, 89–90, 93–99, 173; in scholarship, 19, 28–29; settler colonialism and, 22, 116–17, 174; sexuality and, 130–31, 147–51; in sports, 8; survival, 103, 109; as umbrella term, 2, 69–70; violence and, 10, 178–79; visibility and, 3–6, 8, 10, 13, 16–17, 22, 67–68, 70–71, 74–75, 78–82, 85–86, 100–101, 110–13, 115–16, 142–43, 168, 173–75, 179–80, 186–88, 190; vulnerability and, 88–89, 189; world-making and, 88–89, 138–39, 142–43, 145, 147, 149–51, 155–56, 158–59, 164–65, 175–80, 182, 188–90. *See also* genderfluid; nonbinary; queer, queerness

Trans Day of Remembrance, 196–97
transgression, 4–5, 22, 25–26, 116, 128, 132–34. *See also* refusal; resistance; world-making
transitioning, 16, 18–19, 89, 111–12, 118–20, 124–25. *See also* health, health care
transmisogyny, 67
transnormativity, 18–19, 70, 112–14, 118, 120–21, 135
transphobia, 5, 10, 19–20, 40–41, 52, 79, 84–87, 89–91, 94–98, 102–3, 108, 138–39, 143, 155–56, 161, 163, 170–72, 176–78, 184–86. *See also* cisheteronormativity
trapdoors, 16–18, 33–34, 138–39, 143, 146–47, 150–51, 154–55, 163–65, 182, 188–89. *See also* nobodiness; utopia; *and* band hall, tech booth *under* East City High
Travers, 67–68, 70, 91–92, 175
Tsleil-Waututh (səl̓ilwətaʔɬ təməxʷ) Nation, 5
Tuck, Eve, 11–12, 29–30, 178

ungovernability, 139
utopia, 2–3, 18, 139–40, 142, 146, 150–51, 154–55, 158–59, 165, 182. *See also* future, futurity; trapdoors

victimization, 9–10, 56, 96–97, 170–71, 178. *See also* risk
violence, 9–10, 46–47; of assimilation, 21; in education, 69, 86, 89–90, 108; of gender binary, 21; as misunderstanding, 97–98; racialized, 21; sexual assault, 21, 35–36; systemic, 39–40, 42, 52, 60–61, 96–97, 178–79. *See also* harm; risk
Virginia, "Model Policies," 169–70
visibility, 3–6, 8, 10, 13–14, 16–17, 19, 22, 65–68, 70–71, 74–75, 78–82, 85–86, 100–101, 110–13, 115–16, 140–43, 164–65, 168, 173–75, 179–80, 186–88, 190
vulnerability, 3–4, 9–10, 29–30, 65–66, 82, 85–89, 108, 144–45, 154–55, 169–72, 175, 177, 180–81, 189

whiteness. *See under* race
white supremacy, 23, 40, 69
Wilchins, Riki Anne, 28–29
world-making, 2–3, 5, 13, 17–18, 30–31, 138–40, 142–43, 145–47, 149–51, 154–59, 163–65, 175–80, 182, 190
writing, 145–55. *See also* fan fiction

Yang, K. Wayne, 29–30
youth: acts of survival, 2–3, 11, 13, 17, 86, 103, 109, 175–76; adulthood and, 10–11, 24–25, 34, 107–8, 171, 176–77, 179, 193–96, 199–200; building community, 2–3, 11–15, 97–98, 103, 125–26, 140–42, 159, 163–65, 175–76, 179–80; care for, 3–4, 14–15, 97–98, 103, 112, 125–26, 140–41, 163–65, 175–76; childhood and, 21, 28, 107–8, 177, 179, 194–95; development of, 21, 117–18, 176–77, 179; disability and, 4–5, 20–22, 69, 77, 82, 174, 194–95; feelings of not being "enough," 2, 18–19, 112–17, 129–30, 135–36, 147; gender and, 1–3, 8–11, 13, 18, 28–29, 82, 199; labor of, 2–3, 5, 8, 11–13, 16–18, 30–31, 58, 62–63, 86, 90–91, 97–99, 103–9, 112, 114, 124–26, 130–31, 134–35, 138–39, 163, 175–80, 182, 184, 186, 188–90; movement and, 24–25, 30; normativity and, 10–11, 18–19, 66, 111–12, 176–77, 179; as problem to be fixed, 10–11, 66, 82; race and, 8, 20–22, 69, 77, 82, 158–59, 174, 177, 194–95, 199; safety and, 96, 170–71; settler colonialism and, 20–22, 77, 174, 177–78, 194–95; surveillance of, 2, 5, 17–18, 127–28, 138–39, 165; world-making and, 138–40, 145–47, 149–51, 154–59, 163–65. See also adults, adulthood; childhood; trans and gender-nonconforming youth

youth studies, 8

ABOUT THE AUTHOR

LJ SLOVIN is the Martha LA McCain Postdoctoral Fellow at the Bonham Centre for Sexual Diversity Studies at the University of Toronto. They were a Vanier Scholar, and they received the Pat Clifford Award and the AERA Queer SIG Article of the Year Award. Their work has been published in *Curriculum Inquiry*, *Journal of LGBT Youth*, *Sex Education*, and *RERM*.